TRAVELLERS' SONGS

FROM ENGLAND AND SCOTLAND

TRAVELLERS' SONGS

FROM ENGLAND AND SCOTLAND

Ewan MacColl and Peggy Seeger

THE UNIVERSITY OF TENNESSEE PRESS
Knoxville

First published in the United States of America
in 1977 by the University of Tennessee Press,
Communications Building, Knoxville 37916.
This book is published jointly with
Routledge & Kegan Paul Ltd,
39 Store Street, London WC1E 7DD and
Broadway House, Newtown Road,
Henley-on-Thames, Oxon RG9 1EN
Printed in Great Britain.

ISBN 0-87049-191-1

Library of Congress
Catalog Card No.: 76-2854

MacColl, Ewan, and Seeger, Peggy
Travellers' Songs from England and Scotland.
Knoxville: University of Tennessee Press

400 pp.

7611   760303

CONTENTS

CONTENTS

CONTENTS

CONTENTS

CONTENTS

ACKNOWLEDGMENTS

Publication of this book was assisted by the American Council of Learned Societies under a grant from the Andrew W. Mellon Foundation.

To the many people who helped us with this book, we extend our warmest thanks:

To Charles Parker, who took part with us in recording Mrs Caroline Hughes.

To Belle and Alec Stewart of Blairgowrie, for acting as our guides in the tremendously rich and exciting world of the Scots travelling folk.

To Helen Fullerton and Joan and Miller Frondigoun for introducing us to John MacDonald.

To Bob Gale for arranging the recording sessions with Nelson Ridley.

To Tony and Jenny Dunbar, who supplied the documentation on 'The Hop-Pickers' Tragedy'.

To Robert Thompson, for supplying us with broadside references from the Madden Collection.

To David Hammond, for making available to us his copy of the Sam Henry Collection.

To Hamish MacColl for valuable research in the British Museum Broadside Collections.

To Kirsty MacColl, for statistical analyses of material quoted in this work.

To Calum MacColl and Neill MacColl, for proof-reading and checking bibliographical references.

To Mrs Alice Dawson who, by helping to take care of our household and children, made this book possible.

Finally, we are indebted to all the men and women who opened their doors, made us welcome and sang their songs for us. It is a great privilege to be able to refer to them as *our friends*.

The Editors

INTRODUCTION

To compile and edit a book of English, Scots, Irish or Yoruba folksongs is a comparatively straightforward task. Armed with tape-recorder and notebook the collector goes out and finds his singers, records them, transcribes the recordings, organises them according to this or that methodology, writes a commentary and (providing a sympathetic publisher can be found) the collection is eventually published under the title of *English, Scots, Irish* or *Yoruba Folksongs*.

Reviewers and a specialist reading public may greet the book with mild interest, enthusiasm or disdain; criticism may range from an all-out barrage directed at the author's or editor's general thesis to occasional sniping at this or that component in the book's structure. What is *never* questioned is the right of informants to describe themselves as 'English', 'Irish', 'Scots', or 'Yoruba'. The collector is under no obligation to produce proof of the Englishness or Scottishness of this Norfolk or that Aberdeenshire informant. It is unlikely that anyone will question the validity of the collection merely by inferring that the informants are not 'real', 'true', 'genuine' or 'full-blooded' representatives of their ethnic groups.

The situation changes dramatically the moment a collector crosses the *gorgio* culture boundary to record scrap-metal dealers in Perth or itinerant fruit-harvesters in Wisbech. From that time on he finds himself in the position of having to defend the *bona fides* of his informants. He has only to mention that he is engaged in recording Gypsies to elicit an apparently automatic response: 'Are they real gypsies or *didekais*?' Or: 'You can't mean those people down the road! They're not gypsies, not true Romani gypsies!'

The collector may be forgiven if he abandons the scene in despair on discovering that Gypsies themselves, victims of racist feedback, often contemptuously dismiss members of their own fraternity as *mumpers, posh-rats* (half-bloods), or merely as *not proper gypsies*. Even tinkers, those 'ultimate whipping-boys' (Acton, p. 205) in the scapegoat hierarchy, have their lesser breeds, their *bucks, blue-bucks* and *schulas*.

The myth of the 'true', 'full-blooded', 'real', 'proper' Gypsy has its genesis in the numerous apologias written by nineteenth-century gypsiologists. It has flourished and spread unchecked like a virus, infecting and distorting the greater part of the vast literature dealing with British Travellers. The continuing debate among gypsiologists as to which group of people should, or should not, be awarded the title of *true Gypsies* is one in which we have no desire to participate. For the purpose of this collection of songs, we have chosen to designate our informants as Travellers.

> The word may be applied by Gypsies living in England and Wales to the following classes of people: first, any person who is living or has lived on the road, following one of the modes of self-employment or casual labour which are perceived as the 'Gypsy trades' or occupations. Second, any person whose parents or other ancestors were Travellers, and who has inherited (i.e., derived from the socialisation practices of his parents, real or adoptive) elements of travelling culture, particularly Romani or Gammon linguistic elements, or Travellers' economic habits, the 'Gypsy occupations' referred to above (Acton, p. 65).

THE LITERATURE

Of the many collections and anthologies of English, Scots and Irish folksongs published during the last hundred years, only Miss Alice Gillington's *Songs of the Open Road* is concerned exclusively with the songs of British travelling folk. And yet Travellers, with their close-knit family structure, surely provide the classic conditions for the maintenance and continuity of traditions of all kinds. By the same rule, they offer students of folksong ideal opportunities for comprehensive study of traditional songs in a milieu which has, so far, proved remarkably resistant to cultural change.

There can be little doubt that social prejudice has been, to a large extent, responsible for the neglect of the Travellers' repertory of songs and ballads. Hamish Henderson and Francis Collinson, in a recent reference to the Scots folklorist and collector Gavin Greig, write:

> The late Geordie Robertson, who recorded 'Robin Hood and the Pedlar' for the School, knew Gavin Greig quite well; he actually played the pipes at one of the productions of Greig's bucolic comedy *Mains Wooin'*. For years he lived on a croft within easy walking distance of Greig's schoolhouse at Whitehills, New Deer. Yet Greig never made any attempt to collect folksongs from him. The reason was, in all probability, a social one; Greig got the bulk of his wonderful collection from the farming community, and Geordie Robertson was

a tinker – a settled tinker, a crofter and 'made horseman', but still a tinker. In Greig's day this represented a real social barrier (*Scottish Studies*, vol. II, p. 2).

The social barrier between English Travellers and collectors of English folksongs appears to have been equally insurmountable. Only in the recently-published *Folksongs of Britain* (Kennedy) is an attempt made to redress the balance between Traveller and non-Traveller informants.

Even those researchers who specialised in gypsy studies seem to have had little or no interest in the songs and music of English and Scots Travellers. Hoyland, in his *Historical Survey of the Gypsies* (p. 213), makes only a passing reference to their music: 'Their means of subsistence are tinkering and fiddling at feasts and fairs, by which some, I believe, make a good deal of money, which helps them out in the winter, when there is less work and less dancing.' Crabb's sole reference (p. 30) concerns 'a woman of the name of B—— who lived to the reputed age of a hundred and twenty years and up to that age was accustomed to sing her song very gaily.' Morwood (p. 121) in a passage which follows on the heels of an enthusiastic description of the musical talents of Russian, Hungarian and Transylvanian Gypsies, writes: 'Reverting, however, to English gypsies, we may remark that they seldom sing, having but few songs of their own. When the women attempt to sing they never aspire to anything beyond a simple ditty over the washing tub, or a soft, low lullabye to their dark-eyed infants.' Brockie (p. 77), in his account of the Kirk Yetholm Gypsies, confines himself to a single musical reference – in the past tense: 'Many of the gypsy men practised music, and the violin and bagpipes were the instruments they commonly used.'

Simson (p. 306) is a little more informative: 'The young man sang part of two gypsy songs to me, in English; and then at my request he turned one of them into the gypsy language, intermingled, however, with English words; occasioned perhaps by the difficulty of translating it.' A little further on, he writes: 'As far as I can judge from the few and short specimens which I have myself heard, and had reported to me, the subjects of the songs of the Scottish gypsies (I mean those composed by themselves) are chiefly their plunderings, their robberies, and their sufferings. My father in his youth often heard them singing songs in their own language.'

Sampson's 'English Gypsy Songs and Rhymes' is a collection of eighteen Anglo-Romani fragments. With the exception of an Anglo-Romani translation of 'The Gypsy Laddie' (Child 200), the English-language songs of the Travellers remain unexplored.

Francis Groome, one of the best-informed gypsiologists of his day, and no mean folklorist, quotes fifteen song-titles in the text of *In Gypsy*

Tents (pp. 141–57). Six of these are standard pieces from the Welsh national repertory, seven are English or Scots ballads and songs:

'The Unquiet Grave' (Child 78)
'The Butcher Boy' (Laws P 24)
'The Jolly Ploughboy' (Laws M 24)
'Babylon' (Child 14)
'Sir Hugh' (Child 155)
'The Leather Bottle'
'The Poacher's Fate' (Laws L 14)

The two remaining songs are Anglo-Romani pieces written by Groome himself, 'macaronic effects made years ago to meet the literary want'.

In the 538 pages of *The Tinkler Gypsies*, McCormick quotes only four songs actually sung by Travellers:

'The Tinkler's Weddin''
'The Boatman' (a children's fragment)
'The Grey Mare' (a nineteenth-century song of broadside origin)
'Dick Darby the Cobbler' (a cant version)

McCormick's study of border and Galloway Travellers was pursued, albeit intermittently, over a period of some twenty years. It is inconceivable that in all that time he should only have heard the four songs mentioned above. Or was he, like so many of his contemporaries, so intent on hearing the elusive Anglo-Romani muse that he became deaf to those songs which the travelling folk had inherited from *gorgio* farm-labourers and the rural poor? His description of an encounter with a group of Travellers' children is not without its amusing side: 'As I squatted by the burnside, the children gathered around and I rhymed to them gypsy songs, in Romanes, which I had learned from the book published by Leland' (p. 247).

Groome's categorical statement 'The Anglo-Romani muse is dead, if indeed she ever lived' would seem to have fallen on deaf ears. One can only surmise that the exotic image of the 'true', 'real' Gypsy demanded an exotic muse; that muse could, apparently, only survive in the Balkans and in the lands skirting the Mediterranean. George Black's *Gypsy Bibliography* includes 120 entries on the songs and music of Travellers. Only 27 of these deal with British Travellers. The overwhelming emphasis is on the music of Hungarian, Rumanian, Transylvanian, Spanish, and Russian Gypsies. There is much in this formidable list of monographs and learned (and not so learned) disquisitions that is of value. At the same time one cannot help regretting that our native gypsiologists failed to take advantage of an opportunity to study the songs of our native Travellers at a time when our traditional music was still in full flower. A brief gypsiological vacation from Transylvania might have furnished us with valuable data on how songs are transmitted across cultural barriers.

SOME UNANSWERED QUESTIONS

It is generally assumed that the descendants of Romani-speaking exiles from India reached our shores towards the end of the fifteenth century. It is possible, and even likely, that at that time they possessed a body of Romani songs or songs in one or more Romani-inflected languages. Unfortunately, none of these songs appear to have survived; at least none have been reported by British collectors. One can appreciate that songs fall into disuse when those who sing them are engaged in acquiring a new vocabulary. On the other hand, Travellers have shown themselves to be remarkably tenacious in retaining those traditions which reinforce cultural identity. Why, then, was the Romani song repertoire lost? And when, roughly, did the Travellers begin to assimilate the songs and ballads of the working people of Great Britain and Ireland? How was this assimilation effected? The Travellers were – and still are – members of a pariah-group in a society which has always been hostile to them. Who, then, were *their* informants? The evidence which would enable us to answer these and other questions lies now, alas, beyond our reach. Without it we are reduced to mere speculation.

A SUMMARY OF CONTENTS

English contributions

The English songs in this collection were recorded from seven Anglo-Romani speaking Travellers – three women and four men. Five of them were members of the same camping group temporarily located on a piece of waste ground in Dorset. Another was a Kent Traveller and the seventh claimed Surrey as his birthplace. Collectively, they contributed 87 items to this book. Of this total, 13 are Child ballads, 68 are songs representative of the standard English song-repertoire, and 5 are either in Anglo-Romani or are songs sung exclusively by English Travellers. Fifty-one of the 87 songs were contributed by three women singers.

Scots contributions

The Scots items came from eleven Travellers – seven women and four men. Three were natives of Aberdeenshire, two came from Banffshire, two from Perthshire, two from Argyll and one (though hailing originally from Argyll) regarded himself as a Lanarkshire man. Together, they contributed

71 songs. Fifteen of these are Child ballads, 54 are songs characteristic of the standard Scots repertoire and 2 are cant pieces sung exclusively by Scots Travellers. Fifty of the 71 items were contributed by seven women singers.

Comparisons

All our English singers were caravan dwellers. Only two of our Scots Travellers belonged, strictly speaking, to this category; the others, with the exception of a bow-tent dweller, were *grounded*, or housed – that is, they occupied fixed dwellings during the winter months and travelled throughout the rest of the year.

Our English Travellers were, without exception, illiterate. The Dorset group were members of a camping community numbering forty-eight men, women and children, only three of whom had attained a small degree of literacy. At the same time, all of them gave the impression of being fluent in the *pocardi-jib* (the broken language of Anglo-Romani).

Of the eleven Scots Travellers, seven could both read and write. All of them had fairly extensive cant vocabularies and two of them professed to have a good working knowledge of Anglo-Romani. On the whole, the Scots gave the impression of being more sophisticated than the English Travellers. They were generally more forthcoming, though this was probably due to the fact that our first meetings with them were usually effected through the good offices of a third person already known to them. They were impressively articulate and both men and women appeared to take considerable pleasure in manipulative word-play. Their descriptions of craft processes were particularly vivid and detailed and their ability to correlate and verbalise their experiences made our recording sessions with them a constant delight. We occasionally visited them in the company of English, American and Italian friends. On these occasions their verbal agility was given full play – they would jump from Scots to English, from English to Scots-English, from there to English-Scots and back to broad Scots whenever they felt the need to emphasise a conversational point. Similes, metaphors, proverbs and occasional rhymes enriched the speech of all of them.

Our English Travellers were, on the whole, less ebullient and more reluctant to accept the overtures of strangers. This was particularly true of the Hughes group, all of whom were living in conditions of considerable poverty. They gave the impression of having had little or no social intercourse with *gorgios*. In conversation they would frequently refer to people, events and customs without bothering to explain or identify them for the benefit of outsiders. Their verbal delivery, whether they were being laconic or passionately vehement, was always full-voiced. At first we attributed their apparent aggressiveness to a natural hostility towards *gorgios*. Later, after friendly relations had been established between us, we realised that it was merely the vocal style of a people who spend the greater part of their lives out of doors. Their vocabularies, while on the whole less extensive than those of Scots Travellers, were rich in dialect words, middle-English usages, Anglo-Romani words and, occasionally, invented words. Their dialect was the old speech of rural Dorset.

Levi Smith and Nelson Ridley both possessed the curious accent common among Travellers who hail from the Home Counties – an odd mixture of Kent, Surrey and other dialects, with occasional West Country inflections and the whole overlaid by a kind of rural Cockney.

TRAVELLING STYLES

There were differences in the travelling habits of the two groups. Our English singers tended to confine their wandering to two or three southern English counties. Indeed, Caroline Hughes said emphatically: 'I never been across the water and I never intend to.' She was referring to the Thames, not the English Channel. The Hughes family and their neighbours, the Bakers, were, incidentally, still using horse-drawn caravans. Nelson Ridley, the most widely-travelled of our English singers, had never been further north than Carlisle or further east than Wisbech in Cambridgeshire. Like Levi Smith, the greater part of his travelling life had been spent in Kent, Surrey and Essex.

Our Scots singers, despite the fact that most of them were housed for part of each year (or perhaps *because* of it), had all travelled extensively on the Scots mainland. Three of them had visited Orkney, four had travelled in the Western Isles and all but one had travelled in Ireland. Eight of them had been as far south in England as London. All but one of them possessed motorised caravans.

Nevertheless, the two groups had much more in common than either one was prepared to admit. For both of them the large family unit with its mosaic-like patterning of blood-ties represented the ultimate in social organisation. Then, again, the recent history of the two groups has been almost identical. Both have seen their traditional crafts made redundant by the development of commodity production. The tin pans, kettles, washtubs, pails, etc., which for centuries were part of the tinkers' craft, have been swept aside by a flood of mass-produced stainless steel and aluminium kitchenware. Similarly, the heather-besoms, birch brooms, baskets, creels, scrubbers, clothes-pegs and other wooden products of Traveller craftsmen, have been superseded by plastic and man-made fibre products. Even the harvesting of fruit and vegetable crops, traditional seasonal occupation of travelling folk, is being more and more taken over by machines. Finally, the usurpation of the horse by the internal combustion engine has transformed a small army of horse-copers, farriers, bloodstock dealers and fine judges of horseflesh into scrap collectors, car-boshers, engine-fakers and second-hand car-dealers.

THE TRAVELLERS AS HISTORIANS

In the course of acquiring considerable mechanical expertise, the Travellers do not appear to have abandoned traditional attitudes, nor has their feeling of group identity become in any way diminished. That their identity is threatened must be obvious to everyone. Perhaps it is the consciousness of the threat and the fear of an imminent dreadful 'final solution' that gives the Travellers such a strong sense of history. In the course of the last ten years the editors of this book have interviewed more than a hundred Scots and English Travellers, and all of them could talk intelligently, if not always accurately, about the origins of their respective groups.

Mrs Charlotte Higgins, of Blairgowrie, Perthshire, in response to a question concerning the history of the Scots tinkers, made the following answer:

> 'The real tinkers, y'know, not maybe the generations now but the generations that come from far back after the Battle of Culloden and after the Massacre of Glencoe . . . the people, y'know, so many of them being murdered in their houses by the English, being murdered in their houses and all their little places . . . many of those people, hundreds and hundreds, fled to the Lowlands of Scotland. Well, they'd no home, no chattels or anything with them. And they started to live in dugouts or in caves, away down as far as Orkney, where there still is caves, and where the McPhees mostly lives: in Wick and Thurso and the Orkney Islands. And then some of them went into dugouts and some of them made places away in the hills. But all these peoples, it doesn't matter where they come from, they're the remnants of the Highland Clans: McPhee, Stewart, MacKenzie, MacLean, every name you can get. The remnants of the clans of long ago. . . .'

Gilbert Boswell, a Lincolnshire Gypsy whose grandfather, 'Dictionary Boswell', had 'tutored George Borrow in the gypsy language', spoke to us about the history of the *Gypsy* people:

> 'So far as the educated person has studied the Gypsy people, they believe that they come from India. But my father's teaching that has been brought to him from his father – my grandfather, Wester – and therefore, he would get it from his father, Tyso Boswell; and Tyso Boswell would get this information from his father again, which was

Shadrack Boswell. . . . If you refer to Genesis in the Bible, you will
find Abraham and Sariaye at this time. And they didn't get any
children, those two people. But Sariaye had a maid-servant, and the
Lord told Abraham to go into the tent with the maid-servant. And it
seems that Sariaye was agreeable to this. And she conceived, it says in
the Bible, and there was a child. Well, eventually, Sariaye become
jealous of this girl and the baby and she told Abraham she'd have to
go. And of course, she did drive the girl and the child off. And you
read further on that the Lord found her crying beside a well and
he put his hand on her head and told her to arise and she would go
into a far country and she would accumulate a family or a tribe
and they would deal in cattle and sheep – and they would be a
despised race but a clever race.'

The more immediate past was evoked for us by William Baker, a
Hampshire Traveller, when he spoke about the nineteenth-century
enclosures:

'My grandfather, he looked at me one morning while we was setting
down minding the horses and he said, "My son, years ago," he said,
"we used to stop there two year at a time. Till a lord come along," he
said, "and he put a bit of fence up. Bit by bit, that's how they got their
land! That's how they got it – by pinchin' it! Bit by bit!" And that's
how you come to be a squire or lord. They men have no more right to
that bit of ground than what you or I have.'

This account of an important historical process is one that we have heard
frequently from Travellers; such commentaries, along with the songs and
the folk tales, appear to be regarded as part of a single body of knowledge
owned collectively by an entire community.

SONG-HUNTING

The physical conditions in which the recordings were made varied a good
deal. Maggie McPhee, Wilhelmina MacAllister, Ruby Kelby, Maria
Robertson and Jeannie Thompson were all recorded in their own homes,
or in the homes of friends or relatives, within the space of a single week.
The events which led to their being recorded were as follows.

In the early part of 1960 we were engaged in recording that
remarkable family of singers and storytellers, the Stewarts of Blairgowrie.
(The many songs recorded on that occasion are to be included in a book
dealing exclusively with the Stewart family.) We mentioned to Belle Stewart
that we were interested in finding 'The Twa Sisters' in a version containing
the swan-refrain. Several months later, she phoned us from Blairgowrie

with the news that she had just heard the song sung by an Aberdeenshire
Traveller, Christina MacAllister, who was working as a berry-picker in the
raspberry fields. We left London the following morning and headed north.
It was late evening when we reached Blairgowrie, only to discover that
Christina had left for Aberdeen. We were, naturally, disappointed but the
Stewarts assured us that it would be a simple matter to discover her
whereabouts.

Accompanied by Alec and Belle Stewart, we left the next morning and
headed north again. In the three days that followed we were given an
insight into the extraordinary way the grapevine operates among Scots
travelling folk. Our first port of call was the home of Alec's sister, Jeannie
Thompson of Montrose. Within minutes of our arrival the table was set
with tea, scones, cakes, ham sandwiches and all the things with which Scots
Travellers greet their visitors. Unfortunately, Mrs Thompson knew
nothing of 'Auld Teenie's' movements – and as for the song, one of her
neighbours knew it well but 'he's awa' noo traivelling'. However, in order
that our journey should not be a complete waste of time, she sang 'Young
Beichan' for us and three or four other songs, finally capping her
performance with a forty-minute version of the traditional tale, 'The
Black Bull of Norrowa'.

Two hours later we were driving through the centre of Aberdeen when
Alec hailed a young man riding a bicycle. He came over to us and, with
scarcely any hesitation, pointed at Alec and said, 'You're a Stewart!' Alec's
response was equally direct: 'You're a White!' In the brief conversation
that followed it was established that at some early point in history the
Stewarts and the Whites had become related. We also learned that Auld
Teenie had passed through Aberdeen earlier that day. We were advised to
make enquiries from 'The Iron Man' who, we were told, could be found
'ootside the pub, on the left and doon a bit'. Sure enough, The Iron Man
was there, looking like the classic Gypsy of English romantic fiction. In
response to Alec's signal, he sauntered over to us, looked at Alec, pointed a
finger and said, 'You're a Stewart!' Alec's finger pointed back at him:
'You're a Robertson!' After a further investigation of family relationships,
we were instructed to proceed to 'Wilhelmina's place'.

At Wilhelmina MacAllister's apartment in the Bridge of Don (a district
of Aberdeen where many grounded Travellers may be found) we faced
another array of scones, cakes, biscuits, sandwiches, etc. Our hostess was
mortified at not being able to produce Auld Teenie for us. 'She's awa' to
MacDuff. At least, I think that's where she was gaun. But ye ken whit Auld
Teenie's like.' On being asked whether she herself knew any songs, she
protested, 'I was never much o' a hand at singing.' She was, however, eager
to help and offered to take us to meet 'an auld body that kens mair auld
sangs than ye could hear in a month o' Sundays'. It was decided that the

Stewarts, Peggy and our hostess would visit 'the auld body' while MacColl stayed behind to fix a microphone lead-plug which had developed a crackle. Mrs MacAllister, whose notions of hospitality belonged to a Golden Age, invited a neighbour in to keep MacColl company.

The neighbour, Maria Robertson, was painfully shy and was, apparently, in the throes of a personal emotional crisis. The attempt to engage her in conversation was a miserable failure. Furthermore, she denied knowing any songs at all. The silence that followed was so painful that finally out of sheer desperation she began to sing. The song was 'The Dowie Dens of Yarrow'. It was followed immediately by 'My Son David' and by the time the reconnaissance party returned she had sung five songs, three of which were long ballads.

The auld body had elected not to sing that day. Wilhelmina was very apologetic. Just before we left, she said, 'Here, get that thing oot again [the microphone]. Here's a sang that's gey auld.' And she sang 'The Courting Coat'.

We continued to search for Mrs MacAllister throughout the following day, stopping now and again to sample the tea, cakes, scones, songs and traditional tales provided by the innumerable friends of the Stewarts living along the A-947 and A-749. We finally landed that evening at the Kelby household in MacDuff, where we learned that Auld Teenie had gone back to Blairgowrie. There was nothing for it but to set up our recording gear and start recording Ruby Kelby. Later we were joined by her mother-in-law, Maggie McPhee, who entertained us until the small hours with the kind of songs that rarely find their way into print. Our search for Christina MacAllister and her song had been unsuccessful, but in the course of it we had collected more than forty songs and ballads and six traditional tales.

THE HUGHES CAMP

We first visited the Hughes group in 1963. At that time, they were living on a temporary camping site situated on a piece of waste ground some twenty yards off the Wareham Bypass, five miles outside Poole, Dorset. Our visit was ill-timed. The Ratepayers' Association of a nearby private housing development had just initiated a campaign against the Travellers and feelings were running high. A petition had been drawn up which called for drastic measures to be taken. It included the following passage:

> We feel that our elected representatives on the borough council were elected to bring progress and prosperity, happiness and a sense of well-being to the population as a whole. And it is not understood why there should be so much time wasted and trouble caused by a handful of dirty, filthy, unhygienic, scrounging non-entities.

Not unnaturally, the Travellers at first greeted us with suspicion and hostility. Nevertheless, they were prepared after some argument to discuss our request to record them. After a short debate they decided that we should be allowed to record the matriarch of the tribe, Mrs Caroline Hughes, or Queen Caroline, as they called her.

This remarkable old lady who, several years earlier, had been permanently crippled by a hit-and-run driver, was carried down the steps of her horse-drawn caravan and seated on a mound of cushions placed on the ground. She was immediately surrounded by several younger women, some of whom were her daughters, and by a score of young children. A short distance away, three or four men were dickering for a horse, a process in which ritual disinterest and a sharp exchange of insults alternated with disconcerting suddenness. Another nearby group was engaged in dismantling an old car, while on our left several women were busy sorting out a huge pile of rags into three separate heaps. And, of course, there were the dogs and the endless roar of passing traffic.

When we visited Mrs Hughes four years later her health was such that the interview had to be conducted at her bedside. The reduction in the number of onlookers was merely a relative one. In addition to ourselves and Mrs Hughes, nine other people were packed into the interior of her little caravan. This kind of communal participation characterised all the recording sessions which involved English and Scots Travellers. Essentially, there was no 'audience–performer' relationship established during these sessions. Indeed, there was virtually no 'audience'. Instead, there were a number of individuals each of whom could, on occasion, act as custodian of the group's collective memory. As far as the singers were concerned, we – the collectors – were entirely incidental to the proceedings, mere observers of a community rite.

The high esteem in which Mrs Hughes was held was due, to some extent, to the fact that she was the oldest woman in her community and grandmother to more than half the children on the site. But it was also because she was regarded as the Singer of the group – though as far as we could judge almost everyone else in the community knew the stories and themes of her songs well enough to prompt her with an opening line or to supply a missing stanza. Occasionally, particularly when a long, narrative song was being sung, a debate would develop among those present concerning 'the right order' or sequence of action. These moments of disagreement, in which as many as half-a-dozen voices might be heard simultaneously reciting different parts of the story, often ended with Mrs Hughes declaiming *her* verse in a loud voice and then, everyone having been silenced, she would begin to sing again.

It was our impression that Mrs Hughes, and the community to which she belonged, possessed a group of stories and a group of melodies which could be brought together in any kind of combination the singer might find satisfying. One can see the way in which this works in Mrs Hughes's 'Famous Flower of Serving-Men'. This song has a number of pivot-points at which events, common in balladry, take place. For instance, in stanza 3, a man gets killed. In 'The Three Butchers', also, a man is killed. So Mrs Hughes switches, in the space of one stanza, from 'The Famous Flower' to 'The Three Butchers'. In theory, it would be possible to continue and finish with 'The Three Butchers' or she might (as she does in our text) come back to 'The Famous Flower' in stanza 4. In stanza 6, this happens again, but this time the second half of the verse belongs to 'Lord Thomas' (Child 73) and the pivot-point subject is a woman travelling from one place to another. Verses 7 and 8 contain emotional and atmospheric substitutions from other songs, slotted in with astonishing facility. Yet the overall story of the 'Famous Flower' is dominant over these intrusions. Sometimes the results of such dovetailing are unsatisfactory and, occasionally, unintelligible, but a surprising number of these mutant texts possess both dignity and their own kind of dramatic sense.

We asked Mrs Hughes if she knew the ballad 'Lord Thomas and Fair Ellender' (Child 73). Without hesitation, she launched into the following recital in which two ballads are inextricably intertwined. In order to aid the reader we have set this section out as follows:

UPPER CASE LETTERS INDICATE MATERIAL FROM CHILD 73

lower case letters indicate material from Child 53 ('Young Beichan')

italics indicate passages which were spoken rather than sung.

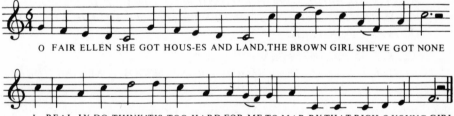

O FAIR ELLEN SHE GOT HOUS-ES AND LAND, THE BROWN GIRL SHE'VE GOT NONE

I REAL-LY DO THINK 'TIS TOO HARD FOR ME TO MAR-RY THAT RICH-O YOUNG GIRL.

WEREN'T HE A CLEVER YOUNG FELLER, LORD THOMAS, to wed two brides all in one day? HE GOT MARRIED TO ELLEN, HE GOT BACK AND THE BROWN GIRL LOOKED AT HIM SO SAD AND HE STUCK HER RIGHT THROUGH WITH A SWORD.

*IS YOU BLIND OR CAN'T NOT SEE
YOUR OWN HEART'S BLOOD RUN DOWN BY YOUR SIDE?*

COME RIDDLE, COME RIDDLE, MY BOLD FORESTER
HE IS THE KEEPER OF OUR QUEEN'S DEERS,
O, wasn't Lord Bateman the cleverest young fellow
THAT EVER THE SUN SHONE ON?

to wed two brides all in one day.

The pivot-point between the two ballads is, of course, one man and two women in a marriage situation. The second time we recorded this sequence from Mrs Hughes she gave it to us in the following format:

O FAIR ELLEN SHE GOT HOUSES AND LAND
THE BROWN GIRL SHE'VE GOT NONE:
O RATHER YOU LOVED HER LITTLE FINGER
NOR YOU DID HER WHOLE BODY.

WELL THE BROWN GIRL NOW SHE SET TO ONE SIDE
BECAUSE SHE WAS NOW VERY POOR
WASN'T SHE THE HANDSOMEST YOUNG WOMAN THERE
THAT EVER THE SUN SHONE ON?

WELL, FAIR ELLEN SHE HAD HOUSES AND LANDS
SHE STEPPED RIGHT INTO THE LORD'S ARMS,
SHE WENT TO THE WEDDIN' BOBBIN' RED WHITE AND BLUE

WHEN SHE WENT TO THE WEDDING', ELLEN COME BACK. THE BROWN GIRL WAS ONE OF THE BRIDEMAIDS, THE BROWN GIRL COME IN AN' LORD HALLERTON SAID HE'S SOONER HAVE THE BROWN GIRL. WELL, THEY SAID, GO AND KISS YOUR BRIDE. BEFORE HE KISS HIS BRIDE, SWEET ELLENDER, HE DRAWED THE SWORD FROM HIS SIDE AND HE STUCK HER THROUGH THE SIDE. THEN HE LOOKED UP AND SAID,

*IS YOU BLIND OR CAN'T YOU SEE
YOUR OWN HEART'S BLOOD A-RUNNIN' DOWN BY THE SIDE?*

In the course of these recitals, Mrs Hughes went directly, without pause, from the spoken to the sung passages.

The comments of those present at the Hughes recording sessions generally concerned the songs rather than the manner in which they were sung, and singers and audience, as a rule, made the same kind of comments: 'That's a *true* song, that is.' 'That's an *old* song.' And 'true' and 'old' appeared to be equally significant measures of praise. Of 'Barbara Allen', 'Geordie', 'Little Sir Hugh' and other long narrative pieces Caroline Hughes said, 'Them's our *relegends*.' Thinking we had mis-heard, we questioned her about the word: 'You mean like going to church and singing hymns?' A dozen voices were raised in dissent. Billy Cole, a thirty-year-old Traveller, explained: 'Relegends is our history, like. Take 'em away and what we got? We got nothing.'

Since that first recording session with Caroline Hughes, we have visited a number of caravan sites occupied by English Travellers and on each occasion we have observed the same phenomenon: the existence of a body of traditional songs and stories known to the entire group and used to maintain and reinforce the Travellers' identity. The fact that the greater part of this traditional repertory was made originally by *gorgios* is unimportant, since the *gorgios* have, on the whole, abandoned it. As with the scrap cars, obsolete sewing machines and old radios which litter their sites, the Travellers have taken whatever was retrievable of that abandoned repertory and made it their own. It is interesting to note that all our English singers held the view that the songs they sang had actually *originated* among Travellers. When it was pointed out to Nelson Ridley that non-Travellers also sang them, he said: 'Not the old songs, the real old songs. They just sing these modern things.'

It may be argued that we are guilty of exaggeration when we suggest that the travelling people have become the real custodians of English and Scots traditional song. But the evidence, in the form of innumerable tape collections recorded in the course of the last twenty years, is overwhelming. In our view, a significant part of our national heritage has passed into the hands of the Travellers and is dependent upon them for its survival. We are not saying that there are no traditional singers left in Britain other than those who are Travellers. Obviously, there are; indeed, there is a surprisingly large number of them. But most of them are old and nearly all of them live in communities which have, for the most part, relegated the old songs – and their singers – to the lumbershed along with the reaping-hook and the Rotherham plough. As often as not, their only audience is the visiting collector, folklorist or city folk-club enthusiast.

Among the Travellers, old age is not penalised. The old man or woman is an honoured and still-useful member of the community. Their songs and stories are regarded as important contributions to the group and the possession of them benefits each individual within the group.

THE SCOPE OF THIS WORK

In several recent works dealing with Travellers, attention has been focused on what would appear to be an occupational hazard among gypsiologists – the tendency to make far-reaching generalisations on the basis of the most slender evidence. The editors of this work wish to avoid that particular pitfall and would, at the outset, point out that this collection of songs cannot, in any way, be considered a definitive work on the songs and ballads of Scots and English Travellers. Such a work would necessitate a comparative study of songs recorded from hundreds of Travellers throughout the British Isles.

We have attempted to present our material as faithfully and accurately as we know how. We have resisted the temptation to 'improve' or amplify broken-down texts or to regularise irregular melodic structures. Our objective has been merely to provide a truthful record of the kind of songs which were being sung by two small groups of Scots and English Travellers in the years between 1960 and 1975.

MUSIC NOTE

Folkmusic is always difficult to notate. Folksingers tend to alter melodies at each performance with the result that the tunes are always in a state of flux. There is, after all, nothing to tie the singer down, no 'dots', no composer's blueprint as in formal music. A singer may, if he chooses, give more attention to the story than to the musical line; or he may concentrate on the tune, exploring it, adding here and subtracting there as the mood takes him. Whatever the reason, or reasons, for these constant changes, they present a problem for the music notater, who has the choice of producing a near-accurate record of what he hears or presenting the reader with a comprehensible manuscript.

Where we have been confronted with this kind of problem, we have attempted to arrive at an 'average' melody, based on one or two stanzas in which the musical line seems to have become stable. Our ultimate choice of stanzas depended on the specific nature of the type of variation(s) employed by the singer in the course of a song. These variations are neither accidental nor incidental. They are extremely important, not merely because each performance is unique but because they represent a singer's attitude towards his or her craft and towards the transmission of an inherited oral culture.

VARIATION AND DECORATION

We found that there were four different categories of variation employed by our singers.

1   Tonal

These consisted almost entirely of speaking tones, i.e. half spoken and half sung. These formed the basis of the vocal styles of Caroline Hughes and Maggie McPhee. Both women were conscious performers and neither had a 'good' voice. They would enhance a song by dropping into speech, swinging back into melody at will, not as an actor does (with histrionics and gestures) but in an almost conversational manner. The borderline between speech and song was often so tenuous that we did not realise the transition had been made until the new form of expression was well-established. We have not indicated where this occurs unless it is a constant characteristic or dominant feature of a singer's style.

2 Structural

We use this term to cover those variations which keep within the time-values normally found in the given metre, but which actually alter the pitch arrangements within the melodic structure. In the terminology of formal music, these would be called *passing notes, auxiliary tones, echappée, cambiata, appoggiatura, anticipation*, etc. They usually employ melodic material already present in the tune itself. Our best example of this kind of variation was in the singing of Nelson Ridley, who appeared to be able to improvise at will on the melody, without altering its basic identity, and without shifting its cadences or mid-phrase notes. We have done a complete transcription of Mrs Hughes's 'All Fours' as an example of this type of variation.

3 External

We use this term to cover those variations which are usually grouped under the general definition of *grace notes*, that is notes or note-combinations with smaller time-values than those generally found in the tune itself. Only one of our singers, Maria Robertson, used external variation with any consistency.

4 Rhythmic

There is a multitude of these variations in the performance of any folksong: the added beat at the cadence, the held high note at mid-phrase, the addition of an extra beat or two in any bar, the change of metre as a regular feature in a song, and so on. They may depend on what section of the text the singer wishes to emphasise or to hurry past. They may even depend on how much breath the singer has at the end of a line or verse. Many such rhythmic irregularities (a word which we hesitate to use, as it suggests that music should be regular, a one song—one metre concept evolved by formal music) are very predictable. For instance, a number of 6/8 tunes went into 9/8 at each cadence; or occasionally a 2/4 tune with a basic unit rhythm of ♫ would soften into a basic 6/8 rhythm of ♩ ♪ as the text required. We have by no means notated such rhythmic variations exhaustively.

[18]

From a number of singers we recorded the same song several times. We discovered that certain of the variations were present in one rendition and absent, or shifted to different positions in the stanza, in the next performance. On the other hand, certain of the improvisations, always present at the same point, had been wedded to particular words or phrases in the text. Others, involving an actual melodic change due to a textual irregularity, had crystallised in that way even though the set verse-form had been violated (see 'The Jolly Barber Lad', and stanzas 3–6 of 'Too Young'). It is our opinion that singers do not do this because they have forgotten the words or because they are unable to fill in by improvisation the exact footage required by the laws governing formal poetry. We feel that, to a certain extent, it may be a device consciously employed by the singer in order to startle and surprise the listener. It may also arise from the way in which a singer 'gets into' a song, so that the characteristic melodic pattern does not emerge until the second or third stanza.

In short, these variations are not introduced to make the tune more interesting: they *are* the tune. If you ask a singer like Nelson Ridley to lilt the tune of 'The Oyster Girl', he will lilt it first one way, then another, and to him this *is* the tune, even as a diamond is a diamond with many facets. When words accompanied the tune, however, it appeared that the main attention of our singers was on the story and the tune was taken for granted or allowed to go its own way.

Before we leave the subject, we would like to comment on the fact that certain songs within the repertoire of a creative singer were not given the same treatment as other songs. For instance, both Mr Ridley and Mrs Hughes sang 'Twenty-One Years' with almost none of their characteristic improvisation. 'Green Grows the Laurel' was rarely decorated by any of our singers. These are semi-popular songs, sometimes learned from recordings or from the radio, songs which are understood to exist in one version only. They seem to remain unchanged, unaffected by a singer's creativity, although they are widely sung.

WHO IS A SINGER? WHO IS NOT?

John MacDonald, after singing several dozen songs, confessed, 'Of course, I'm no' the singer in the faimily. It's my dochter that sings.' Nelson Ridley said as much about himself. There is a recognised set of criteria used among Travellers as to what makes a Singer as opposed to a singer. The music is still a fluid and malleable medium, can be well or badly interpreted, and in a society where it is still one of the most important forms of entertainment – and education – it is imperative that your Singer is a good one.

Of our informants, Jeannie Thompson, John MacDonald, Henry and

William Hughes, Maria Robertson, Sheila Hughes, Big Willie McPhee (a splendid stylist despite his self-deprecation), Emily Baker, Jock Higgins and Ruby Kelby did not regard themselves strictly as Singers. They were merely the best that were to hand at the time, knew a version of a song that had been asked for and sang it in the spirit of 'well, any singer is better than no Singer'. Had a Singer been present they probably would not have sung at all.

Where there were several Singers resident in the same area and where the repertoire was shared, the songs were often parcelled out. The Stewart family, Travellers grounded in Blairgowrie, Perthshire, has three excellent Singers in its older generations: Belle and her two daughters, Sheila and Cathie. Belle has taught her songs to the girls but if she feels that one of them sings a song better than she herself does, she will not sing it. In the Stewart family, there are 'my mither's sangs' (generally the big ballads, the bawdy songs, certain of the love-lyrics), 'Sheila's songs' (some of the ballads, a number of Irish songs, the sad love-lyrics) and 'Cathie's songs' (the Irish and the more popular material). We did not find this approach to singing among non-Travellers, who have fewer Singers in their midst.

It is interesting to note that when our Singers were performing and they happened to forget a line or a tune, other members of the surrounding group would supply it. Everyone seems to know the songs. John MacDonald's wife, Betsy, who is tone-deaf, knows *all* the words of his songs as well as the words of many pieces which he does not sing. She herself never sings, cannot sing. But she has a wealth of texts in her head and is a sort of walking memory bank. The children sitting at the feet of Caroline Hughes could recite 'Sir Hugh' with her – including the interpolated prose section.

So – a Singer can handle the old songs, the real songs; can improvise; can sing what Caroline Hughes called the 'relegends', the 'heavy' songs; can recreate for the community its own past and present history. In other words, many of the Travellers are singers – and almost every travelling community has its Singer.

IS THERE A TRAVELLER SINGING STYLE?

These days it is not easy to be a vocally versatile singer in a community of Travellers. Contrary to popular belief, it is not the healthiest outdoor life. Whatever the situation may have been in the past, the overwhelming majority of Travellers today are the victims of almost continual harassment. Overcrowding on the few available camping sites, lack of facilities for even the most elementary hygiene, and an inadequate diet, combine to produce a poor state of health among Travellers. Almost all our English singers suffered from chest and respiratory disorders. It is difficult for a singer suffering from catarrh or bronchitis (or both) to sing with agility or delicacy. Does this explain why there is so little external and tonal variation in the singing of English Travellers? Again, to what extent is a singer's choice of repertoire determined, or at least affected, by the condition of his vocal apparatus?

William Hughes suffered so badly from bronchitis that his 'Little Chimney Sweep' sounded as if it were being sung by an English Louis Armstrong. Maria Robertson and Ruby Kelby sang in a hoarse whisper. Caroline Hughes, a semi-invalid, was forced to adopt a continual reclining posture which affected her breathing to such an extent that she rarely sang a long phrase without breathing at mid-phrase. Her light vocal effort, lavish use of speaking tones, and fairly up-tempo delivery may well have been due to the same cause.

The most common singing style among both Scots and English Travellers is an open-throated, direct delivery. Our English singers tended to use more *portamento* and occasional diphthongs at the ends of lines and sustained notes. Their tone was sharp and slightly nasal. Both groups of Travellers used an underlying pressing effort resulting in intensity rather than in volume. Charlotte Higgins, for instance, a small and gentle woman, sang with a small and gentle voice. Even though she was recorded in her own parlour, she employed the same kind of attack that a street singer might use. John MacDonald spoke gently but sang with tremendous pressure which gathered volume as the song took him over. There is an almost heroic quality in the singing of Travellers, a desire to declaim, to demand attention, an assertion of oneself as a Singer. It is a quality that we have not often encountered among *gorgio* singers.

Singing style also seems to be affected by whether or not the singer regards himself as a Singer. Maria Robertson sang almost to herself, painfully shy and withdrawn. She sang for us chiefly because she could not stand the silence which followed the question 'Do you know any songs?' Her style of singing was introspective, dreamy and almost apologetic – but intense. Jeannie Thompson, a gay and admittedly non-musical element, almost threw the songs away in a fit of good humour. Both she and Maria Robertson began the recording session by declaring that they didn't sing and didn't know any songs. Sheila Hughes, singing her mother's song in her mother's presence, constantly cast glances at her mother to check if she was singing it correctly. Such hesitancy and lack of confidence and practice in performance must affect the singing style.

The function of the song often determines the manner in which the song is sung. Emily Baker, who usually sang 'The Little Beggar Boy' to her children, crooned, as if singing to children, in a gentle and monotonous tone of voice. Caroline Hughes, when diddling for dancing, kept the volume down so that she could maintain the breathing for the full phrase of music. Songs which were quicker in tempo, or humorous, were given a lighter – but still intense – treatment.

The singing style seems to reinforce a social position. It is assertive, bordering upon the aggressive. It is often violent and always passionate. In his delivery, the Singer is saying 'This is me. This is *us*. This is our history and our heritage. So listen!'

HABIT AND HABITS

Certain habits and tendencies among our singers were obvious, and worthy of further comment and study. These may cast light on why certain songs are passed down; on how versions arise; on how the oral tradition survives, and so on.

1   Many of the singers would *get into* a tune gradually, arriving at a definitive melody by perhaps a second or third stanza. If the song had only two or three stanzas, this stability might never be achieved. Where this introductory melody did not fit the stanzas which followed, we have given the stable melody as well. Only occasionally have we given a composite 'average' tune, made up of the most consistent patterns found throughout the song.

We did not interview the singers in depth as to why the first stanza is treated in this manner. We did notice, however, that musical elements from the previous song were frequently present in this elusive stanza – that is, the singer was still immersed in the song he had just sung and was bringing elements of it into the piece which followed. The most extreme example of this was in John MacDonald's rendition of a complete song – with a few awkward points in the singing – followed by the remark, 'Of course, I dinna sing that tune to it normally.' It was the tune of his previous song! Occasionally, if a singer could not recall the correct melody he would substitute another tune of the same metre, mode and general feeling. This is not a practice confined to Travellers. We recorded a fisherman in Norfolk who sang *five* songs in a row to the same melody.

2   Avoidance of strict rhyme appears throughout the songs in this book often enough to warrant more than a passing comment. We use the word 'avoidance' advisedly as it really often does seem that the singers are loth to use words which sound alike at cadences. The use of assonance instead of rhyme is fairly consistent in our songs. A number of our texts differ radically from many printed versions in this respect. This apparent disinclination to make rhymes takes different forms. Charlotte Higgins, for instance, in 'Jamie Raeburn', has the opportunity to rhyme the word *Caledonia* with *awa', a', Broomielaw* – but she quite clearly and concisely sings *Caledonio* every time.

Our English informants went even further, as may be seen by the number of mixed and ABCD text-forms (see the table on p. 26). It would seem that as long as a story is told, nothing need rhyme at all. Most of the collections with which we are familiar appear to have avoided such texts, preferring to show a constant form or recognisable poetic structure. Singers like Caroline Hughes and Nelson Ridley tend to regard such structures as mere departure points and it is perhaps because of this that their texts are so reduced, having no substantial poetic framework on which to hang the images and ideas.

3   Our collection contains several texts in which the story is so attenuated as to hardly make sense at all. A number of items in even more debased condition were omitted from this book yet were important to their singers. The retention of broken-down texts, their transmission from generation to generation, has always been of interest to students of folklore. Reed Smith, in his *South Carolina Ballads*, refers to it as 'The Road Downhill', in a chapter which should be read by anyone wishing to understand the word-idea-music culture of the southern English Travellers. When we say that a text doesn't make sense or is badly fragmented, this is only *our* opinion. It is not the opinion of those who sing songs like our 'Bonnie Bunch of Roses' or 'All Over those Hills'. The singers of both these pieces (and their normal audience) knew the story or understood its mood, and their imaginations seemed to fill out what was lacking in the text.

4   Our Scots texts were more complete, more coherent, more structurally sound than our English ones. The Scots singers were more articulate, had a fuller vocabulary than their English counterparts, but both groups approached certain aspects of language and communication in the same manner. For instance, we asked Nelson Ridley why he sang 'As I was pervoiding among the sweet pimeroses', or why certain verses, seemingly unrelated, were grouped under one tune as one song. His answer would be 'That's the way I learned it'; or he would give a perfectly rational explanation which in itself made sense, but which made no sense when applied to the song or when applied to everyday situations. 'Pervoiding among the sweet pimeroses' meant 'walking among the sweet primroses'. When asked the meaning of 'pervoiding', he said 'rambling, wandering'. When asked if he ever used that word in speech or in any other song, he said no – only in that one song, that one line.

We had similar experiences with other singers. John MacDonald sang the word 'moneyward' at one point. When we asked its meaning, he said 'homeward'. We asked why he did not sing 'homeward' in the song. He said, 'I *did* sing moneyward.'

The possibilities are staggering when you contemplate language used in this way. It means, among other things, that language can become gibberish in a split second. Caroline Hughes's rendition of 'Clementine', which she learned from the radio, shows how the substitution of words of a similar sound can affect a song:

> Whip me varmint, whip me varmint
> Whip me varmint, clever times;
> O, I kissed my little sister
> When I lost my valentine.

This free-association in pronunciation and meaning can provide us with rich new words and phrases, like 'relegend' for ballad, and 'improving a child by thee' for 'proving with child by thee'. It may also affect the continuity in a story-telling situation, in that a singer may dart with bewildering ease from one song to another – without stopping singing. Furthermore, large textual diversions may bring their music with them, explaining perhaps why a person like Mr Ridley has such rich structural 'decoration' in his singing. Is he merely allowing his mind and voice to wander from one musical section of the repertoire to another, even as Mrs Hughes, in 'The Famous Flower of Serving-Men', uses focal points in the plot to swing from one ballad to another and back again – without stopping singing? Thought-processes such as these make one realise how very different oral transmission is in a non-literate society.

    5   Telescoping a melody from a four-line to a two-line form may be seen in about a dozen of our songs (e.g. 'My Love Lays so Cold Below My Feet', 'Caroline of Edinburgh Town', 'Wild Rover') and would seem to exist as a practice among both Scots and English Travellers. It occurs most frequently in ABBA tune forms and in songs in which the first two lines of a quatrain have disappeared so that the song goes automatically into couplets.

ANALYSIS OF THE SONGS

This table contains a very basic breakdown of some of the more obvious ingredients which go to make up a song. Remembering that our informants come only from two main areas of Britain – southern and northeast Scotland and southern and southeast England – it is clear that no sweeping generalisations can be made other than about these songs and these singers. The terms used are as follows:

mixed metre	refers to a song which changes metre internally from duple to triple time. Those which change from, for instance, 6/8 to 9/8 or from 2/4 to 4/4, are not considered as *mixed*.
major basis modes	Ionian, Lydian, Mixolydian.
minor basis modes	Aeolian, Dorian.

borderline modes	possibly major, possibly minor, depending on the inclination and orientation of the listener.
text forms	there were fourteen different forms used, but we give only the four most common. We regard a word as a rhyme if it is either exact or close. Close assonance has been regarded as an acceptable rhyme.
mixed text form	meaning that some of the verses in a song may have remnants of a poetic structure but this structure does not play a dominant part in the poetry of the song.
ABCD text form	refers to those songs in which the stanzas do not contain a significant number of rhyming lines.
tune forms	these are based on the formation of a line and on its cadence. An ABBA form, for instance, has two identical or very similar lines sandwiched between two other identical or similar lines. Occasionally, the second B-line will be identical except as regards the final cadence. Contrary to usual practice we have regarded this second line in such a case as 'identical or similar', as our comparisons are for rough generalisations only.

For explanation of range and mode terms, see pp. 28–9 in this Music Note, *The Transcriptions*.

From even such a simple table as the one given on p. 26, a number of trends may be observed as regards these singers and their songs.

The emergence of triple-time and major-orientated tunes came as quite a surprise, as we were under the impression that our tune-types were more varied. The paucity of pentatonic tunes amongst the Scots singers, whose culture has produced so many grand pentatonic melodies, the high incidence of pitch-inflected tunes among the English singers, the fact that only six of the 158 songs contained text forms which correlated to the tune forms – all these are matters for speculation and investigation. It is certainly obvious that, for the most part, the Scots singers may have more of a sense of the form of the texts, but their approach to the tunes is less elastic and uninhibited than that of the English Travellers, whose tunes produced more pitch and structural variations, more internal modulations and more final cadences on a non-tonic note.

It became quite clear when making this analysis that certain singers definitely prefer certain tune and text forms. Of the major singers, the following might be said.

Mrs Higgins had no bawdy songs (at least none that she would sing to us). Her main stock was lyric love songs. Her favourite mode was authentic

SONG ANALYSIS TABLE

		Scots	English
	Number of songs collected	70	88
	Child ballads	13	7
	Number of Child ballad variants	15	13
Metre	triple	40	62
	duple	21	30
	5/4	1	1
	mixed	7	4
Range	authentic	28	43
	plagal	22	30
	mixed	21	15
Mode	major basis	47	72
	minor basis	13	16
	pentatonic	7	none
	borderline	2	none
Most common text forms	AABB	25	21
	ABCB	23	16
	ABCD	none	6
	mixed	none	33
Most common tune forms	ABCD	20	35
	ABBA	13	14
	ABCA	9	5
	ABAC	17	7
	Tune-text correlations	1 (on ABAC)	5 (on ABCD)
	Tunes with pitch inflections	10	37
	Tunes ending on a non-tonic note	5	8–10
	Gapped tunes (hexatonic)	25	9

Ionian and most of her songs are in triple time. All her songs were nearly within the compass of an octave, save one which was, incidentally, her only minor tune. Her favoured text form was AABB, her dominant tune-form was ABCD.

Mrs Hughes had the greatest variety and the largest number of pieces. She provides songs for every category in this book. Almost all her pieces were in major; two-thirds were in triple time and just under half of them contained pitch-inflections. Her favourite text format was mixed, her dominant tune format was ABCD.

John MacDonald possessed the classic northeast Scotland agricultural repertoire. He preferred songs with a story, and triple time governs half of his songs in this book. Two-thirds of his songs were in major and he did not produce many pitch inflections. His most dominant format was an ABBA text wedded to an ABCA tune. Half of his tunes were in hexatonic scales.

Maggie McPhee preferred lighter material. Her repertoire gives this book but one ballad and a number of light, humorous and bawdy songs. Two-thirds of her songs are in major, of which half are in plagal range. A third of her pieces are in ABCB text format joined to an ABAC or ABCD tune form.

Nelson Ridley had in his repertoire a wide variety of songs and ballads with some real melodic treasures. Two-thirds of his songs are in triple time and half his tunes are in authentic major modes. The number of pitch-inflected pieces is high and, like Caroline Hughes, he leaned towards a mixed text form and an ABCD tune form.

THE TRANSCRIPTIONS

1 Pace and spirit markings

These are to be found in the upper left-hand corner of each notation. They represent the manner in which the singer sang the song, not how the editors feel the song should be sung. The word *free* is frequently applied and is not to be interpreted as meaning that the song should be sung slowly. It merely means that the song is not sung *strictly in rhythm*. A good two-thirds of our songs were sung in this manner, but we have marked about half with the word *free*. Few of our singers sang in absolutely strict time. Often the free songs were sung quite fast, almost conversationally, with halts at cadences, at mid-phrase and at places required by the sense and emphasis of the text.

Frequently songs marked *slow, free* were performed so slowly as to make casting them into a metre a matter of conjecture alone. In such cases, we used the text as a guide, speaking the song out loud as verse and casting it into a poetic metre. It should be noted that those wishing to sing the songs may want to change the speed as marked and we would like to comment that while certain of our informants sang them too slowly to carry the sense, *none* of them sang too fast, a common tendency amongst present-day revival folksingers.

2   Decoration and variation

In the notations, we have given below each melody the variations which appear most frequently or those which carry a line of text which would otherwise not fit into the given tune. These alterations are numbered according to the bar in which they occur.

3   Keys

We have cast the songs into what we consider singable keys, not the keys in which the songs were originally sung or all in a standard key. While this makes it difficult for those wishing to compare one tune with another, it does make it simpler for those wishing to sing the songs. As is now common in collections such as this, we mark sharps and flats in the signature only if they appear consistently in the tune.

4   Modes and scales

We have put a range and mode marking in the upper right hand corner of each notation. The *range* covered by a melody is expressed by the lower-case letters *a*, *p* or *m*.

> *a*   authentic, in which the tune lies within the range between the tonic note and the octave above it. In the key of C, this would place the tune between middle C and the octave C above.
>
> *p*   plagal, in which the tune lies within the range between the fifth above the tonic and a fourth below it. In the key of C, this would place the tune between G below middle C and G above middle C.
>
> *m*   mixed, in which the tune has a range which is either a combination of those above or which crosses the two octave areas or covers more than the compass of a ninth.

The *mode* in which the melody is cast is expressed by the upper-case letters *I*, *D*, *Ly*, *M* and *Ae*.

> *I*   Ionian, a major-based mode (C–D–E–F–G–A–B–C)
> *D*   Dorian, a minor-based mode (D–E–F–G–A–B–C–D)
> *Ly*   Lydian, a major-based mode (F–G–A–B–C–D–E–F)
> *M*   Mixolydian, a major-based mode (G–A–B–C–D–E–F–G)
> *Ae*   Aeolian, a minor-based mode (A–B–C–D–E–F–G–A)

A number of gapped or hexatonic scales, lacking an interval, could be possibly one of two modes and, where there is any doubt as to which mode it could be, we use Bronson's system:

> A tune containing the first six notes of a major scale but lacking the VII degree could be either Ionian or Mixolydian. Hence I/M.
>
> A tune containing the first three notes and the last three notes of a major scale but lacking the IV degree could be either Ionian or Lydian, hence I/Ly.
>
> A tune containing the first five notes of a minor scale but lacking the VI degree could be either Aeolian or Dorian. Hence Ae/D.
>
> A tune which contains all the intervals characteristic of Mixolydian or Dorian but lacking the decisive III degree is labelled M/D.

The *pentatonic*, or five-note, scales are marked π followed by a small number to show which of the five possible inversions of the scale is applicable, helping to place the tonic note.

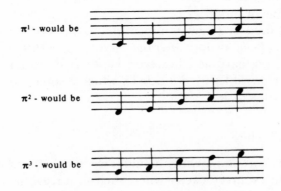

and so on.

In any folkmusic work there are borderline tunes where it is difficult to decide which mode is being employed. A concept of tonality is built up through experience and inclination. We have not got many major-*or*-minor alternatives in this book – perhaps the most questionable case is that of the 'Twa Sisters'. One listener might feel that A is the tonic, in which case the tune is in the m Ae/D (ending on III) category. Another person might hear C as the tonic, in which case the tune would be identified as an a I/Ly scale. In these borderline cases we brought in singers and asked, 'Where is the home-tone in this song?' Where there was a difference of opinion we marked the song with both alternatives.

Wherever the range-mode marking contains the word *inflected*, this merely means that a certain interval may be raised or dropped a half-tone occasionally, but that the mode is, for the most part, consistent.

GENERAL ARRANGEMENT

Titles and categories

The first nineteen items in this book are traditional ballads, the titles and numbers of which follow the system formulated by Professor Francis J. Child. Thereafter we have attempted to arrange the songs according to their type, theme or mood.

Titles followed by a Laws number refer to the appropriate category in *Native American Balladry* and *American Balladry from British Broadsides* (see Bibliography). We have not, however, kept strictly to Laws's titling but have, wherever possible, used a title by which a song is most commonly known in the British Isles.

Bibliographical references

In the references accompanying the notes we have avoided duplication of Professor Child's sources, except where such a source is mentioned only in the body of one of his notes. We have followed the same procedure with specifically American references given by Bronson, Coffin and Laws.

Punctuation

Quotation marks have not been used in the notes where it is obvious that a passage is a direct quote – instead, we have inset the piece to separate it from the body of a note. In the songs, we have used quotation marks only when a passage of direct speech follows a designated speaker with an active verb (i.e. he said, she cried, and so on).

Stanzaic sequence

Bracketed stanza numbers indicate the order of stanzas given by the singer. Due to the fact that half-forgotten songs were often brought out at a moment's notice, stanzaic order was frequently sacrificed in the interest of performance continuity. Where the singer's stanzaic sequence seemed illogical, we have re-ordered the stanzas but have indicated, in brackets, the original order.

Glosses

Bracketed words in the body of a song indicate words or phrases which were garbled or did not seem to make sense. We have left them as sung but have suggested, in matching brackets in the right-hand margin, what the meaning or sense might be.

Copyrights

The modern practice of copyrighting traditional songs is a subject of continuing controversy. It is our opinion that if copyright *must* be assigned, then it should be to the singers.

THE SINGERS

EMILY BAKER

Emily Baker was born in the Poole district of Dorset in 1894. 'I'm a proper Romani born and bred, been a-travelling all my days . . . different towns – Ramsgate, Margate, Whitstable, Herne Bay, Sandwich, Deal, Folkestone, Canterbury, Chatham, right down to Devonshire, Cornwall, Plymouth, Bristol. All parts I've a-been, in a horse-drawn caravan.' She learned her songs from her mother and has contributed 'The Little Beggar Boy' (No. 122) to this collection. (Collected 1962)

WILLIE CAMERON

Willie Cameron (known as 'Pipe-Empty') is the youngest son of Sandy and Maggie Cameron, Argyllshire Travellers. Both his parents are fine story-tellers; indeed, Mrs Cameron is one of the most gifted narrators of tales that we have ever encountered. We recorded them one cold, wet night late in September at the Cookson Field, near New Alyth, Perthshire. They had spent a long, hard day in the potato-fields and they were all tired and wet. They made us welcome, however, and soon we were sitting huddled along with another eighteen people in the long tunnel-like bow-tent which was their home. We heard the story of 'The Black Bull of Norroway', and tales of headless spectres and a dream of long-tails (rats) harnessed to a coffin which they were drawing through a quarry of tears.

The hissing of the oxyacetylene lamp made recording almost impossible, so it was turned off and we sat there in the darkness and listened to 16-year-old Willie Cameron play his piano-accordion – an almost magical feat in that confined and crowded space. He has contributed 'The Tattie-Liftin'' (No. 105) to this collection. (Collected 1962)

CHARLOTTE HIGGINS

Charlotte Higgins (née Riley) was born in Perkmass, Lumphanon, Aberdeenshire, in 1893. Her father, Thomas Lucas, hailed from Bristol, as did her mother, Mary Paul, who died shortly after Charlotte was born. The father, in order to pursue his trade as a deep-sea fisherman, arranged for his infant daughter to be brought up by a family of Travellers called Riley, whose name Charlotte finally adopted. 'My foster-parents were good to me and they brought me up decent. They learned me a lot I never would have learned. She was an auld woman and she believed in the young girls being early to bed and away to your calling in the morning.'

Of her formal schooling, she said, 'I believe I only got as far as Standard One. But I was a great one for books. I remember we used to go over the alphabet both forwards and backwards to keep ourselves entertained.'

At the age of twelve, Charlotte was initiated into the ancient trade of street-hawking. 'We used to leave New Deer in the morning and maybe travel to Ethlick (that's about six miles). Or we'd hawk Strichen and come back at night. Or maybe we'd ca' at the fairms, and on the cotters. The cotters o' that day, 1912 or 19 and 14, they didna have much. They'd only a pound a week and their meal, milk and tatties. Even though they had five and six bairns. A pound a week! And yet they'd take you in sometimes and they would say, "Come awa' noo, sing a bit song and I'll gie ye your tea".'

In addition to becoming a proficient hawker, Mrs Higgins also learned 'to read hands and to tell fortunes by the white of an egg'. She became fluent in the use of the cant and had a profound knowledge of the customs of Travellers. In 1911, she married a Traveller called MacGuire and bore him two children. 'He was a piper and was killed in France during the First World War.' She contracted a second marriage to Jock Higgins, who has also given a number of songs to this collection.

'My husband and I did farm work. We shawed the turnips, thinned the neeps, lifted the potatoes. During the Second World War, we workit in the flax. And we'd go to Blairgowrie to the berries. You could make good money at the berries if you were a good picker. But you had to be at it since childhood.'

The Higgins family finally settled in Blairgowrie, where Charlotte died in 1971. She has contributed the following songs to this collection:

82	Alan MacLean	94	Jamie Raeburn
92	The Boston Burglar	113	The Wild Rover
93	Van Dieman's Land	131	Hi, Bara Manishee
			(Collected 1963)

JOCK HIGGINS

Jock Higgins was born in Portree, Skye, in 1897. His mother, Kirsty Stewart, was daughter to John Stewart of Kinlochrannoch. Jock Higgins married Charlotte Riley, who bore him two sons. He has contributed the following songs to this collection:

17 The Braes o' Yarrow
79 Locks and Bolts
88 MacPherson's Farewell

(Collected 1963)

CAROLINE HUGHES

Caroline Hughes (née Bateman) was born in 1900 in a horse-drawn caravan in Bere Regis, Dorset. 'My mother's name was Lavinia Batemen and my father was Arthur Hughes. I was one of seventeen children. My parents worked all their lifetime to bring we up clean and respectable. My father was a rat-and-varmint destroyer. We could bide anywhere, and was respected with anybody. My father had a good name and a good character. My mother worked hard, use to go hawking to get a living in a straightforward way. Never done no wrong. Never been had up for stealing, robbing, lived a straight life. . . . I started to go hawking with my mother time I got up old enough, then I went to school till I was ten year old. Then I took off with my mother to get my living, just like all my sisters did. And I grew up to get married and I knew how to get my living. I met my husband arter he done three years in France a-fighting. When he come back he had a long tarry in hospital. We never courted long before we got married. I was married two years and five month before I had my first child. After that I had three children in three year and seven month. I knowed how to take the basket on my arm to get my own living honest. I didn't want teaching. I knowed to get my living working on a farm, doing things straightforward. My children used to help me go out in the field to pull docks. . . . I been out in the fields hoeing all day and come back and done my girt tubs o' washing. I was proud o' that, and done it until I turned fifty-three. Then I met with an accident, which turned me an invalid for nine years. This car-driver, he ran straight on and never stopped. Never mind . . . I left that to God.

'Don't I wish they old times would come back again . . . where we used to go and have a drink at a public house, all come back on the old common, singing, hang on our pots of girt big suety puddings, hocks o' bacon, pigs heads . . . we done nice then. We was all healthy, never much illness amongst the family. Farmers come round, talking with our fathers and mothers. We children playing with their children. Dancin', playin' gramophone records, tap-dancin', clog-dancin'. You could stay anywhere . . . not today. The world's turned upsidedown part, you can't do as you like. It's a different law. I reckon to myself the Lord Almighty he died to save all we in this world. God wasn't a proud man. He liked every form of mother's child. He liked mine and other children too. He sent this world for we poor people. Sent the mountains for us, sent everything for us all to have a share o't, everything. The Lord send bushes, he send trees, birds, comfort, greens, swedes, potatoes, flowers, everything in the world for one another. Not for one, for the lot.

'My name is Caroline Hughes. I'm a principled woman. I can't read but I tell you I got my knowledge. I got my little wooden caravan, and I got my eight nice children and my thirty-five grandchildren and I love to hear the birds in the morning and get to the copses and woods and set round the old camp-fire. I don't want no saucepans to cook with. I want to follow my great-great-great-grandmother with the old-fashioned three-gallon pot. My great grandmother had a grandmother lived till she was 104. The next was 101. The next one again was my grandmother, she was 103. That was Alice Bateman, my father's mother. His father was more than a hundred when he died, but my mother was only seventy-two and my father eighty-two, so they didn't follow on their families. But I want to reach there if I can.'

Of her songs, she said, 'My mother sang all the time. When she were making clothes-pegs or making we children's bloomers, shifts and petticoats. We be all around the fire singing these old songs, and I been with my mother listening, listening, and I made her sing them over and over till I learned the lot. Many a time my father and mother have come back with a glass of beer in their hands and they'd say to we children, "Would you like to hear a song?" "Yes," says we. And my father and mother they've sat and sung songs, and there've been local people out in the road a-listening. That was my father and mother, the bestest singers in the world. And there was my brother, he used to play a fiddle and he would sing.'

At this point, one of Caroline's daughters interrupted to say, 'My mother done the same with us. She would always sing when she was making tea or to keep we kids quiet. And she always sang to us at bed-time. On Sundays too, when the men came back from the pub, that would always be a time for singing.'

Caroline Hughes concluded the story of her life with these words: 'Where you going to find a good mother when she's gone? One who's worked, slaved hard, runned and raced for you, been through bitter frost and snow, finding snitches of wood, buckets of water, through all the ups and downs. The young girls today don't know the meaning of it. What do they do today? Wear their clothes above their knees so you can almost see their fanny. And there's paint and powder. They're not like the gals what's fifty years ago, nothing like they was thirty, forty years ago. I'm a gal, my name is Caroline Hughes. I been out a-beggin' for my bread. I wish I could do it now. . . .'

Queen Caroline Hughes died in 1971 and was given a gypsy funeral. As is the traditional way among older gypsies, her caravan and all her possessions were burned in the presence of her tribe. She contributed the following songs to this collection:

7	The Broomfield Hill	62	Green Grows the Laurel
11	Bonny Barbara Allen	65	The Girl I Left Behind
13	The Famous Flower of Serving-Men	66	Green Bushes
		67	Too Young
14	Sir Hugh	68	The Banks of Sweet Primroses
20	Brake of Briars	70	Sheep-Crook and Black Dog
22	Mother, Mother Make My Bed	71	The Fatal Snowstorm
23	Long A-Growing	73	The Butcher Boy
24	The Three Butchers	74	Oxford City
27	The Sailor's Return	75	The Wexford Girl
31	If I Was a Blackbird	80	All Over Those Hills
36	All Fours	86	McCaffery
40	Ring Dang Doo	89	The Highwayman Outwitted
44	Seventeen Come Sunday	98	The First Day in October
45	The Lady and the Soldier	100	Twenty-One Years
50	The Bird in the Bush	103	We Dear Labouring Men
54	The Seeds of Love	118	The Jolly Herring
55	Died for Love	119	Paddy Backwards
56	The Blacksmith	123	Little Poppa Rich
57	The Cuckoo	125	The Two Gypsy Girls
58	The False-Hearted Lover	126	Diddling Songs
59	Blue-Eyed Lover	128	Jal Along
61	My Love Lays Cold Beneath My Feet	129	Mandi Went to Poov the Grais
		130	The Atching Tan Song

(Collected 1962 and 1966)

HENRY HUGHES

Henry Hughes was born in 1904. Brother to William Hughes, he contributed the ballad 'Geordie' (No. 16) to this collection. (Collected 1962)

SHEILA HUGHES

Sheila Hughes is one of Caroline Hughes's daughters. She contributed the following items to this collection:

4   Lord Randal
31   If I Was a Blackbird

(Collected 1962)

WILLIAM HUGHES

William Hughes, brother to Henry and husband to Caroline, was born in 1895 in Dorset, in a horse-drawn caravan. 'All my life I been on the road. Earned my living at anything I could lay my hand to. Harvesting, bird-snaring, chair-making, baskets, dolls, wooden clothes-pegs, mat-making, horse-breaking, pullin' beets, scrap-collecting. Never harmed nobody and brought my childer up as decent as I know how.' He contributed the following songs to this collection:

76   Camden Town
121 The Little Chimney Sweep

(Collected 1962)

RUBY KELBY

Ruby Kelby (née Stewart) was born in Aberdeen in 1918. Her father was a Stewart of Kinlochrannoch and her mother is Christina MacAllister, who has contributed several songs to our collection. Her husband bears a name famous among Scots Travellers, Frank Kelby, who is son to Maggie McPhee. Mrs Kelby gave us No. 63, 'I Went to Mass on Sunday'. (Collected 1962)

CHRISTINA MACALLISTER

Christina MacAllister ('Auld Teenie') was born in 1895 at Crooten Bay, Peterhead, Aberdeenshire, one of sixteen children born to Margaret Hutchison and Donald Stewart of Carney, near Huntly. Her father was a prize-fighter of some note and is reputed to have been a skilful Highland dancer. Christina is the mother of Ruby Kelby. She gave us the following songs:

3 The Twa Sisters
53 The Braes of Strathblane
60 False, False Hae Ye Been to Me, My Love
99 The Prisoner's Song

(Collected 1962)

WILHELMINA MACALLISTER

Wilhelmina MacAllister, 'Auld Teenie's' sister, first saw the light of day in a quarry near Turriff, Aberdeenshire, in 1910. Her early childhood was spent in the Aberdeenshire fishing village of Rosehearty. Later, the family moved to Fraserburgh where she met her husband, Peter MacAllister. She now lives in Bridge of Don, Aberdeen. Her sole contribution to this collection is No. 34, 'The Courting Coat'. (Collected 1962)

JOHN MACDONALD

John MacDonald, on the occasion of our first meeting with him, described himself as a Lanrickshire (Lanarkshire) Traveller, although he was born at Tarbert, Lochfyne, a small fishing village on the coast of Argyll. Of his forebears, he said, 'As far as I'm led to believe, they all travelled – my father, my grandfather, great-grandfather and great-great-grandfather.' It was from his mother that Mr MacDonald learned his songs: 'She was a great singer – in the winter nights when you hadnae very much doing . . . they used to sit round a big fire, sheltered (for we used to put up quite a barricade) and we would sing these songs. And they'd be saying, "D'ye know this one?" or "D'ye know that one?" But it was only the ones you really took to you that you learned yoursel'. They would keep you going all night.'

Mr MacDonald continued: 'It's not that long ago since the auld men used tae gang roond Scotland – and they went from one farm to the other farm. They wore badges and ribbons in their hats. They were comedians to some extent and they told stories, played the pipes and the chanter, and they sang songs. And the fairmer would tell the cotters – the working people – to come at seven o'clock maybe and he [the auld man] would keep them going there to ten or eleven o'clock. An' ye made him a bed in the byre and in the morning the cotters would gang and prepare his breakfast.'

John MacDonald's descriptions of bothy life are based on personal experience both as a hawker who called at the bothies in order to sell his wares and as a farm-servant who, from time to time, lived in them. 'You got a pound from the fairmer for the best-groomed horse and a pound for the best-kept set o' harness. So instead of going to picters or concerts or onything like that i' the evening, you stayed in and sorted your harness and brushed your horse. That was in your ain time – no' the fairmer's time. Well, when they were a' finished wi' that, they'd jist get in the bothy and ye had boxing gloves, a set o' bagpipes, and an accordion (there wasnae sae much o' they guitars in they days) and ye had to play some o' them. And if *we* come roond aboot, we hawker-lads that sell't razors and shavin' soap and onything that would suit – well, when ye went to the door, it was, "Ah, come awa' in, man, and hae a cup o' brose!" Well, they'd gie ye brose, y'see, there'd be a great big bowl and they poured some oatmeal intae it, ta'en a kettle aff the hob and mebbe put a bit o' butter intae it and poured hot water intae it, stirred it, filled it up wi' milk, and ye supped that. And then it was, "Well, noo. Can ye sing us a sang?" "No, I'm sorry, I cannae sing." "Well, can ye play a tune on the pipes?" "No, I cannae play." "Can ye play a tune on the melodeon then?" "No." "Can ye fecht (fight)?" Well, ye got a lickin' if ye couldnae dae nane o' those things. You just had to be able to dae *something*. Mebbe ye'd tell them a joke and make them laugh and then ye'd open your pack and mebbe sell them a pair o' laces or a cake o' shavin' soap. That was Forfarshire and Angus-shire in they days if ye were a hawker-lad.'

John's wife, Betsy, is a MacDonald by birth as well as by marriage. They had fifteen children, eleven of whom survived. Mr MacDonald has contributed the following songs to this collection:

1	The Elfin Knight	78	My Father's Servant Boy
4	Lord Randal	81	Bogie's Bonnie Belle
6	Babylon	84	Jamie Foyers
14	Sir Hugh	85	The Bonnie Bunch of
17	The Braes o' Yarrow		Roses
28	MacDonald's Return to Glencoe	95	The Isle of France
37	The Jolly Barber Lad	104	The Feein' Time
43	Rosemary Lane	107	Nicky Tams
47	The Overgate	108	The Dying Ploughboy
51	Caroline of Edinburgh Town	112	Erin-go-Bragh
72	The Banks of Red Roses	127	The Moss o' Burreldale

(Collected 1969)

MAGGIE MCPHEE

Maggie McPhee (née Stewart) was born in Peterhead, Aberdeenshire, in 1889. Her father, James Stewart, was a cousin of the Stewarts of Kinlochrannoch; her mother, Betty McPhee, belonged to that large family of Travellers among whom the ability to play bagpipes is regarded as an inherited gift. 'Ay, and there were some o' the McPhee *women* played them, tae!'

In 1906, Maggie was married to William Kelby, a Traveller to whom she bore eight children and who was killed in France during the First World War. A few years later, she was married again, this time to Isaac McPhee, a cousin. To him, also, she bore eight children. One's first impression of Mrs McPhee is of a frail old lady, but that impression is banished when she opens her mouth to tell a story or sing a song. From that moment on, one is conscious only of her tremendous, irrepressible zest for living.

She has contributed the following songs to this collection:

19	The Gaberlunzie Man	42	My Father was Hung for
21	The Laird of the Denty		Sheep-Stealing
	Doon Bye	46	Where Gadie Rins
25	Sweet William	69	The Bonnie Green Tree
27	The Sailor's Return	79	Locks and Bolts
29	The Lass o' Glencoe	90	Whiskey in the Jar
39	Featherin' Oot and In	106	The Hash o' Bennygak
41	Aye She Likit the Ae Nicht	109	Sheelicks
		127	The Moss o' Burreldale

(Collected 1962)

BIG WILLIE MCPHEE

Big Willie McPhee (known as 'The Blacksmith') was born in Helensborough, a coast town of Dunbartonshire, in 1910. He was one of thirteen children, only five of whom survived infancy. From his father he learned basket-making and tinsmithing: 'I done that for years. I still make baskets yet, but I dinna mak' tin stuff any more because ye canna sell the stuff noo, there's too much plastic. It's twenty-five years since I stoppit making tin but I've still got my tools.'

Willie started work when he was ten years old, 'helpin' my mither, hawkin', gaitherin' tatties and shawin' turnips, and so forth. I've been at it ever since and I'm no richer.' He claims to have done every kind of farm work 'even plooin' [ploughing] though I've never plooed wi' tractors, aye horses. I've gaithered clover-stones for a shilling an acre. It's surprising the amount of ground that stones take up in a clover-field. I worked for a mairket-gairdener grawing' a' kinds o' vegetables. I've built stacks [haystacks], picked berries and in Dunfermline I workit as a blacksmith.'

In the summer months, Willie earns a precarious living as an itinerant piper. His beat covers a large area – from Aberfoyle in Perthshire to Ross and Cromarty in the northwest. He is married and has seven children, one of whom plays the pipes and often accompanies his father busking. Mr McPhee contributed two songs to this collection:

52 The Maid of the Sweet Brown Knowe
97 Big Jimmie Drummond

(Collected 1975)

NELSON RIDLEY

Nelson Ridley was born in 1913 in Wineham, Kent. His father, Alfred Ridley, and his mother, Louisa Jems, were both Kent Travellers. Nelson was one of sixteen children, all but one of whom reached adult age. Their names roll off his tongue like a litany: 'Ingmay, he was the oldest, we lost him three years ago. Then there was Noah, then Absalom, then Joseph – my oldest brother still alive. And there was Isaac and Valentine. The girls were Mary, Ina, Fanny, Jane, Mary-Anne, Louise, Betsy and Charity. Isaac played the jews-harp and the mouth-organ and Noah, he played the violin. He just went out one day and bought a violin and learned it hisself. But we could all sing, my father used to set and sing to us when he had a pint or two and we would set and listen to him and we picked up his songs.'

Nelson said that his considerable repertoire of songs was learned before he reached the age of twelve and he hadn't learned a song since then. Of the eight sons and seven daughters born to him and his wife, eleven are still alive and, like their parents, they are all Travellers. Most of Nelson's travelling had been in Surrey and Kent. He was living on a municipal caravan-site in Harlow New Town, Essex, and he died there in late 1975. He has contributed the following songs:

2	Lady Isabel and the Elf Knight	38	The Molecatcher
8	Young Beichan	45	The Lady and the Soldier
11	Bonny Barbara Allen	48	The Oyster Girl
16	Geordie	49	Eggs in her Basket
18	The Jolly Beggar	56	The Blacksmith
20	Brake of Briars	68	The Banks of Sweet Primroses
23	Long A-Growing	76	Camden Town
25	Sweet William	77	Erin's Lovely Home
26	The Dark-Eyed Sailor	83	*The Rainbow*
32	The Yellow Handkerchief	85	The Bonnie Bunch of Roses
35	The Walnut Girl	87	The Deserter from Kent

(Collected 1974)

MARIA ROBERTSON

Maria Robertson was born in 1930 in Bridge of Don, Aberdeen. Her father, David Robertson, a brother of Jeannie Robertson (the well-known Aberdeen ballad-singer) is known among Travellers as 'The Iron Man', a title bestowed upon him during the time he worked the boxing booths at fairs and markets. We met Maria at the home of Wilhelmina MacAllister and only recorded her for an hour, during which she sang us five traditional songs and 'yen I made up the day'. She has contributed the following items to this book:

(Collected 1962)

LEVI SMITH

Levi Smith was born on Epsom Downs in 1915. His family, he says, has always been associated with Epsom and one of his brothers was christened 'Derby' in honour of the famous horse-race of that name. Like most of the southern English Travellers he prefers to travel in a comparatively small area. In his case, this is mainly Surrey and Kent. When we recorded him, his caravan was parked on the grass verge of the Croydon–Westerham road. Since that time he has been evicted and is now almost certainly constantly on the move. He has contributed two songs to this collection:

(Collected 1971)

JEANNIE THOMPSON

Jeannie Thompson was born in 1904, one of eleven children born to John Stewart, a small-holder of Kinlochrannoch, and Nancy Campbell, a travelling woman. The Stewarts of Kinlochrannoch produced many distinguished pipers; Jeannie's great-grandfather was piper to the Duke of Argyll and John Stewart, her father, served the Duke of Athol and, later, Lord Dudley in the same capacity. All who knew her mother, Nancy, agree that she was a singer of tremendous ability and a compelling story-teller. It was from her that Jeannie, like her brother Alec and his wife Belle, learned many of their songs and stories. Jeannie married Sammy Thompson, a Traveller from the Belfast area, and finally settled in Montrose, Perthshire, where she died in 1972. She has contributed the following pieces to this collection:

8   Young Beichan
12   The Lowlands of Holland
124   Twa and Twa

(Collected 1962)

THE SONGS

CHILD BALLADS

1   THE ELFIN KNIGHT
(Child 2)

Professor Child emphasises the antiquity of riddling and setting impossible tasks by putting the riddling ballads at the beginning of his collection. His work on 'The Elfin Knight' quotes antecedent stories and ballad analogues. Frazer summarises the function of riddling as 'the expression of the conflict between a life-force and a death-force in a potentially fertile situation' (i.e., courtship, planting, harvesting, and so on). In most versions of the ballad the contest does, indeed, take place between two lovers. Despite the fact that seven of Child's texts are given the title 'The Devil's Courtship', the devil himself does not appear as a protagonist in any of them although there *are* elements of the supernatural in the person of an *elphin knight* or an 'old, old man'. John MacDonald's actual naming of the devil is unusual.

The ballad first appeared in print in this form in 1670. So many versions have been printed and so much research has been done since that time that even to give a short précis of the folkloristic content, the proliferation of secondary and children's forms, the alliterative alterations of both verse and refrain poetry, would run into volumes. MacDonald's song stands out chiefly for its mention of the devil and for certain turns of phrase such as 'the sting of an adder' and 'one blink o' sun'. Despite the variety of tasks mentioned in the Child texts, these particular ones do not appear in them. It is possible that they are transliterations of such phrases as 'strap of leather' or 'one peppercorn', but if that is so, then MacDonald's text has the effect of making the impossible task even more difficult.

The 'plaidie awa'' motif, which appears in so many Scots songs, usually signifies the loss of virginity.

BIBLIOGRAPHY

Child 2 (see also Additions and Corrections); Bronson, vol. I and Appendix; Coffin, pp. 23–4.

British Bruce and Stokoe, pp. 79–80; Greig, No. 100; Halliwell (1), No. 475; *JFSS*, vol. I, p. 83; also vol. II, pp. 212–13; also vol. III, pp. 12–16 and 274–5; *JEFDSS*, vol. VIII, p. 26; Kennedy, p. 656; Kidson, pp. 42–4 and 172; Kidson and Moffat (1), p. 48; O'Lochlainn (2), pp. 196–7; Opie (1), pp. 108–9 and 165; Reeves (1), p. 243; *Rymour*, vol. I, p. 201; *Scottish Studies*, vol. IX, pp. 4–8; Sharp (1), pp. 119–21; Sharp and Karpeles (2), vol. I, pp. 1–3; Stokoe and Reay, pp. 54–5.

North American Carey, p. 93; Moore, pp. 6–10; Peacock, vol. I, pp. 6–8; Thompson, pp. 422–3.

General Frazer (under Riddling); Wimberly (under Riddling), also pp. 294–5.

'Blaw, Ye Winds, Blaw', sung by John MacDonald. This tune is almost identical to Bronson's 'Twa Sisters' (Child 10), Group A, No. 4. See also his Appendix to Child 10, No. 13.2. The most distinctive feature of our tune is its final cadence, which is not common to those versions of the melody which share the form, the first three cadences and the mode.

1 For there once was a fair maid went a-walk,
   Blaw, blaw, blaw ye winds blaw;
  Ay, between yon salt sea and yon sea strand,
   And the dreary wind's blawed my plaidie awa'.

2 For as she met a devil by the way,
   Blaw, blaw, blaw ye winds blaw;
  And to her he did give a task,
   And the dreary winds did blaw her plaidie awa'.*

3 For you'll make to me a holland shirt (etc.)
  Without either seam or needle-work (etc.)

4 For you'll wash it up in yon draw-well,
  Where there never was water or a dew-drop fell.

5 For it's when I do that task for you,
  Surely you'll do one for me.

6 For you'll fence to me three acres of land,
  Ay, between yon salt sea and yon sea strand.

7 For you'll plough it up wi' a double ram's horn,
  Sow it o'er wi' one peck o' corn.

8 For you'll harrow it o'er wi' a tree o' black thorn,
  And ye'll reap it up wi' one blink o' sun.

9 For you'll shear it down wi' a pea-hen feather,
  And you'll stook it up wi' a stang o' a nether,   (sting of an adder)

10 For you'll yoke two sparrows in a match-box,
  And you'll cart it home to my own farmyard.

11 For it's when you do that task for me,
  You come back and you'll get your sark,
   And the dreary winds'll blaw my plaidie awa'.

* The use of 'my' and 'her' in the final line of the refrain, and the tense of the verb 'blaw', seem to depend on the sense of the verse-lines. Occasionally Mr MacDonald omitted the first refrain line, the verse thus consisting of a rhymed couplet and the final refrain line, as in verse 11.

2 LADY ISABEL AND THE ELF KNIGHT
(Child 4)

The earliest printed text of this ballad, which is commonly known as 'The Outlandish Knight', is a German broadside (c. 1550). The story is, of course, much older and most European countries have yielded variants of it either in the form of a ballad or a folktale. The most exhaustive and definitive work dealing with it has been done by Holger Hyard. Subsequent research inevitably refers the reader to this study, and useful notes are to be found in the definitive collections. Having enjoyed a long life in print the ballad is widespread throughout the English-speaking world, and numerous parodies of it may be found. Our fragment does not tell the whole story, that of a girl outwitting and killing her lover whose intention is to murder her.

BIBLIOGRAPHY

Child 4; Bronson, vol. I and Appendix; Coffin, pp. 25–8.

British Bell (Robert), pp. 142–4; Bruce and Stokoe, pp. 48–50; Dixon and Bell, pp. 61–4; Greig and Keith, pp. 2–4; Hamer, pp. 50–1; *Henry Collection*, No. 163; *JFSS*, vol. II, pp. 282–5; Kidson, pp. 26–9; Morton, pp. 21–3; Sharp (2), vol. I, pp. 29–31; Stokoe and Reay, pp. 130–1; Williams, pp. 159–61.

North American *Folklore Fellows* Communication No. 169 ('The Ballad of Heer Halewijn', by Holger Hyard); Fowke, pp. 102–4; *JAF*, vol. 85, No. 335, pp. 32–41; Karpeles (2), pp. 23–4; Peacock, vol. I, pp. 206–7.

General Wimberly, pp. 137–8.

'Don't Prittle Nor Prattle', sung by Nelson Ridley. The tune is characteristic of those found in the Bronson A-category (roughly between numbers 26 and 40), but none of these similar versions contain our two odd second and third phrases which end on the II interval. Some of the later A-category types contain a mid-cadence ending on II (notably Nos 75–90) but these tunes are not very similar to Ridley's.

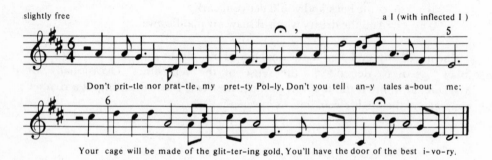

slightly free   a I (with inflected I)

Don't prit-tle nor prat-tle, my pret-ty Pol-ly, Don't you tell an-y tales a-bout me;

Your cage will be made of the glit-ter-ing gold, You'll have the door of the best i-vo-ry.

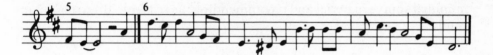

1   Don't prittle nor prattle, my pretty Polly,
     Don't you tell any tales about me;
     Your cage will be made of the glittering gold,
     You'll have the door of the best ivory.

2   Now, you go and get me your father's bright gold,
     Then likewise your own mother's money;
     Your cage will be made of the glittering gold,
     You'll have a door of the best ivory.

3   Now you go and get me your father's bright gold,
     (To the stables remounted I'm told);
     For the gold it will waste and your silver may shine,
     You'll have the door of the best ivory.

3   THE TWA SISTERS
(Child 10)

Bronson has suggested that versions of this ballad with the rare 'swan swims' refrain are associated with Celtic communities. Our text lacks certain vital story elements, notably the basic conflict of jealousy between sisters. In most versions, there is a young man (seemingly intended for the older sister) who prefers the younger sister. Our text begins instead with the invitation to walk and omits the high point of the action in which the younger sister is pushed into the water. This omission is balanced by the presence of the 'singing bones' motif which is absent from many other texts.

The earliest printed version of the ballad, in English, dates back to 1656, a broadside entitled 'The Miller and the King's Daughter'. Of Norwegian extraction, this ballad is full of vestigial primitive beliefs, ritual and superstition. Wherever it has travelled, it has picked up the speech-patterns and social mores of the communities in which it is sung. It exists as a folktale, a ballad and a children's piece. It is found in Great Britain, North America, the Scandinavian countries, the Balkans and throughout western Europe. It has so many variations in poetic style, presentation, length, characterisation and general structure that we are only listing minimal source material and recommending the reader to Brewster's main study.

BIBLIOGRAPHY

Child 10; Bronson, vol. I and Appendix; Coffin, pp. 32–6.

British Bell (Robert), pp. 206–10; Bruce and Stokoe, pp. 61–3; Ford (2), vol. II, pp. 189–94; Greig and Keith, pp. 9–13; *JFSS*, vol. II, pp. 283–6; also vol. VIII, pp. 249–50; Ord, pp. 430–2; *Rymour*, vol. I, p. 200; *Scottish Studies*, vol. I, pp. 126–7.

North American Carey, pp. 93–5; *Dusenbury MSS*, No. 41 11a; *Folklore Fellows* Communication No. 147 ('The Two Sisters', by Paul G. Brewster); Moore, pp. 18–21; Peacock, vol. I, pp. 179–80.

'The Swan it Swims Sae Bonnie, O', sung by Christina MacAllister. The text type of this ballad is in Bronson's D-group, but the tune type is his A-category. The cadences, however, are not generally in keeping with the A-group tunes. Strangely enough, the closest match in fourth-line cadence is in Group E No. 89. This, however, is an aI tune, so that ending on the C would be a natural ending. None of Bronson's pAE or pAE/D tunes end, as ours does, on the lower III.

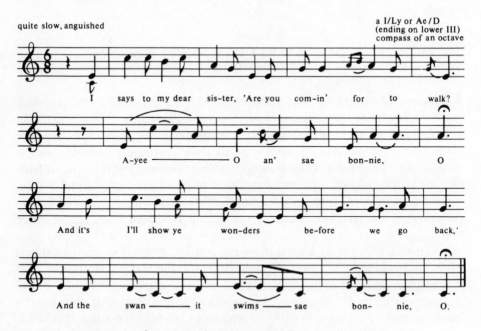

1   I says to my dear sister, 'Are ye comin' for to walk?
           Ayee, O an' sae bonnie, O;
       And it's I'll show you wonders before we go back,'
           And the swan it swims sae bonnie, O.

2   Put your foot on (like) a marble stone
        Ayee, O an' sae bonnie, O;
    And I'll show ye wonders before ye go home,
        And the swan it swims sae bonnie, O.

3   But miller, O miller, come dry up your dam (etc.)
    For I see a maid all white like a swan (etc.)

4   But the miller he quickly, he dried the dam,
    And he took out the maid all white like swan.

5   He took out the maid and he hung her up to dry
    And there was three fiddlers passin' by.

6   There was one of them that took three lengths o' her hair
        Ayee, O an' sae bonnie, O;
    There was anither of them took her breast bone,
        And the swan it swims sae bonnie, O.
    There to make a fiddle-head to play a tune upon,
        And the swan it swims sae bonnie, O.

7   But those three fiddlers was playing' gaun along
    Until they come to the castle so high.

8   But fiddlers, sweet fiddlers, and let them be gaun,
    Out then it speaks her father, the king,
        Ayee O an' sae bonnie, O;
    And out then it speaks her father, says to Jean
        And the swan it swims sae bonnie, O.

Note: From Willie Kelby and a Mr White, on a different occasion, we obtained an almost identical text until verse 8. Their text concluded thus:

8   There sits my father the king (etc.)
    And there sits my mother, the queen (etc.)

9   And there sits my false sister, Jean
    Wha drowned me against the stream.

4   LORD RANDAL
(Child 12)

This is perhaps one of the most popular and varied of all the Child ballads. Anne Gilchrist, in an interesting note (*JFSS*, vol. III), suggests a possible connection between the ballad and the story of Ranulph (Randal III) the Sixth Earl of Chester, who died in 1232 and was succeeded by his nephew, John, whose wife (according to legend) attempted to poison her husband.

Versions of the ballad have been found in Italy, Spain, Czechoslovakia, Hungary, Germany, Holland, Iceland and Sweden. The forms in which it is found vary greatly in matters of detail. It is a masterpiece of the stychomythic form and its splendid economical structure must have played no small part in the ballad's struggle for survival.

In the Anglo-American tradition, the ballad occurs in a number of distinct forms. These are:

1   The 'Lord Randal' type (Child A, B and C), of which our A-text gives a skeletal example. A young man is questioned by his mother as to where he dined and with whom. He usually says that he was with his sweetheart. It transpires that he has been poisoned, as have his dogs who ate the leavings of the meal. Before dying he bequeaths his belongings to his father, mother, sister, brother – and some deadly gift or legacy to his sweetheart.

These versions generally go under a title involving some form of the hero's name (Lord Donald, Ronald, Jimmy Randolph, Lordeno, etc.). Occasionally there are such titles as 'O Mak My Bed Easy', 'Three Drops of Poison', etc.

The complete plot as given above has been reported from England, Ireland and North America, but it is from Scotland that the most comprehensive texts have been recovered.

2   The 'legacy' type, most common to North America. In this form, the naming of the food, the identity of the poisoner and enquiry regarding the fate of the dogs are generally absent. The core of the ballad lies instead in the distribution of the dying man's property. The titles in this group are as in the 'Lord Randal' family.

3   The 'Henry, My Son' type, of which our B text is a good example. Here the treatment is neither completely serious nor wholly comic. It deals in a simplified way with the pre-deathbed dialogue and names the poisoner as grandmother, step-mother, gypsy, mother, but rarely sweetheart. In some cases there is no poison, the death being by misadventure. This form is most commonly found among urban children in England.

4   The 'lullabye' type, of which Child's J to O texts are examples. As

with 'Henry, My Son', these deal with the questioning concerning the poisoning, the death of the dog, the identity of the poisoner, who is either a step-mother or grandmother. The mood of the piece is one of sadness and resignation. Titles for this group are usually variants of 'Wee Croodlin Doo', 'Willie Doo', etc. Most examples of this type are Scots, although occasional texts turn up in North America.

5   The 'Billy Boy', type, which Bronson describes as 'a spirited parody of "Lord Randal"'. In this family, the young man, questioned by his mother about his courtship, describes his sweetheart's knack for creating havoc in house, kitchen, sewing-box and bed. There is no poisoning, no legacy, only laughs.

There are, in addition, types which combine elements from all these categories. The most consistent features are the question and answer motif, the eating and poisoning, the legacy and death.

BIBLIOGRAPHY

Child 12; Bronson, vol. I and Appendix; Coffin, pp. 36–9.

British   Bell (Robert), pp. 210–11; Greig, No. 112; Halliwell (1), No. 476; Halliwell (2), pp. 252–7; Hamer, pp. 76–7; *Hammond MSS*, D–134; *Henry Collection*, No. 814; *JFSS*, vol. II, pp. 29–32; also vol. III, pp. 43–4; also vol. V, pp 117–23 and 244–8; *JEFDSS*, vol. V, pp. 15–16; also vol. VI, p. 15; also vol. VIII, p. 210; Joyce (2), No. 812; *Museum*, vol. IV, No. 327; Opie (1), p. 75–80; Purslow (3), p. 69; *Rymour*, vol. I, pp. 200–1; *Scottish Studies*, vol. XIV, pp. 39–40 and pp. 162–3; Sharp (2), vol. I, pp. 98–9; also vol. II, pp. 2–3; Sharp and Karpeles (2), vol. I, pp. 17–26; Sharp and Marson, pp. 46–9.

North American   Carey, pp. 114–15; Creighton and Senior (1), pp. 22–4; *Dusenbury MSS*, No. 57 17b; Moore, pp. 21–4.

A. 'Lord Ronald', sung by John MacDonald. This tune is of the 'Villikens and Dinah' type mentioned by Bronson as the basis for his subgroup Ab. It is unusual in two of its features: (a) it is a three- rather than four-line form, and the telescoping of the usual format gives an effect of starkness and urgency; (b) all three lines end on the tonic. Several of the Bronson Aa-group versions contain three tonic cadences, usually on the first, second and fourth lines. Our tune is closest in cadential similarity to Bronson's Appendix versions Nos 43.2 and 69.1, both from Scots sources, but if a close similarity had to be drawn to any one Bronson tune it would be in the Aa-group between Nos 13 and 19.

B. 'Henry, My Son', sung by Sheila Hughes. This tune belongs in Bronson's Bb-category.

A.

1 Where have you been hunting, Lord Ronald, my son?
I've been hunting wild geese, Mother, make my bed soon.
For I'm weary, weary hunting, and I fain would lie doon.

2 What had you for your supper, Lord Ronald, my son?
I'd a cup full of honey, Mother, make my bed soon.
For I'm weary, weary hunting, ay, and fain would lie doon.

3 What brought ye to your mother, Lord Ronald, my son?
All my household and furniture, Mother, make my bed soon.
For I'm weary, weary huntin', ay, and fain would lie doon.

4 What brought ye to your sweetheart, Lord Ronald, my son?
I brought a rope for to hang her, Mother, make my bed soon.
For I'm weary, weary hunting, and fain would lie doon.

B.

1   Where have you been all day, Henry my son?
     Where have you been all day, my beloved one?
     Fields, dear mother,
     Fields, dear mother;

Chorus: I have pains in my head and I want to go to bed,
         And I want to go to sleep.

2   What have you had to eat, Henry my son?
     What have you had to eat, my beloved one?
     Snakes, dear mother,
     Snakes, dear mother; (chorus)

3   What do you want to drink, (etc.)
     Poison (etc.), (chorus)

4   How many pillows, (etc.)
     One (etc.), (chorus)

5 EDWARD
(Child 13)

Child prints two texts of this ballad. His A-text, from Motherwell, is a story of fratricide and the killer is 'son Davie'. His B-text deals with parricide and the killer is named 'Edward'. This second text is rather literary and appears not to have entered the oral tradition. Nevertheless, it has given its name to the ballad family.

The A-text is similar to ours, but its final verses are reminiscent of those that conclude 'Lord Randal' (Child 12). Legacies, not of property but of woe, are bequeathed to Davie's wife and son. The worst fate is reserved for his mother who, it is implied, was the original instigator of the crime:

> What wilt thou leave to thy mother dear,
> > Son Davie, Son Davie?
> A fire o' coals to burn her, wi' hearty cheer,
> > And she'll never get mair o' me.

This text changes form in verses 7, 10 and 12. Instead of one speaker per verse throughout (as in Mrs Robertson's set) it changes to the stychomythic form at key points.

On the whole, 'Edward' is a somewhat rare ballad. It has been reported infrequently from Britain and Ireland but rather more often from North America. Child mentions that 'the ballad has been familiarly known to have an exact counterpart in Swedish' with Finnish derivatives. Archer Taylor, in an oft-quoted article entitled 'Edward and Sven I Rosengard' (see Coffin), has advanced the theory that the Scandinavian analogues owe their origin to British texts.

A quick glance over the Bronson texts provides an insight into what has happened to the ballad in the course of its migration. All but one of the versions quoted are North American. In all of them the subject is fratricide. The name of the son is not given, the form of the burden nearly always being 'My son, come tell to me', 'Son, pray tell it to me', etc. The chief variations are in small details, such as the excuses given by the son as to the source of the blood (a grey hawk, a hound dog, an old grey mare, a gross hog, etc.). In these versions the boy-murderer leaves his child(ren) to his parents. Accompanied by his wife, he sets foot in a bottomless boat, swearing to return 'When the sun and moon shall set in yonders east', or a similar nevermore-concept. These verses are more common to the incest ballad 'Lizie Wan' (Child 51), which shares several plot and motif features with 'Edward'. None of the American versions implicate the mother as a catalyst in the fraternal conflict.

BIBLIOGRAPHY

Child 13; Bronson, vol. I and Appendix; Coffin, pp. 39–40.

British *JEFDSS*, vol. VI, p. 99; also vol. VII, p. 38 and pp. 128–30; *Scottish Studies*, vol. XIV, pp. 41–2 and 170–1.

North American Moore, pp. 24–5.

'My Son David', sung by Maria Robertson. This tune is almost identical to Bronson's Appendix version 3.1, which puts the melody in his A-category. It would seem not to be a common tune for the ballad.

Note: Mrs Robertson uses many mordants and often slides up to a note. Bar 5 is often omitted completely.

1   What's the blood that's on your sword?
      Hey son David, Ho son David,
  What's the blood that's on your sword?
      Come promise, tell me true.

2   That's the blood of my grey mare,
      Yes lady Mother, ay, lady Mother,
  That's the blood of my grey mare,
      Because it wadna rule by me.

3   That blood is far too clear,
         Hey son David, Ho son David,
    That blood is far too clear,
         Come promise, tell me true.

4   That's the blood of my hunting hack,
         Yes lady Mother, ay, lady Mother,
    That's the blood of my hunting hack,
         Because it wadna rule by me.

5   That blood is far too clear,
         Hey son David, Ho son David,
    That blood is far too clear,
         Come promise, tell me true.

6   That's the blood of my brother John,
         Yes lady Mother, ay, lady Mother,
    That's the blood of my brother John,
         When he drew his sword to me.

7   What way did youse fall out?
         Hey son David, Ho son David,
    What way did youse fall out?
         Come promise, tell me true.

8   It was the cuttin' o' a silly wand,
         A silly wand,
   'Twas the cuttin' o' a silly wand
         When he drew his sword to me.

9   I'm gaun awa' in a bottomless boat,
         In a bottomless boat,
   I'm gaun awa' in a bottomless boat,
         And a good scholar I'll come hame.

6 BABYLON
(Child 14)

Child reports variants of this story from Denmark, Sweden, Iceland, Norway and the Faroes. His five texts of the ballad are all Scots, all quite complete and all in roughly the same form as that given here. From his A-text (in which the brother's name is 'Baby Lon') comes the rather confusing title above. Of the five versions, it is this A-text which has a refrain most similar to ours: 'On the bonnie, bonnie banks o' Fordie'. The other four texts have burdens in which the main motif is 'dew on the woods', or dew on a tree or flower.

Coffin states that the ballad is rare in North America. In the last five or six years, Scots collectors have encountered it with increasing frequency. In form, the ballad has been fairly consistent since Child and usually consists of four basic dramatic units: (1) the setting of the scene, (2) the approach of the robber, (3) the repeated sequence of question-and-answer between the robber and the sisters, (4) a repentance, or suicide, verse acting as dénouement. The variations from version to version seem to have centred on the name and description of the robber, on the dénouement (either suicide or repentance of the robber or his death at the hands of the girls' brother), and on the actual wording of the refrain lines.

In nearly all the versions, a quatrain consists of verse-lines interlaced with refrain-lines. John MacDonald has substituted a repeated verse-line for the first refrain-line, a form unprecedented in any of the printed texts.

BIBLIOGRAPHY

Child 14; Bronson, vol. I and Appendix; Coffin, pp. 40–1.

British   Buchan and Hall, pp. 82–3; Greig and Keith, p. 15; *Rymour*, vol. II, pp. 77–9; *Scottish Studies*, vol. IX, pp. 19–22.

North American   Karpeles (1), pp. 78–82; Karpeles (2), pp. 27–9; Peacock, vol. III, pp. 809–11.

(untitled), sung by John MacDonald. This tune is almost identical with Bronson's A-group No. 6. It also is closely related to many of the 'Hind Horn' tunes (Bronson, Child 17).

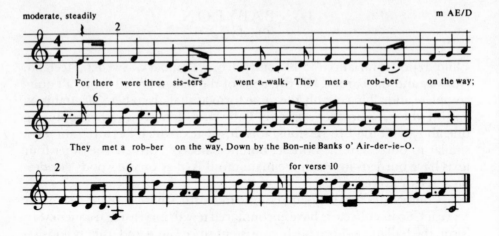

moderate, steadily   m AE/D

For there were three sis-ters went a-walk, They met a rob-ber on the way;

They met a rob-ber on the way, Down by the Bon-nie Banks o' Air-der-ie-O.

for verse 10

1   For there were three sisters went a-walk,
     They met a robber on the way;
     They met a robber on the way,
        Down by the Bonnie Banks o' Airderie-O.

2   He took the first one by the hand,
     He twirled her round till he made her stand;
     He twirled her round till he made her stand,
        Down by the Bonnie Banks o' Airderie-O.

3   It's will you be a robber's wife?
     Or will you die by my penknife?
     Or will you die by my penknife?
        Down (etc.)

4   It's I'll no' be a robber's wife,
     But I will die by your penknife,
     O, I will die by your penknife, (etc.)

5   He catched the second one by the hand,
     He twirled her round till he made her stand,
     It's will you be a robber's wife? (etc.)

6   It's I'll no' be a robber's wife.
     But I will die by your penknife;
     But I will die by your penknife, (etc.)

7   He catched the third one by the hand,
     He twirled her round till he made her stand;
     He twirled her round till he made her stand, (etc.)

8   It's will you be a robber's wife?
Or will you die by my penknife? ·
Or will you die by my penknife? (etc.)

9   If my two brothers was here this night,
You wadna be sae keen and bright;
If my two brothers was here this night, (etc.)

10   What does your two brothers do?
The one is James and the other is John;
The one is a minister, the tither's like you, (etc.)

11   Ah, my God, what have I done?
I've kilt my three sisters all but one;
I've kilt my three sisters all but one, (etc.)

7 THE BROOMFIELD HILL
(Child 43)

This ballad has a long and intricate history. It has been developing in this form since the mid-1500s and has hidden treasures of folk-belief and superstition. It is related to a large family of songs and stories found throughout western Europe.

To match our text with any of Professor Child's would prove an almost impossible task. Even to understand the basic story from our five verses would mean juggling lines from stanza to stanza, changing tense and gender, inserting absent verses and motifs. The full story tells of a girl who has been challenged to meet her lover on the top of a hill and return home a virgin. In some versions she consults a witch before embarking upon her task. In other versions she administers a sleeping-potion to her lover and then goes off to the hill armed only with her own courage. Upon arriving at the trysting-place, she finds her lover asleep, lays broom at his head and feet, then walks three (seven, nine) times around his feet or head. After leaving a token to prove she has met the terms of the wager, she hides behind a bush of broom in order to observe her lover's reaction. The young man, on discovering the token, turns enraged upon his steed, his hawk, his hound, and demands to know why they did not wake him. They reply that their attempts to do so elicited no response. He laments that had he been awake instead of asleep he would have had his will of her or else the small birds would have had their fill of her blood. Sometimes a final verse depicts the girl running merrily back to town.

This basic plot (which does not pretend to give all the details found in various texts) has naturally undergone considerable modifications in the many variants found in Britain, Ireland and North America. Such modifications involve substitutions, subtractions, additions and alterations such as can only be produced by the same forces in the folk process that have wrought such havoc in Mrs Hughes's set.

Our final verse is a curious one. It does not appear in any of the Child texts and is rarely found in British texts, with the notable exception of the Gillington text, recorded from Hampshire gypsies. It would seem at first to have been borrowed from another song – but this murder-motif has also been found in several American versions of 'The Broomfield Hill'. In these latter texts, the speaker is the *girl* who, from her hiding-place, upon hearing her lover threatening to dispense her body to the wild birds, comments:

> O, hard-hearted young man, O hard-hearted youth,
> Your heart is just as hard as any stone;
> For to think of killing one who has loved you so long
> And would mourn o'er the grave you lie in.

BIBLIOGRAPHY

Child 43; Bronson, vol. I and Appendix; Coffin, pp. 51–2.

British Bell (Robert), pp. 297–300; *Gardiner MSS*, Hp-725 and Hp-546; Gillington, pp. 18–19; Greig and Keith, pp. 31–32; *Henry Collection*, No. 135; *JFSS*, vol. III, p. 69; also vol. IV, pp. 110–16; also vol. VII, pp. 31–3; also vol. VIII, pp. 127–8; *JEFDSS*, vol. IX, pp. 187–8; Purslow (4), p. 11; Sharp and Karpeles (2), vol. I, pp. 35–40.

North American see Coffin.

General Wimberly, pp. 300–1 and 354—5.

(untitled), sung by Caroline Hughes. This tune fits into Bronson's C-group and is almost identical with No. 15, collected from Hampshire gypsies by Alice Gillington. It is unusual in this group to have the second and third cadences ending on the II interval.

fairly fast, lilting
Verse 2*   m I

O, for I laid my-self down in a bon-nie bunch of (blue)

And lis-tened to what my true- love had to say,

In- stead of be-ing a- sleep, love, you should have been a- wake,

I'd have known the deeds the false young man had done.

*The melody does not stabilise until the second verse.

1   O, a wager, a wager, a wager I'll bet on you,
I'll bet you fifty guineas to your one:
That you sha'n't rise and kiss her before she's gone to clay
For (her) true love's been here, but now (he's) gone.   (your?) (she's?)

2   O, for I laid myself down in a bonnie bunch of (blue)   (broom?)
And listened to what my true love had to say,
Instead of being asleep, love, you should have been awake,
I'd have known the deeds the false young man had done.

3   O, it's three times that he walked around the soles of her shoe,
Three times around the crowning of her hair;
O, it's you I'm going to kill and your blood I'm going to spill,
And let the little wild birds have their fill.

4   O, where is he now, my running faithful dog,
The dog as I been running with before?
It's you I have killed and his blood I'm going to spill
And we'll let these little wild birds have their fill.

[65]

5   O, what a hard-hearted young man, what a heart he must have had,
    He must have had a heart like any stone!
    For murdering of the young girl that he dearly, dearly loved
    And he doted on the green grass she walked on.

8   YOUNG BEICHAN

(Child 53)

Mrs Thompson's version of this well-known ballad begins in the middle of the story, the antecedent action of which runs thus: a young lord, thirsting for adventure, goes abroad and is taken prisoner by the Turks. He complains of his fate and is overheard by the daughter of his captor, who frees him and supplies him with provisions, a horse and a dog. They exchange vows of love and loyalty, swearing that neither will marry other partners for seven years. At the end of the allotted time she sets out to find him and arrives at his door on his wedding day.

The ballad has affinities with 'Hind Horn' (Child 17) in which the hero returns after years of absence only to discover that his love has just married another. There are European analogues in which story elements cross and combine with each other. The Child texts vary considerably not only in length but in specific content; in motifs and poetic style as well, these versions display considerable variety. There is, for example, an amusing turn in Child's M-text, in which Young Bondwell offers the girl a substitute:

> Five-hundred pounds to you I'll gie
> Of gowd an white monie
> If ye'll wed John, my ain cousin
> He looks as fair as me.

In a Tennessee version this sum has been inflated to £90,000!

In two of Child's texts there is a magical personage: Billy Blin, or a woman in green, awakens the Turkish girl and announces that her love's wedding day has arrived and that she must go and claim him. The girl is told to dress herself in her finest clothing and proceed to the shore where a ship awaits her. She is immediately transported to her love's door. This feature does not appear to have survived in any of the traditional versions.

BIBLIOGRAPHY

Child 53; Bronson, vol. I and Appendix; Coffin, pp. 58–60.

British   Bell (Robert), pp. 144–51; Broadwood, p. 43; Broadwood and Maitland, pp. 62–3; Bruce and Stokoe, pp. 64–70; Christie, vol. I, pp. 8–9; Crawhall, pp. 3–25; Greig, No. 78; Greig and Keith, pp. 40–3; *Henry Collection*, No. 470; *JFSS*, vol. I, pp. 240–1; also vol. III, pp. 192–200; also vol. VII, p. 315; *JEFDSS*, vol. VIII, pp. 23–5; Joyce (2), No. 617; Kidson, pp. 32–6; Kidson and Moffat (2), pp. 8–9; Logan, pp. 11–18; *Rymour*, vol. I, p. 114; Sharp (2), vol. I, pp. 17–19; Sharp and Karpeles (2), vol. I, pp. 43–51; Williams, pp. 147–9.

North American   *Dusenbury MSS*, No. 42 11b; Karpeles (1), pp. 88–92; Karpeles (2), pp. 42–6; Moore, pp. 41–3; Peacock, vol. I, pp. 210–13.

General   Davis (3), pp. 158–71.

A. 'Lord Bateman', sung by Jeannie Thompson. The melodies for this ballad are extraordinarily consistent, as may be seen by these two tunes collected 600 miles apart, one from an Englishman, the other from a Scot. Bronson, in his introductory note to the ballad, virtually lumps all the tunes together, making his distinction between them chiefly on the cadence of the second phrase. Both our versions end their second phrase on the II interval, this being the second most popular mid-cadential ending. Mrs Thompson's tune is to be found in Group Ab (between Nos 64 and 85).

B. (untitled), sung by Nelson Ridley, whose tune is in Group Aa, between Nos 19 and 34.

A.

moderate, rather free
p I (with inflected VII)

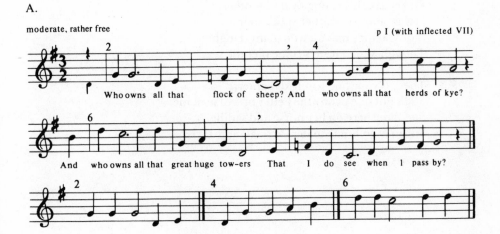

Who owns all that flock of sheep? And who owns all that herds of kye?
And who owns all that great huge tow-ers That I do see when I pass by?

1   Who owns all that flock of sheep?
And who owns all that herds of kye?
And who owns all that great huge towers
That I do see when I pass by?

2   Lord Bateman owns all these flocks of sheep,
Lord Bateman owns all these herds of kye;
Lord Bateman owns all these great high towers
That we do see as we pass by.

3   What news, what news, now, my little page?
What news, what news do you bring to me?

. . . .

. . . .

4   There are a lady all at your gate, sir;
And the beat of her I did never see,
For there are as much gold all around her body
As would buy your kingdom and another three.

5   She said to send out one bit of your wedding bread,
And one glass of your wedding wine;
And to ne'er forget of a fair young lady
That did release you from close confine.

6   He kicked the table all with his foot,
The cups and saucers he made them flee;
I'll bet any man now my lands and kingdom
It's Susie Pirate from o'er the sea.

7   Out speaks his young bride's mother,
'Twas news to hear her speak so free:
'For you may make a wife o' my daughter
Though Susie Pirate's come o'er the sea.'

8   There is your fine young daughter,
She's not one penny the better or worse of me.
She came here on her horse and saddle,
She may go home in her carriage-and-three.

B.

moderate

p I (with inflected IV, VII and ending on lower V)

Lord Bate-man was a no- ble lord,

And a no- ble lord of the high de- gree;

When she stole the key of her fa-ther's pri- son,

And she thought Lord Bate-man she would set free.

1-for verse 2   6 –for verse 3

1   Lord Bateman was a noble lord,
     And a noble lord of the high degree;
     When she stole the key of her father's prison,
     And she thought Lord Bateman she would set free.

2   She sailèd east and she travelled water,
     Round till she came to Lord Bateman's house;
     If this is what they call Lord Bateman's (harbour)
     I saw him taking his new bride in.

3   She may came in on her horse and saddle,
     She may came in on her coach and two;
     When she stole the key of her father's prison,
     And she thought Lord Bateman she would set free.

9 LORD LOVEL
(Child 75)

In recent years this romantic ballad has been but seldom reported from Britain and Ireland. In North America, on the other hand, it has flourished in a host of variants, as a tragic ballad, a lyric song, a comic piece and in many parodies. It became a popular London music-hall song in the early nineteenth century and possibly owed its popularity to its circulation on broadsheets and in songsters, chapbooks and garlands. Most of the major North American collections contain a set of the ballad, usually derived from Child's H-text (a London broadside, 1846).

The earliest recorded printed version is in the *Percy Papers* (1770). Child prints this as his A-text. Our version contains most of the basic plot material but lacks the rose-and-briar motif which usually rounds off this and other related ballads.

BIBLIOGRAPHY

Child 75; Bronson, vol. II and Appendix; Coffin, pp. 72–3.

British   Bell (Robert), pp. 134–6; Greig, No. 159; Greig and Keith, pp. 57–8; *JFSS*, vol. VI, pp. 31–3; also vol. VII, p. 315; *JEFDSS*, vol. I, pp. 134–5; *Scottish Studies*, vol. XIV, pp. 45–6 and 159–61; Sharp (2), vol. II, pp. 22–3; Sharp and Karpeles (2), vol. I, pp. 81–2; Williams, pp. 145–6.

North American   Carey, p. 97; Moore, pp. 56–8; Thompson, pp. 380–1.

General   Barry, Eckstorm and Smyth, pp. 139–49.

'Lord Lovett', sung by Charlotte Higgins. Bronson notes the melodic tradition of the ballad as 'unusually compact and consistent', and comments that the tune has been 'remembered almost note for note by multitudes, we must suppose'. Most of the versions are in 6/8 time, our 3/4 version being so notated because of the pace at which Mrs Higgins rendered the ballad.

This tune belongs in the Aa-group and is quite standard except for its fourth cadence, which appears very rarely in the Bronson versions (this line usually ending, in its group, on the mediant).

fairly slow, smoothly

a 1

Lord Lo-vett he stood at his own sta-ble door,

Brush-ing doon his milk- white steed;

When who passed by but La—dy Nan— cy Belle,

16
Wish-ing her lov- er good speed,——

O, wish-ing her lov- er good speed.

16- Alternative, and more common, ending:

(La-dy Nan-cy Belle, I'll come and see ye. La-dy Nan-cy Belle, I'll come and see.)

1   Lord Lovett he stood at his own stable door,
     Brushing doon his milk-white steed;
     When who passed by but Lady Nancy Belle,
     Wishing her lover good speed,
     O, wishing her lover good speed.

2   'O, where are you going, Lord Lovett?' she said,
     'I pray you will tell me.'
     I'm going over the seas, strange countries to see,
     Lady Nancy Belle, I'll come and see ye,
     Lady Nancy Belle, I'll come and see.

3   He hadn't but sailèd a year or two,
     Two years but scarcely three;
     When a curious dream came into his head,
     Lady Nancy Belle I'll go and see,
     Lady Nancy Belle I'll go and see.

[71]

4   As he rode down by Chappleton Court
And in by Mary's Hall,
Three times he heard the dead-bells ring
And the ladies all weeping all,
And the ladies all weeping all.

5   'O, who is dead?' Lord Lovett he said,
'I pray you will tell me.'
Lady Nancy Belle died for a true lover's sake,
And Lord Lovett it was his name,
And Lord Lovett it was his name.

6   He ordered the coffin to be opened up
And the dead sheets they rolled down,
Three times he kissed her merry cold lips
And the tears came falling down,
And the tears came falling down.

10   THE LASS OF ROCH ROYAL
(Child 76)

In his discussion of this ballad, Bronson writes: ' "The Lass of Roch Royal" must have been circulating freely before the middle of the eighteenth century, because Child's A-text from a manuscript of the second quarter of that century, is in a state obviously disordered by traditional transmission.' This is borne out by Mrs Higgins's text, which is in a somewhat confused state. The most obvious disorders are:

1   The breakdown of the quatrain form.
2   The loss of the opening stanzas, which usually identify the ballad. In these stanzas, the girl asks 'Who will glove my hand/shoe my foot/comb my hair/bind my waist/be father to my child until Lord Gregory comes home?' It is these stanzas which have endured the passage of time and geographical transplantation, and which have caused many an American collector to rejoice at having 'found a Child ballad'. In reality, they are often two more recruits to the army of floater verses which make up so many generalised American love-laments, and most of the New World texts in which they are found have no other connection with 'The Lass of Roch Royal'. Coffin gives a list of pieces in which these verses are commonly found.
3   The intermediate action prior to our first stanza is missing. This

describes the girl making a sea voyage in order to find her lover and finally arriving at his door with her child in her arms. There she is involved in a dialogue with her lover's mother who, posing as her son, drives the young woman from the door.

4   The section which closes the ballad, stanzas 11–14, really belongs elsewhere in the Child canon. Stanzas 13 and 14 are, of course, common to many ballads of ill-starred love. Stanza 11 is reminiscent of 'Lord Lovel' and stanza 12 of both 'Lord Thomas and Fair Eleanor' and 'Fair Margaret and Sweet William'.

Regarding the layout of Mrs Higgins's recited text: the stanzas would appear to be laid out arbitrarily, but as the piece was recited sometimes as poetry and sometimes as prose we have ended the 'verses' where pauses were made.

BIBLIOGRAPHY

Child 76; Bronson, vol. II and Appendix; Coffin, pp. 73–5.

British   Bell (Robert), pp. 211–16; Greig and Keith, pp. 59–63; *Museum*, vol. I, No. 5.

North American   Fowke, pp. 106–7; Moore, pp. 58–61.

'Lord Gregory', recited by Charlotte Higgins.

1   O, open the door, Lord Gregory,
     O, open and let me in;
     For the rain rins doon my bonnie yellow hair,
     And the dew falls on your son.

2   O, open the door, Lord Gregory,
     O, open and let me in.

3   O do you mind, O do you mind, Lord Gregory
     When we sat on the hill together?
     We exchanged the rings off one another's hand,
     But I vowed that the best was mine,
     Ay, I vowed that the best was mine.

4   Mine was o' guid gold,
     And yours was o' silver fine.

5   O, do you mind, Lord Gregory,
     When we exchanged the cloaks off one another's back,
     And I vowed that the best was mine.

6 O, open the door, Lord Gregory,
  O, open and let me in.
  For the rain rins doon my bonnie yellow hair,
  And the rain falls on your son.

7 Go 'wa', go 'wa', you ill woman,
  Go 'wa', go 'wa', you ill woman.

8 He says, 'O mother dear, I dreamed a dream,
  I hope it won't come true;
  I dreamed that the lass of Lochinvar
  Was knocking at the door for me.
  Ay, knocking at the door for me.'

9 She said, 'The lass of Lochinvar
  Was knocking at the door for you
  More than three-quarters of an hour ago.'

10 O woe be unto you, mother,
  Wae be unto you again,
  And woe be unto you, mother,
  That did not let her in.

11 Go saddle to me the black or the brown,
  Go saddle to me the grey.
  He rode and he rode and he faster than rode
  Till he come to the nearest town.
  And there he spied two men,
  Carrying a corpse away,
  And the water rinning down,
  And the water rinning down.

12 'O lay down, O lay down this corpse,' he said,
  'And lay them down wi' care.
  You will drink a strong drink over them,
  But you'll drink far stronger over me.'

13 They were both buried in the one grave,
  There was a red rose grew out of one lover's grave,
  And a briar out of the other.

14 They twisted and twined and better than twined,
  Till a true-lover's knot they made.

11   BONNY BARBARA ALLEN
(Child 84)

The theme of this ballad occurs frequently in European folktales and dates, in balladry, from the mid-1600s. Versions found in Britain are usually fuller than our two texts. It is in the opening line of the first stanza that most of the textual variations occur, the name of the town or place changing with the locality in which the song is collected. We have printed the verses of our A-text in the singer's sequence, although stanza 2 would seem to make more sense if placed at the end.

BIBLIOGRAPHY

Child 84; Bronson, vol. II and Appendix; Coffin, pp. 82–5.

British   Buchan and Hall, pp. 64–5; Chappell (2), vol. II, pp. 538–9; Christie, vol. I, pp. 86–9; Greig, Nos 165 and 166; Greig and Keith, pp. 67–70; *Henry Collection*, No. 236; *JFSS*, vol. I, pp. 111–12 and pp. 265–7; also vol. II, pp. 15–18 and pp. 80–1; *JIFS*, vol I, p. 45; Joyce (1), p. 79; Kidson, pp. 36–40; Sharp (2), vol. I, pp. 20–1; Sharp and Karpeles (2), vol. I, pp. 94–105; Sharp and Marson, pp. 44–5; Williams, pp. 206–7.

North American   Carey, pp. 97–8; Fowke, pp. 60–1; Moore, pp. 68–70; Peacock, vol. III, pp. 649–61; Seeger, Charles ('Versions and Variants of Barbara Allen', *Selected Reports*, published by The Institute of Ethnomusicology, University of California at Los Angeles, vol. I, no. 1 (1966, pp. 120–67); Thompson, pp. 377–9.

A. 'Barbry Ellen', sung by Caroline Hughes. The closest tune type to be found in Bronson is in his C-group, No. 97. Various elements of the tune may be found among Nos 84–129, but none of these contain a second phrase ending on the supertonic. It is certainly not one of the most common melodies which accompany the ballad.

B. 'Burber Helen', sung by Nelson Ridley. A very common tune type, to be found in Bronson's A-group between Nos 1 and 15.

A.

1   O, in Reading Town where I was born,
     There's a fair young lady dwelling;
     I picked her out for to be my bride,
     And her name was Barbry Ellen, Ellen,
     And her name was Barbry Ellen.

2   Now, mother dear, you make up my bed,
     You'll make it soft and easy;
     That I might die for the sake of love,
     And that she might die for sorrow, sorrow,
     And that she might die for sorrow.

3   Now, mother dear, you'll look up over my head,
     You'll see my gold watch standing;
     There's my gold watch and my guinea gold ring,
     Will you 'liver it to Barbry Ellen, Ellen?
     Will you 'liver it to Barbry Ellen?

4   Now, mother dear, look at the side of my bed,
     You'll see a bowl there standing,
     It is full of tears that I've lost this night
     For the loss of Barbry Ellen, Ellen,
     For the loss of Barbry Ellen.

5   Now, as I were a-walking across the fields,
       I met a corpse a-coming;
       (O, you put down, my six young lambs)   (O, put him down, my six
                                                              young lads?)

       That I might well gaze on him, on him,
       That I might well gaze on him.

6   While (strollily) I walkèd on,   (strollèd I, strolling there?)
       I heard the (knell a-telling),   (bell a-tolling?)
       And as it tolled, O, it seemed to say:
       'Hard-hearted Barbry Ellen, Ellen,
        Hard-hearted Barbry Ellen!'

B.

slightly free   a I

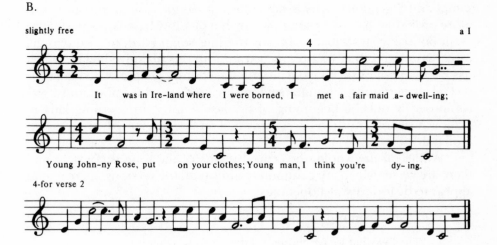

4-for verse 2

1   It was in Ireland where I were borned,
       I met a fair maid a-dwelling;
       Young Johnny Rose, put on your clothes,
       Young man, I think you're dying.

2   Look at the side of my bedside,
       You'll find a vase a-standing;
       There's a gay gold watch and a diamond ring,
       That's left for Burber Helen.

3   O, clerky, clerky, dig me my grave,
       And dig it long and narrow;
       My true love died for me last night,
       I'll die for her tomorrow.

[77]

12   THE LOWLANDS OF HOLLAND
(Child 92, Appendix)

The first printed text of this song appeared in Herd's *Scottish Songs* (1776). Child mentions it in his short note to 'Bonny Bee Hom' (No. 92), a ballad with which it shares a formula verse which is missing in our text:

> No shoes nor stockings I'll put on, nor comb go through my hair,
> No firelight nor candle bright come in my chamber more;
> Nor never will I married be until the day I die,
> For the low, low lands of Holland parted my love and I.

There is room for argument as to what constitutes a 'derivative' or 'secondary' form of a ballad and it is our view that the sharing of a single stanza and a general theme is not sufficient. In the case of this song, it is more probable that a new song was created possibly based on a particular event but using stock material from an older song. Ford, in a note to the piece, says 'according to a popular tradition, this plaintive ballad, which has been an established favourite with the country people of Scotland for several generations, though seldom printed in the collections, was composed about the beginning of the last century, by a young lady in Galloway whose husband was drowned in the course of a voyage to Holland.'

While, on the whole, the central theme of the song is constant and there are verses which are common to almost all the versions, there would appear to be four distinct openings:

1   Most commonly found in Scotland:

> The love that I have chosen I'll therewith be content
> The saut sea shall be frozen before that I repent;
> Repent it will I never until the day I die,
> But the Lowlands of Holland hae twined my love and I.

2   Found in North America and Scotland (but sometimes as a second verse in Scotland and England):

> My love he built a bonnie ship and set her on the sea,
> Wi' seven-score brave mariners to bear her company;
> Three-score gaed to the bottom and three-score died at sea,
> And the Lowlands of Holland hae twined my love and me.

Occasionally this verse begins 'I built my love a bonnie ship'.

3   Most commonly found in Ireland and occasionally in England:

> On the night that I was married and lay in my marriage bed,
> (and so on, as in our text)

4   Most commonly found in England and occasionally in Ireland:

> As I walked out one May morning down by a riverside,
> There I beheld my lovely fair, O then to be my bride;
> O then to be my bride, my boys, and the chambers to behold,
> May the heavens above protect my love for a jolly sailor bold.

With one exception, all the printed versions known to us begin with one of these four stanzas and are followed by floaters peculiar to this particular song, but which may be omitted without altering the sense of the piece. The texts divide into two types:

(a) The entire narrative, beginning with the third or fourth opening. These texts describe the arrival of the captain, the bedside conversation of the lovers, with the following typical opening lines:

> . . . I throwed my arms around him, imploring him to stay

> . . . Lie still, lie still, my bonnie bride, lie still and take your ease

> . . . O daughter, dearest daughter, what makes you so lament?

> . . . No shoes nor stockings I'll put on, no comb go through my hair.

(b) The second part of the narrative, generally beginning with the first and second openings. These texts are not so strong in narrative continuity and their stanzas have the following typical opening lines:

> . . . My love lies on the saut sea and I am on the side

> . . . I built my love another boat and sent her to the main

> . . . Holland is a pretty place, most pleasing to be seen

> . . . Says the mother to the daughter, 'What makes you so lament?'

> . . . There's not a coif go on my head, nae combs come in my hair.

These forms probably owe their stability to particular broadsides, for the song was very popular as a penny-sheet in Britain. On the whole the song has been improved by its passage into the oral tradition. It has become shorter, more economical, more effective as a piece of story-telling and the language less inflated.

North America has yielded few versions, but those which have appeared show how the song has adapted itself to the New World:

> . . . Lie low, the lily of Arkansas has parted you and me.

> . . . Rise you up, dear William, come go along with me
>   To the lowlands of Missouri, we'll fight for liberty.

BIBLIOGRAPHY

Child 92 (Appendix); Bronson, vol. II; Coffin, p. 89.

British Ashton (2), p. 59; Baring-Gould and Sheppard (2), pp. 210–11; Chambers (3), pp. 412–13; Christie, vol. I, pp. 236–7; Ford (2), vol. I, pp. 54–6; *Gardiner MSS*, H-1040; Greig, Nos 83 and 135; *Henry Collection*, No. 180; Herd, vol. II, p. 2; Hughes, vol. II, pp. 70–5; *JFSS*, vol. I, pp. 97–8; also vol. III, pp. 307–9; also vol. V, pp. 170–1; also vol. VII, pp. 63–6; Joyce (1), p. 65; Joyce (2), No. 404; Logan, pp. 22–5; *Museum*, vol. II, No. 115; O'Lochlainn (2), p. 223; Ord, pp. 328–32; Purslow (2), p. 54; Reeves (1), pp. 180–2; Reeves (2), pp. 151–2; Ritson (3), vol. I, pp. 216–17; Sharp (2), vol. II, pp. 16–17; Sharp and Karpeles (2), vol. I, pp. 108–13.

North American Eckstorm and Smyth, pp. 80–1 and 134–9; Flanders and Olney, pp. 113–14 and 118–19; Randolph, vol. I, pp. 339–40; Sharp and Karpeles (1), vol. I, pp. 417–18.

'The Lowlands of Holland', sung by Jeannie Thompson. Bronson has no really exact match for this tune, although in his Aa-group, Nos 1 and 5 contain similar melodic substance and/or similar cadential formations.

moderate, in strict rhythm but smoothly   m I/Ly

The first night that I got mar-ried and lay on my mar-riage bed,

There came a bold sea-cap-tain and he stood at my bed-side.

Say-ing, 'A-rise, a-rise, my mar-ried man, and come a-long with me,

To the low, low-lands of Hol-land and face your e-ne-my.'

1 The first night that I got married and lay on my marriage bed,
There came a bold sea-captain and he stood at my bedside.
Saying, 'Arise, arise, my married man, and come along with me,
To the low, lowlands of Holland and face your enemy.'

2 Lie still, lie still, my bonnie bride, lie still and take your ease,
For if I must go with these young men wherever that they please;
For if I was at my liberty, as I have been before,
I would stay with you all night, my love, and plough the seas no more.

3 My love he's built a mighty ship, a ship of noted fame,
With four-and-twenty seamen bold to steer her o'er the main;
But the night being dark and stormy and the seas begun to roar,
Down went the ship with all her crew, at last to rise no more.

13 THE FAMOUS FLOWER OF SERVING-MEN
(Child 106)

The oldest printed version of this ballad is 1660, but subsequent anthologists and historians have endeavoured to tie later versions down to border feuding and the Massacre of Glencoe (1692). Professor Child, who gives only one set, held that: 'The English broadside, which may reasonably be believed to be formed upon a predecessor in the popular style, has been held to have a common origin with the Scandinavian ballad "The Maid and the Stable Boy"' (see Child's note to 'Child Waters' (No. 63). Scott remade the ballad into 'The Lament of the Border Widow' but subsequent generations of singers appear to have preferred the longer and more complicated traditional version.

 The most complete text we have seen is the one found in Percy's *Reliques*. Its story runs thus: A girl of good family is happily married. One night 'there came foes so fierce a band, that soon they over-run the land.' Her young husband is slain and she is deserted by her servants. (In later versions she buries him alone, using for a shroud the sheets in which he was slain.) She then cuts her hair, changes her name to Sweet William, dresses as a boy and is found weeping in the woods by the king out hunting. He offers the 'boy' a choice of service in his house, and the boy chooses to be chamberlain. One day, the king goes hunting and our heroine, overcome with sorrow, dresses herself once again as a woman and sings, accompanying herself on the lute. The king, who has returned from hunting, overhears her song and, struck with her beauty, asks her to be his mistress. She refuses 'to act so base a part'. The king proposes marriage and the 34-verse piece ends with the couplet which adorns most of the later versions of this ballad:

> The like before was never seen,
> A serving-man to become a queen.

Percy said that the song was ' . . . given from a written copy, containing some improvements, perhaps modern ones, upon the old popular ballad titled "The Famous Flower of Serving-men: or the Lady Turned Serving-Man".'

The ballad has been reported infrequently from Scotland, southern England and the northeastern sections of the United States; it has, however, enjoyed considerable popularity on broadsides and in chapbooks. The texts collected from oral tradition are invariably shorter, less contrived and with interesting variations on the story. The most notable of the variations are:

1   The nameless foes become a definite number of thieves, usually sent by the girl's stepmother, less commonly by her jealous mother and, in one version, by the king himself.

2   The girl is not discovered in the forest weeping but, instead, goes to solicit work at the king's door, often giving a ring to the porter as a bribe to get him to plead her case.

3   Sweet William rarely dresses again as a woman before taking up the lute/flute/harp/fiddle to sing – instead 'he' is overheard by an old man who then reports back to the king.

In our text, the repeated use of the words 'alone, alone' does not occur until verse 11. In other texts, it forms a basic part of the young bride's lamentation from the point where her servants leave her to bury her young husband.

Mrs Hughes's text is an excellent example of how a ballad-story can attract motifs, lines and complete stanzas from other ballads and songs without losing its continuity. A cursory examination of the unusual features in her text is most illuminating:

Stanza   2   The brother does not appear in any other texts, to our knowledge. It is, possibly, a transliteration of 'mother'. Furthermore, in only one other text have we found 'babies' mentioned. 'Slave my life' is possibly a transliteration of 'slay my knight', a phrase which appears in many texts.

Stanza   3   Lines 3 and 4 are reminiscent of 'The Three Butchers', a story of a highway murder. In all the other printed versions of Child 106, the knight is slain in his bower.

Stanza   4   These two lines would normally form the second half of stanza 3.

Stanza   5   The first two lines are reminiscent of 'The Butcher Boy' and 'Sweet William'.

Stanza   6   The most common names for the heroine are Elise, Eleanor, Ellen and Fair Mary – so that Ellender is not unusual. The second half of the verse can also be found in versions of 'Lord Thomas and Fair Eleanor' (Child 73).

Stanza   7   This is not found in any of the other texts. The final line is similar to one that occurs in many versions of 'Earl Brand' (Child 7) and the first three lines are strikingly similar to a stanza of 'I Am a Rover':

> As I crossed over Dannamore
> There I lost sight of my true-love's door
> My heart did ache, my eyes went blind
> As I thought of the bonnie lass I'd left behind.
>
> (Kidson, pp. 147–8)

It is equally possible that the verse has been lifted from 'The Croppy Boy':

> As I was walking on the mountains high,
> I looked all round me at every side
> I looked behind and I looked before
> And my tender mother I will never see more.
>
> (Zimmerman, p. 163)

Stanza   8   This is undoubtedly from 'The Croppy Boy':

> It was early, early in the spring
> When small birds tune and thrushes sing
> Changing their notes from tree to tree,
> And the song they sang was old Ireland free.
>
> (Zimmerman, p. 161)

Stanzas 9 and 10   These are condensations of matters which in the longer text normally require three or four stanzas.

Stanza   12   This, too, can be found in 'I am a Rover' (stanza 7) and in a Shetland song 'The Green Valley'.

Stanza   13   This is a variation on a floater verse mentioned in the note to 'Died for Love' (No. 55).

BIBLIOGRAPHY

Child 106; Bronson, vol. II and Appendix; Coffin, pp. 98–9.

British   Bell (Robert), pp. 192–3; *FMJ*, vol. I, pp. 147–8; *Gardiner MSS*, H-1322; Greig, No. 118; Greig and Keith, pp. 85–6; Purslow (1), pp. 34–5.

North American   Moore, pp. 81–4.

(untitled), sung by Caroline Hughes. This tune does not match any of the variants in Bronson, who prints Mrs Hughes's complete melody in his Appendix section. It is a melody often associated with 'The Croppy Boy' and 'Sweet William'.

1   O, my father he built me a shady bower,
And he covered it over with the shamrock leaves;
'Twas the purtiest bower that ever you see,
What my aged father he built for me.

2   O, could my brother do me a bigger grudge
Than to send nine robbers all in one night?
To send nine robbers all in one night
All to murder my baby and to slave my life.

3   They killed my husband all in my arms,
So sudden we had no time to fly;
But every blow struck him all on the crown,
Left him there on the highway, there to die.

4   . . . .
. . . .
For I had nothing now to wrap it in,
But the linen sheets that my love died in.

5   Now, I catched hold of the pen and I wrote a line,
I wrote it long and I wrote it neat;
But every blow struck him on the crown,
Left him there on the highway, there to die.

6   I'll cut off my hair and I'll change my name,
From Fair Ellender to Sweet William-boy;
And every town, love, that I pass through
They will take me, my love, for to be the queen.

7   As I crossed over the foggy moor,
I soon lost sight of my true love's face;
I looked behind and I looked in front,
But my aged father I will see no more.

8   Now (to Sir Lionel) all in the spring   ('twas early, early?)
While the birds they whistle and they softly sing,
They changed their notes so from tree to tree,
And the song they sang it were 'Home, Sweet Home'.

9   Now, I rung the bell and there comes the lord,
I rung the bell one time and three;
And when he came, I bowed full very low –
O, it's have you any house-duties for me?

10   It's do you want now a house-groom,
Or do you want now a stableman?
No, I want a man-servant to attend the hall
To attend the hall when I am gone.

11   O, I'm all alone, all alone, yes all alone;
Till I took the fiddle and I played a tune:
For once I was a fair lady gay,
And my husband he was once a noble lord.

12   O, it's are you married or are you free,
Or am I bounded now to be your bride?
O, a married life it will as soon suit me,
A contented mind don't breed jealousy.

13   O, it's are you married now, or am I bound,
        Or am I bound to be your bride?
        For a maid again I will never be
        Whilst an apple it grows on an orange tree.

14   SIR HUGH
(Child 155)

After singing his version of the ballad, John MacDonald commented: 'I never could make much sense o' that sang. I never did like it.' The infrequency with which 'Sir Hugh' has been collected in Britain during recent times might suggest that other singers may have also found the subject matter not to their taste. Child gives eighteen versions and in all but one of them the little boy is enticed in by a Jew's daughter. In the United States, where the ballad appears to have been more popular, the trans-literation of 'Jew's daughter' into 'duke's/jeweller's/queen's/king's daughter' is common and in some versions it is an aunt, a grandmother, a neighbour and sometimes even the child's own mother who commits the ritual killing. Since 1255, the date of the alleged murder, a considerable body of legends, songs and tales have circulated throughout western Europe and successive outbreaks of anti-Semitism have all produced 'documentary evidence' concerning the case.

    The Jew's House still stands in Lincoln and there is a plaque in the cathedral where little Hugh is said to be interred. Child virtually dismissed the ballad as a piece of religious witch-hunting, and generations of singers would appear to have done the same either by eliminating the song completely from the collective memory, by excising the Jew's daughter herself, or by transforming the song into a gentle children's piece.

BIBLIOGRAPHY

Child 155; Bronson, vol. III; Coffin, pp. 107–9.

British   Bell (Robert), pp. 189–91; Broadwood and Maitland, p. 86; Groome, p. 145; Halliwell (2), p. 185; *JFSS*, vol. I, pp. 264–5; also vol. V, pp. 253–6; *JEFDSS*, vol. VII, p. 102; also vol. IX, p. 74; Mason, pp. 46–7; *Museum*, vol. VI, No. 582; *Scottish Studies*, vol. IX, pp. 27–32; Sharp (2), vol. I, pp. 22–3; Sharp and Karpeles (2), vol. I, pp. 152–6.

North American   Dusenbury MSS, No. 25 6b; Moore, pp. 89–91.

A. (untitled), sung by John MacDonald. This tune is not among the Bronson variants. It is, however, of popular Scottish stock and seems to be of the same family as 'The Laird of Drum' (Child 236, Bronson's A-group). In that ballad the entire tune structure is very similar although the 1st and 3rd cadences are different. It contains half-cadences which close its 2nd and 4th lines (dictated by the poetry) which in our ballad become authentic cadences. This rhythmic displacement does not mask the definite similarity of the tunes.

B. 'The Jew's Garden', text recited and tune lilted by Caroline Hughes. She said she didn't know the song but could 'tune' the melody (i.e. sing it without words). The melody belongs to Bronson's Ab-category, particularly with the earlier Nos 4 and 5.

A.

slow, stately   mπ¹

There were four-and-twen-ty   mer-ry, mer-ry boys. They were   play-in' at   the   ball;

When oot stepped one of these   mer-ry boys,   The   best play-er   of   them   all.

1 -for verses 3 and 4

1   There were four-and-twenty merry, merry boys,
     They were playin' at the ball;
     When oot stepped one of these merry boys,
     The best player of them all.

2   .   .   .   .
     .   .   .   .
     For he hit the ball a kick and another with his knee
     Till he sent it through the Jew's window.

3   For she wiled him in tae the first braw room,
     And she wiled him in tae twa;
     And she wiled him in tae the third braw room,
     Which caused yon bonnie boy to rue.

4   For she put a mantle below his head
And she dressed him like a (swan);   (swine?)
And she put a basin below his head
Where all his heart's blood run.

B.

fairly slow, deliberate   p I

1   Down in merry Scotland
Where the rain it did come down,
There was two little boys went out one day
To have a game with the ball.

2   He kicked the ball so very, very high,
He kicked the ball so low;
It pitched all over the Jew's garden
Where the Jew lived just down below.

(Spoken)   Out came one of the head Jews. He asked the little boy what he wanted.
He said, 'The ball in the garden.' Well, you shall have your ball again.
He took the little boy and he laid 'm on the table and he stuck him like a
sheep. 'Let me say these last few words before I die.' He said:

3   'You'll dig my grave so very, very deep
Put a marble stone on my grave;
If my tender mother should come this way,
You tell her I'm asleep.'

15 THE BONNIE HOUSE O' AIRLIE
(Child 199)

Airlie Castle is roughly nine miles northeast of Blairgowrie, in Perthshire. Its destruction by the Earl of Argyll's covenanting forces took place on 7 July 1640. For detailed historical references see Ford, and Greig and Keith. The version presented here differs slightly from the four sets given by Child. It is only in Child's D-text that Montrose is mentioned, and there he is merely a remote source of the decision to burn the castle. In the second stanza of our text he is represented as being actually present on the scene.

Child's A-text states correctly, in the eighth stanza, that the Earl of Airlie 'is with *King* Charlie'. In the other Child texts, events have moved forward a century and Airlie is now away with *Prince* Charlie. This historical time-transfer occurs also in the opening stanza of our version where it is stated that 'the clans were awa' wi' Charlie'.

The final transformation of the Covenanting War into the Jacobite Rebellion was achieved in the final stanza of a text given by Ford, when Cameron of Lochiel enters, ready for revenge and crying

> We'll kindle a lowe round the fause Argyle
> And licht it wi' a spark out o' Airlie.

This element of retribution is a motif absent not only in all of the Child texts but in almost all of the versions recorded since.

BIBLIOGRAPHY

Child 199; Bronson, vol. II; Coffin, pp. 118–19.

British Christie, vol. II, pp. 276–7; Ford (2), vol. II, pp. 167–9; Greig, No. 58; Greig and Keith, pp. 123–5; MacColl, p. 17; Ord, p. 470; *Scottish Studies*, vol. IX, pp. 49–50 and 176–8.

North American Moore, pp. 95–7.

'The Bonnie Hoose of Airlie', sung by Charlotte Higgins. Bronson comments that 'the earlier form has tended to be supplanted by a plagal tune, melodically akin, and universally familiar today with the more modern text of "The Bonny Banks of Loch Lomond".' It is into this, his B-category, that our tune fits, although *his* variants all end the first phrase not on the lower V but on the lower VI.

1   It fell upon a day and a bonnie summer day,
    When the clans were awa' wi' Charlie,
    For there arose a great dispute
    Between Argyll and Airlie.

2   The Duke o' Montrose has ridden fast and hard,
    To reach Dunkeld in the morning,
    To lead in his troops by the back o' Dunkeld,
    To plunder the bonnie hoose o' Airlie.

3   Lady Ogilvie she looked fae her high castle wa',
    O, but she sighed sairly
    To see the false Argyll and hundreds o' his men
    Come to plunder the bonnie hoose o' Airlie.

4   'Come doon, come doon, Lady Ogilvie,' he said,
    'Come doon and kiss me fairly.'

I wadna kiss ye, ye false Argyll
Though ye wadna leave a stannin' stane in Airlie.

5   O, I have reared seven bonnie sons,
The eighth ne'er seen his daddy;
But if I wad hae as mony ower again
They would a' gang and fecht for Charlie.

6   He took her by the middle sma',
Throwed her on the banks o' Airlie,
O, it's tell me, Lady Ogilvie,
Where is your dowry?

7   Its up and doon and doon and up,   (A)*
It lies in the bowlin' green o' Airlie.   (B)
For they socht it up and they socht it doon, (C)
They socht it late and early,   (B)
And they found it below a bonnie balm tree (C)
That spread ower the bowlin' greens o' Airlie. (D)

8   If my guid lord had been at hame,
As this nicht he's awa' wi' Charlie,
There's nae Campbells in a' the land,
Wad have burned the bonnie hoose o' Airlie.

* The letters in parentheses indicate which line of music is used.

16   GEORDIE
(Child 209)

Child gives fourteen texts of this splendid ballad, all of them Scots.
Bronson has sixty-eight versions, twenty-nine from England, twenty-eight
from the United States, ten from Scotland and one from Nova Scotia. The
ballad has declined in popularity in Scotland since Child made his
collection but it is still fairly common in southern England and the eastern
United States.

    There are conflicting theories as to the true identity of Geordie. Child
places him in 1554 as a victim of political intrigue and revenge; Buchan, on
the other hand, puts him in the reign of James VI as part of a love-triangle.
The Scots versions all end happily: the wife rides to court, pleads for her
husband who has been convicted of a crime meriting capital punishment,
begs money from judge, jury and bystanders and rides off behind her love.

She occasionally calls for 'balants' (ballads) to be made celebrating her victory. The English and American forms, in which the hero is nearly always hanged, are thought to be based on the death of George Stoole, who was executed in 1610 in Northumberland, convicted of theft. Other theories involve a broadside entitled 'The Life and Death of George of Oxford' (c. 1691). Kidson writes: 'The whole series of "Geordie" ballads sprang, I think from one original now lost. The notes by the early commentators fixing the identity of the particular Geordie are valueless. . . .' He declares that the English and Scots versions are 'totally distinct, yet here and there having a verse in common'.

Child remarks that his A- and E-texts are 'the purer forms of the ballad'. His F-J-texts are, he laments, 'corrupted by admixture'. This phrase sums up what has happened to the story, the poetry and the characterisation in that crucible called 'the folk process'. In southern England, where the ballad is still found in almost every gypsy community, it has been reduced to the state in which (as shown in our two sets) it no longer clearly tells the story.

Unlike 'Bonny Barbara Allen' (Child 84), an equally popular and widespread ballad which has maintained its story-line and poetic consistency, 'Geordie' has taken on the colouring of its surroundings. It has adopted local place names, the language has become more and more reduced, while characterisation and subtleties of personal and social relationships have become obscured.

BIBLIOGRAPHY

Child 209; Bronson, vol. III and Appendix; Coffin, pp. 124–6.

British Broadwood (1), p. 32; Christie, vol. II, pp. 44–5 and p. 290; Gillington, pp. 6–7; Greig, No. 75; Greig and Keith, pp. 130–3; *Hammond MSS*, Nos 213, 393 and 466; Hogg, vol. II, pp. 104–8; *JFSS*, vol. I, pp. 164–5; also vol. II, pp. 27–8 and 208–9; also vol. III, pp. 191–2; also vol. IV, pp. 89–90 and 332–3; *JEFDSS*, vol. VIII, pp. 148–9; Kidson, pp. 24–6; *Museum*, vol. IV, No. 346; Ord, pp. 408–10; Reeves (1), pp. 119–21; Sharp (1), pp. 89–91; Sharp (2), vol. I, pp. 24–5; Sharp and Karpeles (2), vol. I, pp. 174–80; Sharp and Marson, p. 5.

North American Creighton and Senior (1), pp. 18–19; *Dusenbury MSS*, No. 30 7b; Moore, pp. 101–2.

General Buchan (1), vol. I, pp. 130–3 (an excellent historical note).

A. 'Georgie', sung by Henry Hughes. This tune belongs to Bronson's B-group, by far the largest of his categories. It is also found commonly in Scotland carrying the text of 'Andrew Lammie' (Child 233). Bronson gives a number of variants under that ballad in his Aa group.

B. 'Georgie', sung by Levi Smith. This tune is very like Bronson's D-group, No. 50, but the second and fourth cadences are different. There is also a resemblance to Group E, No. 55, but again there are some cadential and modal dissimilarities.

C. 'Georgie', sung by Nelson Ridley. The tune was almost identical to that sung by Mr Smith.

A.

Once I had such a pur-ty lit-tle boy, So good a lit-tle boy as an-y; What would run five miles in one half-an-hour With a let-ter to my Geor-gie.

1   Once I had such a purty little boy,
      So good a little boy as any;
      What would run five miles in one half-an-hour
      With a letter to my Georgie.

2   Now (my) Georgie's going to be hung in some chains of gold, (your?)
      In chains that you don't see so many;
      With the broad, bright sword hanging down by his side,
      Don't I pity you now, gay lady?

3   O sir, what have he done, my good lord judge?
      Have he murdered or killed any other?
      He stoled sixteen of the Queen's fat deers,
      And he sold 'em in yonders-a valley.

4   (Your) Georgie's going to be hung in some chains of gold,   (My?)
      In chains that you don't see many:
      With the broad, bright sword hanging down by his side,
      Won't I fight for the life of my Georgie?

5   There's six pretty babes I've had-a by you,
      And the seventh lays in my body;
      I will freely part from every one
      If you spare me the life of my Georgie.

6 O, once I did live on Shooter's knoll,
   Of vassals I've had plenty;
   I'm a-giving the silver to every man,
   If you spare me the life of my Georgie.

B.

1 Come saddle to me says my lily-white breast;*
   Come saddle to me says my pony;
   For he's willing to ride just before the Lord Judge,
   If you'll spare me the life of my Georgie.

2 For it's what did Georgie done on Shooters Hill?
   Did he stoled or murder by many?
   For he stole sixteen of the Lord Judge's deers
   But we sold 'em down under the valley.

3 For it's George is the father of six babes, love,
   O, the seventh one into (her) body;   (my?)
   For (he's) willing to part, that's all (he) have got (I'm, I?)
   If you spare me the life of my Georgie.

* When Mr Smith repeated the song, he sang the verse thus:
   Come saddle to me says my lily-white breast;
   Come saddle to me says my pony;
   With my guns in my hand and my sword by my side
   For I'll fight for the life of my Georgie.

C. 1 Come, saddle to me my lily-white breast,
       Come, saddle to me, say my pony;
       I am willing to part from that's all I've got
       If you'll gave me the life of my Georgie.

    2 What did Georgie do then on Shooter's Hill?
       He stole the game of many;*
       He stolèd nine of the Lord Judge's fat deer,
       And he sold them under the valley.

    3 I am the father of seven babes,
       And another one in the body;
       I am willing to part, O, from that's all I've got,†
       If you'll spare me the life of my Georgie.

* alternative rendition: *killed* the game of many
† alternative rendition: I am willing to stand before the Lord High Judge

17   THE BRAES O' YARROW
(Child 214)

This ballad, set originally on Yarrow Water in Selkirkshire, is one of the most frequently reported Scots narratives. It has travelled, though not widely, to Canada and the eastern United States. It is found in a number of different types, this being due largely to the practice (common among singers) of lopping off verses and motifs and introducing them into other songs. Most of the changes which take place in this ballad owe their origins to the early hybridisation of Child 214 with Child 215, 'Rare Willie's Drowned in Yarrow'. There are those who believe that the two ballads were originally one and that they separated into two branches which, in spite of fundamental differences, still have motifs in common. These motifs are (a) the girl's search for her lover and her presentiment or knowledge that he is dead (drowned); (b) the finding of his corpse, smoothing his hair and kissing his wounds (lips); (c) the wrapping of her 'long yellow hair' around her lover and carrying him home. In certain versions the two ballads have been so beautifully dovetailed that a new family might well be named Child 214½.

   We present three complete texts all strikingly alike and yet showing subtle differences. After Mr MacDonald had sung his 'Ploughboy Bold from Yarrow', his wife commented that stanza 10 was 'frae anither sang'. This motif (as well as that found in our A-text, stanza 14) is most commonly found in 'Bonny Barbara Allen' (Child 84).

BIBLIOGRAPHY

Child 214; Bronson, vol. III and Appendix: Coffin, pp. 127–30.

British   Greig, No. 57; Greig and Keith, pp. 141–4; *JFSS*, vol. V, pp. 110–16; *JEFDSS*, vol. V, p. 77; Kidson, pp. 21–4; MacColl, pp. 14–15, 30; Ord, pp. 426–7; *Rymour*, vol. I, pp. 44–5; *Scottish Studies*, vol. VII, pp. 115–17; also vol. XVIII, pp. 15–16; Thomson, vol. II, pp. 34–9.

Broadsides   MacNie of Stirling (1824).

North American   Fowke, pp. 62–3; Karpeles (2), pp. 95–6; Moore, pp. 104–6.

General   Cazden, Norman: an article entitled 'Story of a Catskill Ballad' (printed in the *New York Folklore Quarterly*, Winter 1952, pp. 245–66).

A. 'The Dowie Dens of Yarrow', sung by Maria Robertson. This tune does not seem to fit into any of Bronson's categories, although he prints it in his Appendix as No. 41.1, part of his D-group.

B. 'The Ploughboy Bold From Yarrow', sung by John MacDonald. This melody belongs in Bronson's A-category, almost all of which are Scots.

C. 'The Dowie Dens of Yarrow', sung by Jock Higgins. This tune is similar to a number of 'Barbara Allen' tunes (Child 84). Bronson's C-group under that ballad contains similar items. Of the tunes for Child 214, this tune is most like No. 40, in Group D, a tune with which it does not share a similar third phrase.

A.

very freely   a I/Ly

There was a   la-dy   lived in the North Coun-try, You'd scarce-ly find her   mar- row;

She was court-ed by nine   no- ble men,   And a plough- man boy in   Yar-   row.

1 - for verse 2

2.   O will you   tak' your   gun, your   gun (etc.)

1   There was a lady lived in the North Country,
       You'd scarcely find her marrow;
       She was courted by nine noblemen,
       And a ploughman boy in Yarrow.

2   O, will you tak' your gun, your gun,
       Or will you tak' your arrow?
       Or will you tak' your gey broadsword
       To fight your cause in Yarrow?

3   I'll neither tak' my gun, my gun,
       Nor I'll neither tak' my arrow;
       But I will tak' my gey broadsword
       To fight my cause in Yarrow.

4   For he rode up yon high, high hill,
       And to the dens of Yarrow,
       And there he saw nine noblemen
       They were drinking wine in Yarrow.

5   O, did you come to drink our wine?
       Or did you come for sorrow?
       Or did you come your blood to spill
       In the dowie dens of Yarrow?

6   I didn't come to drink your wine,
       I didn't come for sorrow;
       But I come here to fight my cause
       In the dowie dens of Yarrow.

7   It's will you come by one, by one,
       Or will you come by three?
       . . . .
       . . . .

8   It's three he slew and three they drew,
       And three lay dead in Yarrow,
       When her false brother, John, slipped behind the three,
       And pierced him with an arrow.

9   Go home, go home, you false young man,
       And tell your sister sorrow;
       Her true love, John, lies dead and gone,
       In the dowie dens of Yarrow.

10   O father dear, I dreamt a dream,
I hope it won't prove sorrow;
I dreamt I was picking heather bells
In the dowie dens of Yarrow.

11   O, daughter dear, I will read your dream,
I hope it won't prove sorrow;
Ay, your true love, John, lies dead and gone,
On the dowie dens of Yarrow.

12   She wrung her hands and she tore her hair,
And the colour o' it being yellow,
She tied it roond his middle sma',
And carried him oot of Yarrow.

13   O, mother dear, come make my bed,
Come make it long and narrow;
My true love, John, died for me today,
And I'll die for him tomorrow.

14   O, daughter dear, wipe away your tears,
And dry up your sorrow;
We will wed you to a much higher degree
Than the ploughman boy in Yarrow.

15   O, the dead bells they tolled high and sore,
And they will toll tomorrow;
And every toll they seem to say,
'I will die for him tomorrow.'

B.

For there was a la-dy lived in the north, It been hard to find her mar-row;
She was court-ed by nine no-ble lords And a plough-boy bold from Yar-row.

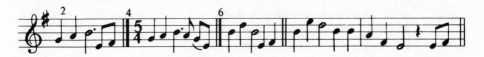

this variant for verses 7-10 (incl.)

1   For there was a lady lived in the north,
    It been hard to find her marrow;
    She was courted by nine noble lords,
    And a ploughboy bold from Yarrow.

2   For as John gaed o'er yon high, high hill,
    Ay, and down yon path so narrow,
    It was there he met nine noble lords
    They were comin' up through Yarrow.

3   For it's have you came my wine to drink,
    Or have you came through sorrow?
    Or it's have you came my broadsword to try
    On the dowie dens of Yarrow?

4   For it's we've not came your wine to drink,
    Nor have we came through sorrow;
    But it's we have came your broadsword to try
    On the dowie dens of Yarrow.

5   For there's nine of youse, but one of I –
    Sure, it is no equal marrow;
    But it's I will fight youse one by one
    On the dowie dens of Yarrow.

6   For it's three he drew and three he slew,
    Ay, and three lay mortally wounded;
    When her false brother, John, came in between
    And he drew his sword and slew him.

7   For as he gaed up yon narrow path
    He met his sister, Saro,
    Sayin', 'Brother dear, I've dreamt a dream
    And I dreamt it all through sorrow,
    That my true love, John, lies dead and gone
    On the dowie dens of Yarrow.'

8   O, it's sister dear, dry up your tears,
Ay, and weep no more through sorrow;
For your true love, John, is dead and gone,
And his blood runs down the Yarrow.

9   For she had long hair, three-quarters long,
And the colour of it was yellow;
And she tied it roond his middle small
And she pulled him out of Yarrow.

10   Sayin', 'Father dear, dig me a grave,
And dig it broad and deep;
For the one that died for me last night
Sure, I'll die for him tomorrow.'

11   O, daughter dear, dry up your tears,
Ay, and weep no more through sorrow;
Sure, I'll have you wed to a higher degree
Than the ploughboy bold from Yarrow.

12   O, father dear, you've seven sons,
All ploughing down in Yarrow,
You may wed them all to your higher degree,
But you'll bury me tomorrow.

C.

slow, with dignity   p I/Ly

There   was   a la- dy   in the north, You'd scarce-ly find   her   mar-row;

She was court-ed by nine gen-tle-men, To fight for her in   Yar-row.

1-most common opening   for verse 10

1   There was a lady in the north,
You'd scarcely find her marrow;
She was courted by nine gentlemen,
To fight for her in Yarrow.

2   For the nine they sat drinkin' wine,
O, drinkin' wine in Yarrow;
They made a vow among themselves
To fight for her in Yarrow.

3   O, she washed his face and she kamed his hair,
For often she's done before, O,
To make him like a knight so bright
To fight for her in Yarrow.

4   For he walked up yon high, high hill
And down in the (downs) of Yarrow;   (dens?)
There he spied nine armed men
Come to fight with him in Yarrow.

5   For three he slew and three he drew
And three were deadly wounded,
When her brother, John, came in beyond
And wounded him sae foully.

6   O, it's father dear, I dreamed a dream,
I hope it does not prove sorrow;
I dreamt my true love lies dead and gone
In the dowie dens o' Yarrow.

7   O daughter dear, I've read your dream
Your dream it does prove sorrow.
For your true love, John, lies pale and wan
On the dowie dens of Yarrow.

8   So she walked up thon high, high hill,
And down in the dens of Yarrow,
There she saw her true love, John,
Lying pale and wan in Yarrow.

9   Her hair it hung three-quarters long
And the colour of it bein' yellow,
She tied it roond (her) middle sma'   (his?)
And carried him home to Yarrow.

10   O father dear, you've reared seven bonny sons,
     You could wed them all tomorrow,
     But the bonniest flooer that ever you had
     I wooed with him in Yarrow.

18   THE JOLLY BEGGAR
(Child 279)

The story-line of this popular ballad falls into three distinct categories, all of which share a roughly identical opening scene: a beggar calls at a farmhouse, is given hospitality and persuades or forces the daughter of the house to lie with him. At this point the narrative takes one of the following paths:

1   The beggar (either on the day following the amorous encounter or after a considerable lapse of time) abandons his disguise, reveals that he is a gentleman of wealth and position and marries the girl. This is the most common form.

2   The beggar abandons his disguise, reveals that he is a gentleman of wealth and position and then (adopting the high moral tone befitting his recently-restored image) castigates the seduced girl for submitting to his advances. At the same time he informs her that by losing her virtue she has lost an even greater prize – himself.

3   There is no disguise motif and, consequently, no revelation. The beggar bids the girl goodbye and departs as poor as he came.

All the English variants, to our knowledge, belong to the third group. The only Scots variant belonging to this group identifies the beggar as 'Davie Faa'. In 'The Farmer and the Tinker', collected by Sharp in Bampton, Oxfordshire (Sharp MSS, printed in Bronson), the beggar is called 'David Fore'. It would seem obvious that these names refer to a single character, a descendant perhaps of that Faa who, in 1540, obtained from James V of Scotland a decree granting gypsies various rights and privileges.

BIBLIOGRAPHY

Child 279; Bronson, vol. IV; Coffin, pp. 150–1.

British   Baring-Gould and Sheppard (1), pp. 52–3; Baring-Gould and Sheppard (2), pp. 200–1; Buchan and Hall, p. 97; Christie, vol. II, pp. 104–7; Farmer (1), vol. I, pp. 5–9; Ford (2), vol. I, pp. 9–11; *Gardiner MSS*, Hp-929; Glen (note), p. 147;

Greig, No. 30; Greig and Keith, pp. 220–3; Kennedy, p. 419; Purslow (4), p. 3;
Reeves (1), pp. 215–16; *Rymour*, vol. I, p. 183; *Scottish Studies*, vol. XIV, pp. 53–4
and 164–6; also vol. XVI, pp. 152–3; Sharp and Karpeles (2), vol. I, pp. 201–8;
Sola Pinto and Rodway, pp. 210–12.

'The Barley Straw', sung by Nelson Ridley. This tune bears some resemblance to
Bronson's D-group, Nos 27 and 36. For a very similar tune, see 'We Dear
Labouring Men' (our No. 103).

1   There once livèd a jolly old farmer, then, he did live somewhere close
        by,
     He thought he wouldn't be happy then until he had a try;
     He disguised himself as a tinker man, he run from town to town,
     Till he came unto some old farmhouse and into there he went.

2   Say, have you any saucepans now or pots and pans to mend?
Or have you got any lodgings here, for I'm a single man;
'O yes,' cried the fair young maid, 'you may sleep here tonight,
O yes, there's a welcome here tonight if you sleep in my father's barn.'

3   Now, after supper was over then she went to make his bed,
But being quick and nimble then he quickly barred the door,
Now being quick and nimble then he quickly barred the door,
And there she slept in the tinker's arms among the wheat and straw.

4   Now, it's early then next morning the old tinker man did rose,
You take this jolly shilling for the damage I have done;
You take this jolly shilling for the damage I have done,
Now if you ever you come this way again then think of my father's barn.

19   THE GABERLUNZIE MAN
(Child 279, Appendix)

This was one of the pieces revised by Allan Ramsay for publication in *The Tea-Table Miscellany* (1724). It was, in Ramsay's words, one of those old verses 'that wanted to be cleared from the dross of blundering transcribers and printers . . .'. It is unlikely that we will ever know how much 'dross' Ramsay felt called upon to clear away, but we can say that the greater part of his published text appears to have sired most of the versions current in Scotland today. Among Scots Travellers it is not unusual to find occasional stanzas of the ballad larded with words and whole phrases in the cant.

BIBLIOGRAPHY

Child 279 (Appendix); Bronson, vol. IV; Coffin, pp. 150–1.

British   Christie, vol. II, pp. 104–7; Farmer (1), vol. I, pp. 1–4; Ford (2), vol. I, pp. 241–3; Glen, No. 226; Greig, Nos 30 and 38; Greig and Keith, pp. 223–6; *Henry Collection*, No. 810; *Museum*, vol. III, No. 226; Ord, pp. 375–7; Petrie, No. 678; *Rymour*, vol. I, p. 183.

North American   Moore, pp. 128–31.

'The Beggar Man', sung by Maggie McPhee. This melody belongs to Bronson's B-group, his largest category.

moderate, a bit free

p I (ending on lower V)

A beggar man cam' ow-er thon lee, He ask- it oot for char-i- ty;

He ask- it oot for cha- ri- ty, Wad ye lodge a beg-gar man?

Refrain:

Lad- die, wi' my tow row ree.

1 -for verses 2 & 4

He wad- na lie in sta-bles, he wad-na lie in byres, He wad-na lie but at my

bon-nie lass-ie's feet;   (etc.)

1   A beggar man cam' ower thon lee,
     He askit oot for charity;
     He askit oot for charity,
     Wad ye lodge a beggar man?

Refrain: Laddie, wi' my tow row ree.

2   He wadna lie in stables, he wadna lie in byres,
     He wadna lie but at my bonnie lassie's feet;
     And through the nicht the twa did creep,
     O laddie, wi' my tow row ree, (refrain)

3   O, a beggar, a beggar I'll ne'er lodge again,
     I aince lodged a beggar and Jimmy was his name;
     And awa' wi' my dochter, Jean, he's gane
     And I dinna ken whit or whaur, (refrain)

4   O, thonder's your dochter, Jean, she's comin' ower the lee,
     Wi' silks and satins a' kilted tae her knee;
     Wi' a bundle on her back and a bairnie in her lap
     And anither on the road comin' hame, (refrain)

[105]

ADDITIONAL
TRADITIONAL BALLADS

20 BRAKE OF BRIARS
(Laws M 32)

The text presented here lacks certain important features found in most of the longer versions of the story, which runs thus: The daughter of a lord/rich man/merchant/farmer is in love with a servant/sailor/ploughboy/apprentice-boy. Her brothers, determined that her dowry will not fall into the hands of a social inferior – or merely incensed by the young man's presumptuousness in aspiring to the hand of their sister – conspire to murder him. Having persuaded him to accompany them on a hunting trip, they lure him to a secluded spot – a brake of briars/bamboo briars/a patch of briars/bramble briars/a lonesome desert/a place of woe – and there they murder him.

On returning home, they are questioned by their sister concerning his whereabouts. They tell her that he has disappeared and will probably never be seen again. The girl dreams that night that she is visited by her lover, who tells her that her brothers are his murderers. After a search she discovers his corpse and, after mourning beside it for three days and three nights, she is driven home by hunger. She accuses her brothers and they, attempting to flee the consequences of their crime, embark on a sea-voyage in the course of which they are drowned. In some versions, they are apprehended and hanged.

The story was popularised in *The Decameron* by Boccaccio (1313–73) and later set into verse by Hans Sachs (1494–1576). In view of the age of the story and the marked resemblances between the English version and the German adaptations, it is somewhat surprising that the ballad does not appear to have been reported from tradition until the present century. Indeed, even the parallel broadside ballad 'The Merchant's Daughter, or the Constant Farmer's Son' was not published until the mid-nineteenth century.

The ballad's distribution in Britain appears to be confined to the southern and southwestern counties of England. In the United States, versions have been reported from a wide geographical area, from Maine to Texas. In only one of the American texts, to our knowledge, is the scene of action identified by an American place-name (Boston). Otherwise, the only real place-names associated with both English and American versions of ballad are Bruton Town (Somerset) – the Brunton Town of a North Carolina text – and Bridgwater (Somerset), the name given in our A-text.

BIBLIOGRAPHY

Laws M 32.

British   Gardiner MSS, H-208 and H-984; Gillington, p. 10; *Henry Collection*, No. 806; *JFSS*, vol. I, pp. 160–1; also vol. II, pp. 42–3; also vol. V, pp. 123–7; Purslow (3), pp. 79–80; Sharp (2), vol. I, pp. 4–5; Sharp and Karpeles (2), vol. I, pp. 280–2.

Broadsides   British Museum, LR 271 a 2, vol. VI, p. 127 (Such).

North American   Fowke MSS (under the title 'The Constant Farmer's Son'); Hubbard, pp. 49–50; Hudson, pp. 154–5; Moore, pp. 159–62.

Alternative titles   The Bamboo (Bramble, Bomberry, Branbury) Briar(s); Bruton (Burlington, Strawberry, Seaport, etc.) Town; The Jealous (Cruel) Brothers; The Apprentice Boy; The Murdered Servant Man; The Merchant's Daughter; Lord Burling's Sister.

A. 'The Bridgwater Farmer', sung by Caroline Hughes.

B. 'There Was a Match of Hunting', sung by Nelson Ridley.

A.

moderate, very free   m I (ending on VIII)

There was a   farm- er liv- ing   near Bridg- wa- ter,

He   had   two   sons   and   one   daugh- ter   dear;

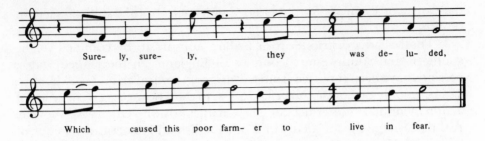

Sure- ly, sure- ly, they was de- lu- ded,

Which caused this poor farm- er to live in fear.

Note: Each line is sung separately, phrased to the inflection of the speech. The above is merely a guide to the melody.

1   There was a farmer living near Bridgwater,
He had two sons and one daughter dear;
Surely, surely, they was deluded,
Which caused this poor farmer to live in fear.

2   Well, our servant man's a-going to wed my sister,
Yes, my sister she have got mind to wed –
. . . .
Surely, surely, that will drive me wild.

3   Three days and three nights she lay demented
And she dreamed, she dreamed of her own true love;
And by her bedside there was tears like fountains,
Covered over and over by gores of blood.

4   She dressed herself and come down to her brothers,
A-crying tears like lumps of salt;
Dear brother, pray tell me where is he?
You've killed my love, and you'll tell me true.

5   Down through the woods she went a-riding,
O, she heard a mournful and bitter cry;
Surely, surely, that's my own dear true love,
In the brake of briars he is thrown and killed.

6   She got off'n her horse and she looked down on him,
Wiping the tears from her eyes like any brine;
My brothers have killed you and ain't they cruel?
Surely, surely, that would drive me mad.

B.

1   There was a match of hunting they was providing,
Down in the grove, that's where briars grow;
O, did ever you hear talk of the young man murdered?
In a bed of briars his body throwed.

2   This match of hunting they was (patruling),   (patrolling?)
Down in the grove, that's where briars grow;
(For keeping of its secret being around two brothers)
In a bed of briars his body throwed.

Child makes a passing reference to this piece while discussing 'The Wylie Wife of the Hie Toon Hie' (No. 290), but it is to 'The Broom of the Cowdenknowes' (No. 217) that Mrs McPhee's song bears the closest resemblance. The story of 'The Denty Doon Bye' is not so complicated as that of Child 217. Its characterisation is less convincing, and its poetry less satisfying. Herd's text has twelve stanzas and is not only less colloquial in style but differs from our set in the following ways:

1   The opening. Our first stanza, and especially the double-entendre in line 3, does not occur in Herd but is reminiscent of a motif in Child 217, in which a maid milking her father's cows – or yowes – is surprised by a mounted troop of gentlemen. Herd's first three stanzas deal with the girl's father sending her out to 'keep the kye'. Instead she goes to the garden of the Dainty Downby to pick thyme, whereupon she is seduced by the laird.

2   The rhyming scheme. It is only in her first stanza that Mrs McPhee departs from the obvious rhyming system of the rest of the text. Herd's text, on the other hand, is quite inconsistent in its rhyming structure.

3   Our verse 2. This stanza, especially line 4, is probably an intrusion from another ballad.

4   Stanzas 5, 6 and 7. These are not found in Herd. Jeannie Robertson, the Aberdeenshire singer, has a stanza in her set of the song which may serve to clarify the meaning of line 1 in the seventh stanza:

> But he took her by the lily-white hand
> He showed her his rooms, they were twenty-one;
> He placed the keys until her hand
> Sayin', 'Ye're the lady o' the Denty Doon Bye.'

BIBLIOGRAPHY

British   Buchan and Hall, pp. 88–9; Child, vol. V, p. 153 (in the note to No. 290); Greig, No. 25; Hecht, pp. 221–3 and p. 324; Herd, vol. II, pp. 232–4; Kennedy, p. 407; *Scottish Studies*, vol. XVI, pp. 146–7.

Alternative title   The Dainty Downby.

'The Laird o' the Denty Doon Bye', sung by Maggie McPhee.

1   A gentleman on horseback he come riding by,
     He saw a bonnie lassie milk her faither's kye;
     O, what wad ye tak' tae come and milk mine?
     I'll mak' ye lady o' the Denty Doon Bye.

2   He took her by the lily-white hand,
     He laid her on tae her ain grassy land;
     He left her on tae her ain grassy land,
     O, never for to rise again.

3   It was on a mornin' in the bonnie month o' May
     When her father had some money for to pay;
     O, when her father had some money for to pay
     Tae the laird o' the Denty Doon Bye.

4   Hullo, good mornin', and how div ye do?
     And how is your daughter, Jannety, noo?
     O, how is your daughter, Jannety, noo
     Since I laid her on the Denty Doon Bye?

5   My dochter, Jannety, she's nae very weel,
       O, my dochter, Jannety she cowps at her kale,
       O, my dochter, Jannety, she's nae very weel
       Since ye laid her on the Denty Doon Bye.

6   He took fae his pocket a broad bunch o' keys,
       To her he said, 'I'll gae doon on my knees,'
       To her he said, 'I'll gae doon on my knees
       And mak' her lady o' the Denty Doon Bye.'

7   (They took him) up to room twenty-one,   (He took her?)
       And there he kneeled doon and he took her by the hand,
       And there he kneeled doon and he took her by the hand
       I'll mak' her lady o' the Denty Doon Bye.

8   Up jumps the auld wife, O what will we dae?
       'O,' says the auld man, 'we'll dance until we dee.'
       'Ay,' says the auld wife, 'and I'll dance tae,
       Seein' she's married tae the Denty Doon Bye.'

22   MOTHER, MOTHER MAKE MY BED

This strange little song is made up of floater-verses from a number of ballads and yet does not appear to be derived from any particular one. Early speculation tied it to 'Lady Maisry' (Child 65) and to 'Lord Lovel' (Child 75). As Mrs Hughes's text omits the normal first stanza and often condenses the contents of two stanzas into one, we also print a text from the singing of E. T. Wedmore (Bristol). We will use this text, entitled 'Come, Mother', in the short discussion below.

    An analysis of the piece shows that practically every stanza, couplet and line in it can be found in one or more of the following Child ballads:

'Lady Maisry' (Child 65)
'Lord Lovel' (Child 75)
'Little Musgrave' (Child 81)
'The Knight and the Shepherd's Daughter' (Child 110)
'Child Maurice' (Child 83)
'Fair Mary of Wallington' (Child 91)
'Bonny Barbara Allen' (Child 84)
'Fair Margaret and Sweet William' (Child 74)
'The Gypsy Laddie' (Child 200)
'Geordie' (Child 209)

There are undoubtedly others. It is generally agreed that the 'connecting links' between 'Mother, Mother' (based chiefly on the Wedmore stanzas 4, 5 and 6) and 'Lady Maisry' are too circumstantial to be regarded as hard evidence of a close relation. What does stand out, and make this song unique, is that a whole series of ballad formulas have been selected and put together in a form which has remained stable. All the reported texts are from southern England.

BIBLIOGRAPHY

British   *JFSS*, vol. I, pp. 43–4; also vol. III, pp. 74–6 and 304–6; also vol. V, pp. 135–7; Sharp (1), pp. 36–9.

Alternative titles   Lady Maisry; Now I Pray You Go Fetch Me My Little Footboy.

(untitled), sung by Caroline Hughes.

moderate, first two lines free, last two lines in tempo

a Ae (with inflected VI, ending on IV)

Verse 2

O, the first three miles that that lit- tle boy run,

And the sec-ond three miles that he walked;

And he walked till he came to a fair ri- ver side,

And he laid on his sweet breast and swum.

<table>
<tr><td>Caroline Hughes's text</td><td>Text from the singing of E. T. Wedmore of Bristol, published in JFSS vol. I</td></tr>
</table>

	Caroline Hughes's text		Text from the singing of E. T. Wedmore

1 O, once I had, O, a good little boy,
   Such a good little boy .   .   .   .
   .   .   .   .
   .   .   .   .

2 O, the first three miles that little boy
      run,
   And the second three miles that he
      walked;
   And he walked till he came to a fair
      riverside,
   And he laid on his sweet breast and
      swum.

3 Well, he swum till he got to the lord's
      front door,
   That he just now as they started
      meals;
   .   .   .   .

   .   .   .   .

4 O, he rung all the bell and out come
      the lord,
   O, what brought you here, my dear
      little boy?
   If you only knew the news that I've got
      to tell you, my lord,
   Not one more bit of food would you
      eat.

5 .   .   .   .

   .   .   .   .
   Now, I'm come to let you know that
      your true love's laying ill
   And will die now before you could
      come.

6 You'll go and saddle to me my milk-
      white steed,
   O, that I now might ride and see;
   That I may go and kiss her two true
      cherry lips,
   Before she has quite gone to clay.

---

1 Come mother, come mother, come
      make up my bed
   And spread that milk-white sheet,
   That I may lie down on a soft bed of
      down,
   For to try whether I could sleep or no.

2 The first that she spied was the little
      boy who went by,
   That was her own dear sister's son,

   Go and tell my true love that I'm
      going to die
   And I shall die long before he come.

3 The first two miles, O he walked,

   The second two miles, O he ran;

   He ran till he came to some fair
      waterside,
   He falled in on his breast and he
      swam.

4 He swam till he came to my lord's
      Highland park,
   Where they was all sitting at tea;

   If you did but know the news that I
      have brought
   You'd eat nor another bit.

5 Up spoke the noble lord, 'What can
      this matter be?
   Is my iron gates up or down?'
   'O no,' says the little boy, 'your true
      love's going to die,
   She'll be alone before you can come.'

6 Come saddle me up my white milky
      steed,
   And put the saddle on the iron-grey,
   That I may go and kiss her rosy cheeks

   Before they are turn to clay.

7 O, the lady she died on a Monday
    morning
Just before the village clock it struck
    twelve;
And the gentleman he died on the
    Tuesday morning
Just before the village bell struckèd
    one.

8 Now, the lady she was buried in a
    vault so deep,
And the gentleman was buried in a
    tomb;

. . . .

. . . .

9 Out of the lady's breast growed a
    purty rose-briar,
And he growed till he got to such a
    height,
Then he twisted and twined till a true-
    lover's knot,
And a rose wrapped around my
    sweet-briar.

7 My lady she died on Saturday night,

Just before the sun went down;

And my lord, O he died on the
    Sunday following,
Just before the morning prayer did go
    in.

8 My lady was buried in my lord's
    chancel,
And my lord was buried in the choir;

And out of my lady's breast there
    sprung a diamond rose,
And out of my lord's there grew a
    sweet-briar.

9 He grows so very high,

Till he could not grow any higher;

And up all on the top grows the true-
    lover's knot,
And the red rose wrapped round the
    sweet-briar.

23   LONG A-GROWING
(Laws O 35)

Baring-Gould hazarded the suggestion that 'this ballad is originally English and not Scotch', and in support of his argument he cites *The Two Noble Kinsmen* (1634), a dramatic work sometimes attributed to Shakespeare. In Act III Scene 5 of the play, the gaoler's love-crazed daughter sings a stanza from 'an old ballad':

> For ile cut my greene coat, a foote above my knee
> And I'll clip my yellow lockes, an inch below mine eie.
> Hey nonny nonny nonny, (etc.)

As evidence, this is less than convincing. The 'old ballad' could just as easily be Scots as English, particularly as the Scots pronunciation of 'eie' (eye) rhymes with 'knee'.

    The earliest reported text of the ballad is a two-stanza fragment in the

Herd *MSS*, entitled 'My Love is Lang a-Growing'. This was used by Burns as the basis of 'Lady Mary Ann', a song written for the *Scots Musical Museum* (1787). In a note to the Burns song, James Dick reports that 'a tune entitled "Long a-Growing" is said to be in Guthrie's *MSS* (c. 1670)'.

The first printed text which contained all the essential narrative elements of the ballad appeared in Maidment. It consists of eight ballad-stanzas with a three-line refrain and tells the story of a twelve-year-old boy (Young Craigstoun) who was married to an older (un-named) girl. After fathering a son on her, the boy died. In Christie's text, the three-line refrain has become the line which ends each quatrain, using the words 'daily/aye/lang (etc.) growing'. In all other respects, this text differs but slightly from its predecessor.

During the last century, versions have been reported from Scotland, Ireland, England and North America. In almost all of them changes have been minimal. The Craigston name has disappeared and the boy, like the girl, is now nameless. The ages of the couple vary from twelve and thirteen to eighteen and nineteen. Where significant change *does* occur, it is generally in the shirt-making stanza where the sark (shirt) has become a shroud.

BIBLIOGRAPHY

Laws O 35.

British Baring-Gould and Sheppard (2), pp. 8–9; Buchan and Hall, p. 71; Christie, vol. II, pp. 212–13; Dick, p. 317; *FMJ*, vol. II, p. 280; Ford (2), vol. II, pp. 183–4; Hecht, p. 145; *JFSS*, vol. I, pp. 214–15; also vol. II, pp. 44–7, 95–7, 206 and 274–6; also vol. V, pp. 190–3; *JEFDSS*, vol. VI, pp. 86–7; also vol. VIII, pp. 20–1; Kennedy, pp. 473–4; Maidment, pp. 21–4; Motherwell, pp. 86–7; *Museum*, vol. IV, No. 377; Ord, p. 112; Reeves (2), pp. 200–2; Sharp (2), vol. II, pp. 20–1; Sharp and Karpeles (2), vol. I, pp. 243–53.

Broadsides British Museum, LR 271 a 2, vol. VI, p. 33; also vol. VII, p. 215.

North American Creighton (1), pp. 81–2; Creighton (3), pp. 100–1; Karpeles (2), pp. 122–3; Peacock, vol. III, pp. 677–8.

Alternative titles The Young Laird of Craigstoun; Young Craigston; Lady Mary Ann; Bonny Boy; My Love (Bonny Boy) is (Long, Still) a-Growing; The Cottage Boy; The Trees they do Grow High (Tall); etc.

A. 'My Father's Castle Wall', sung by Nelson Ridley.

B. 'Young But Growing', sung by Caroline Hughes.

A.

1   Now, as I was a-walking round my father's castle wall,
        I seen one-hundred merry boys a-playing at football;
        It was one out of the hundered he looked so very small
        That I said, 'My bonnie boy, you're young and growing.'

2   Dear father, dear father, do you know what I have done?
        I have married to that young lord, I think he is too young;
        Dear daughter, dear daughter, if you think he is too young,
        We can send him to a college for another year or two.

3   At the age all of sixteen, my boys, he were a married man,
        At the age of seventeen he were the father of a son;
        At the age of all eighteen, my boys, his grave were growing green,
        So that soon put an end to his growing.

B.

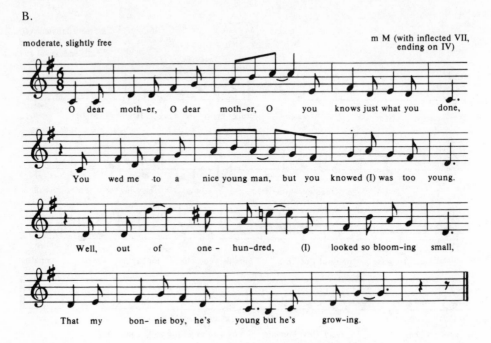

Note: When the singer gave the incomplete second verse the three lines were sung, respectively to the third, the third and the fourth given melodic lines above.

1   O dear mother, O dear mother, O you knows just what you done,
     You wed me to a nice young man, but you knowed (I)   (he?)
         was too young.
     Well, out of one-hundred, (I) looked so blooming small,   (he?)
     But my bonnie boy, he's young but he's growing.

2   . . . .
     At the age of seventeen he was the father of a son,
     At the age of eighteen, love, his grave was growing green,
     And that soon put an end to his growing.

24   THE THREE BUTCHERS
(Laws L 4)

It is odd that Child did not include this popular ballad in his collection as it not only fulfils his definition of a ballad but has also been popular with country singers at least since 1678, when it appeared as a black-letter broadside under the title of 'The Three Worthy Butchers of the North'.

[118]

Subsequent printing by broadside presses tended to reduce the story somewhat, but the general narrative and much of the early poetry has remained. The full story is as follows: two or three butchers are riding along the highway carrying a large sum of money – often given as five hundred pounds. (A more common American opening involves not five hundred *pounds* but a journey of ten thousand *miles*.) The butchers hear a cry and find a naked woman bound to the ground. She explains that she has been robbed and left there by robbers. One of the butchers, usually Johnson, covers her with his coat and takes her up behind him on his horse. As they ride along the highway she screams or in some manner gives a signal, at which a band of robbers springs out in ambush and commands Johnson to halt. A fight ensues in which he kills most of the robbers before being stabbed from behind by the woman. His companions have usually disappeared from the scene by this time. The woman is punished and Johnson's death is lamented.

Few of the traditional versions of the ballad retain all the elements of this plot. The core, however, is always there: the stabbing of Johnson by the woman he has rescued. Small variations with regard to the number of butchers, the number of robbers, the manner in which the plot unfolds, the type of weapon used, the fate of the murderess, etc., are common but do not affect the story line.

Some of the versions have a chorus, the burden of which incorporates a line from the early broadside:

> With a high ding ding, with a ho ding ding
> With a high ding dee, and God bless all good
> people from Evil Company.

These lines, slightly altered, form the chorus of the fullest English text which we have found (*JFSS*, vol. I) and appear in Greig's version, capping his first verse with:

> O dear, Oh keep good people from bad women's company.

North American texts tend to suffer from what Brown calls 'some loss of coherence', something of an understatement. As well as appearing under various hilarious titles, these texts occasionally have a girl as the leader of the band, ending with an exciting chase up a mountain, the killing of the girl and the finding of ill-gotten gains in her saddlebags. Other versions cross with local American pieces such as 'Been All Around This World' and 'The Gambling Man'. One version even transforms the unfortunate hero into a sailor.

BIBLIOGRAPHY

Laws I 4.

British   Ashton (1), pp. 403–5; *Euing*, No. 235; Greig, No. 36; *Hammond MSS*, S-288 and D-666; *Henry Collection*, No. 185; *JFSS*, vol. I, pp. 174–6; also vol. VIII, pp. 2–3; Kennedy, p. 723; Purslow (2), p. 89; Reeves (2), pp. 215–16; *Roxburghe*, vol. VII, pp. 57–63; Sharp and Karpeles (2), vol. I, pp. 274–9; Williams, pp. 275–6.

Broadsides   British Museum, LR 271 a 2, vol. I, p. 21 (Pitts); also vol. IV, p. 276 (Catnach).

North American   Chappell (Louis), p. 83; Davis (1), p. 39; Flanders (2), pp. 14–15; Karpeles (2), pp. 132–5; Leach, pp. 160–1; Moore, pp. 156–7; Peacock, vol. III, pp. 817–18.

General   Flanders, Ballard, Brown and Barry, pp. 238–44 (note).

Alternative titles   alliterative transformations of the names of the butchers (for instance, Ips, Gips and Johnson; Gibson, Wilson and Johnson, etc.); Three (Ten, Two) Jolly (Jovial, Merry, Good, Bold) Boochers (Hunters, Huntsmen, etc.)

'The Three Butchers', sung by Caroline Hughes.

1   'O hark, O hark!' cried Johnson,
     'I heard a poor woman cry.'
     They got her there stark naked
     With her hair pinned to the ground.

2   They floggèd this poor woman,
     They dragged her by the hair of her head,
     They dragged her through forest copses
     And they pinned her to the ground.

3   'Ride on, ride on!' cries Johnson,
     'There sounds that voice again!'
     'O no, O no,' says the other butcher boys,
     'Do let us go away.'

4   Johnson was a clever boy
     And he fought with courage bold,
     'Hark, O hark!' said Johnson,
     'For I hear that woman again.'

5   O, Johnson he was riding,
     He found a woman there;
     Found a woman stark naked
     With her hair pinned to the ground.

6   They dug the skewer through Johnson's back,
     All five he felled at once;
     He was the cleverest butcher boy
     That ever the sun shone on.

FAITHFUL LOVERS

25 SWEET WILLIAM
(Laws K 12)

This nineteenth-century broadside ballad has been widely reported from Great Britain and Ireland, Canada and the United States. Versions vary from fragments of one stanza to full-blown texts of ten quatrains. There are several stock openings:

> 1 A Sailor's life is a merry life,
> He'll rob young girls of their heart's delight;
> Then go and leave them to sigh and moan,
> No tongue can tell when he will return.

This is the most common opening, but in America almost half the versions deal with soldiers rather than sailors and the 'merry life' has become a dreary, or weary life.

> 2 The second most common opening is the one used in our text. This stanza appears in almost all the versions, but not always in the opening position. It may begin in a different manner such as 'I'll go build myself a boat', or 'O build me some little boat' or even 'Mother, mother, build me a boat'. It is definitely one of the most tenacious of the stanzas. Where a fragment only remains, it is likely to contain this particular stanza.

> 3 O early, early all in the spring,
> My love was press'd to serve the king;
> The wind blew high and the wind blew low
> And parted me and my young sailor boy.

This is usually followed by the 'Father, father' stanza and is most common in English and Newfoundland versions. These first two lines are reminiscent of another broadside ballad, 'Early Early in the Spring' (Laws M 1), and as this is not a particularly common opening stanza it is possibly the result of a local hybridisation.

4   As I walked down by the river side,
    Down where the waters gently glide;
    I heard a lovely lady mourn,
    Crying, 'What shall I do? My true-love's gone.'

The appearance of an observer on the scene is confined to the southern United States texts, most of which then proceed to the 'Father, father' stanza.

5   Black is the colour of my true-love's hair,
    His cheeks are as red as the roses fair;
    If he would return it would give me joy,
    For none will I have but my sweet sailor boy.

The opening couplet here is used also in the well-known American song 'Black is the Colour', but the entire stanza is often found in versions of 'Sweet William' in the form of a reply given by the girl to the captain who asks 'What did your Willie look like?' (our stanza 3).

There are other openings, many of which begin in the middle of the story with 'Captain, captain, tell me true / Does my Sweet Willie sail with you?', or 'She run her boat against the main' (etc.).

The various texts are quite consistent in so far as concerns the main story-line. There is one charming version from Virginia (Cox), in which the girl hastens to her love who is 'a-going to die' in the hospital, but arrives there too late. Randolph reports a lumberjack adaptation of the story. For the most part, however, changes are confined to (a) the transformation of the sailor into a soldier; (b) the manner in which the boy dies – drowning, being shot, being lost sight of, and so on.

There exist also some literary versions with some fine poetry but these do not appear to have entered the mainstream of the folk tradition. There a number of variants similar to our B-text which have crossed with or taken elements from other pieces like 'The Lass of Roch Royal' (Child 76), 'The Unconstant Lover', 'Little Sparrow', 'The Butcher Boy' and others. Only by its second and fourth stanzas can our B-text be recognised as a member of the 'Sweet William' family. The opening stanza belongs properly to 'The Croppy Boy' (Laws J 14), while the third is compounded of lines from 'Died for Love' (Laws P 52) and 'The Green Valley'.

BIBLIOGRAPHY

Laws K 12.

British Ashton (2), p. 63; Broadwood and Maitland, pp. 74–5; Christie, vol. I, pp. 248–9; Greig, No. 64; *JFSS*, vol. I, pp. 99–100; also vol. II, pp. 293–4; also vol. VIII, pp. 212–13; Joyce (2), No. 331; Kidson and Moffat (2), pp. 92–3; Moeran, p. 26; Morton, pp. 11–12; O'Lochlainn (1), pp. 112–13; Reeves (1), pp. 254–5; Seeger and MacColl, p. 28; Sharp (2), vol. II, pp. 47–8; Sharp and Karpeles (2), vol. II, pp. 320–3.

Broadsides *British Museum*, LR 271 a 2, vol. VIII, p. 121 (Catnach).

North American Carey, p. 99; Cox (1), pp. 29–30; *Dusenbury MSS*, No. 32 8a; Eddy, pp. 97–103; Henry (1), pp. 188–90; Hubbard, pp. 90–1; Huntington, pp. 272–3; Karpeles (1), pp. 60–2; Karpeles (2), pp. 156–60; Leach, pp. 46–7; Moore, pp. 174–5.

Alternative titles My Boy Willie; Sweet (Lost) Willie; The Sailor Boy (Lad); The Sailor's (Soldier's) Sweetheart (Life); Soldier (Lost) Lover; Father, Build me a Boat; Captain, Captain, Tell Me True; The Deep Blue Sea; The Pinery Boy, etc.

A. 'My Willie Boy', sung by Maggie McPhee.

B. (untitled), sung by Nelson Ridley.

A.

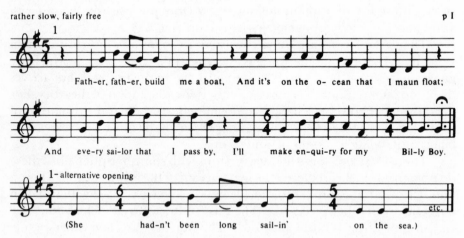

1   Father, father, build me a boat,
      And it's on the ocean that I maun float;
      And every sailor that I pass by,
      I'll make enquiry for my Billy Boy.

2   She hadn't been long sailin' on the sea,
When a homeward vessel she chanced to see;
O captain, captain, come tell me true:
O, is my Willie Boy on board with you?

3   O, what's the colour of your Willie's hair?
Or what kind o' clothes does your Willie wear?
His hair is auburn and his eyes is blue,
And he wears a suit of the navy blue.

4   I doot, I doot, your Willie's no' here,
For he was drownded in yonder pier,
Do you mind thon night when the wind blew high?
It parted us and our cabin-boy.

5   O mother, mother, come make my bed,
Come make it long and come make it wide.
And on my breast put a turtle dove
T'let all world know that I died in love.

B.

1 Early one morning all in the spring,
  Where the birds did whistle and softly sing;
  They changed their note, my love, from tree to tree,
  And the song they sang was 'Old Ireland's Free'.

2 Now, the colour of amber was my love's hair,
  With her ruby lips and her rosy cheeks;
  With her ruby lips and her rosy cheeks,
  O, ten thousand times they've been joined with mine.

3 Now, it's are you single or are you free,
  Or have you came here to marry me?
  For a maid again, O, I never will be,
  Till the apples grow on an orange tree.

4 Now, I passed by one large ship, I passed by two,
  Now, I passed by three large ships, I passed by four;
  Then every large ship that I passed by,
  Then I will enquire for my sailor boy.

26 THE DARK-EYED SAILOR
(Laws N 35)

This broken-token song is widely spread in Britain and North America and the versions are fairly consistent in tune and text. Our set is not complete, does not tell of the sailor returning home nor of the couple happily settling down in a cottage beside the sea.

BIBLIOGRAPHY

Laws N 35.

British Ashton (2), p. 71; Baring-Gould and Sheppard (2), pp. 88–9; Christie, vol. II, pp. 100–1; *Gardiner MSS*, Hp-1265; Greig, No. 112; *Henry Collection*, No. 232; *JFSS*, vol. IV, pp. 129–32; Kidson and Moffat (2), pp. 120–1; O'Lochlainn (1), pp. 10–11; Ord, pp. 323–4; Purslow (1), pp. 30–1; Sharp and Karpeles (2), vol. I, pp. 550–1.

Broadsides *British Museum*, LR 271 a 2, vol. II, p. 197 (Hodges and Pitts); also vol. IV, p. 344 (Catnach); also vol. VI, p. 236 (Disley of St Giles).

North American Creighton (4), pp. 58–9; Fowke, pp. 30–1; Greenleaf and Mansfield, p. 81; Karpeles (2), pp. 184–5; Peacock, vol. II, pp. 513–14.

Alternative titles Fair Phoebe and Her Dark-Eyed Sailor; The Dark-Eyed Canaller; The Broken Ring (Token), etc.

'The Brisk Young Sailor', sung by Nelson Ridley.

1 I once courted a brisk young sailor,
   And then he roamed away from me;
   I will roam no more with that brisk young sailor,
   Lest a brisk young sailor prove my downfall.

2   The ring was broke and shared between 'em,
I have got one young man waiting for me;
Seven long years, now I've been waiting,
Till my sailor boy he return to me.

3   Seven long years I have been waiting,
He may be drownded, he may be dead;
I will roam no more with that brisk young sailor,
Lest the dark-eyed sailor prove my downfall.

27   THE SAILOR'S RETURN
(Laws N 42)

The Roxburghe Collection contains an interesting but undated broadside by one Cuthbert Birket, in which a young girl lamenting for her absent love is accosted by a stranger. He presents her with a token which she recognises as the one which she gave to her love. The stranger declares that the lover, as he lay dying on the battlefield, asked him to return it to her. He goes on to say that it was her lover's last wish that she should transfer her affections to him that delivers the token. The girl declares she will never love another, at which point the stranger reveals himself as the 'dead' lover. The somewhat stilted language of this broadside has little in common, apart from its theme, with the traditional song.

Wherever the song is found, and it is perhaps one of the most common of the returned lover-broken token songs, it is easily identified by its opening stanza: a lady is walking in her garden and a young man approaches her, proposing marriage. Our A-text is fairly complete and contains most of the standard motifs, the presence or absence of which would appear to be dependent on where the song has been collected. The high castle, for instance, common in Scots versions, is rarely found in texts from England, Ireland or North America. Again, the broken token itself is frequently absent from American versions but rarely from British and Irish sets. Whether or not the sailor returns laden with material wealth appears to be quite arbitrary. He is often welcomed explicitly for himself alone. In some American versions, the 'patient Grissel' motif is to be found:

I wish him rest if he be drownded,
I wish him peace if he be slain;
But if he's to another pretty girl married
I'll love the girl that pleasures him.

BIBLIOGRAPHY

Laws N 42.

British   Christie, vol. I, pp. 264–5; also vol. II, pp. 200–1; Greig, No. 23; *JFSS*, vol. IV, pp. 127–35; also vol. VI, pp. 272–3; *Hammond MSS*, B-393 and D-566; *Henry Collection*, No. 818; O'Lochlainn (1), pp. 4–5; Ord, pp. 326–7; Purslow (2), p. 29; Reeves (2), pp. 64–5; *Roxburghe*, vol. III, pp. 127–31; Sharp and Karpeles (2), vol. I, pp. 552–5.

Broadsides   *British Museum*, LR 271 a 2, vol. I, part 1, p. 98 (Catnach); also vol. IV, pp. 231 and 272 (Catnach); also vol. VI, p. 63 (Such).

North American   Creighton (2), pp. 57–8; Creighton and Senior (1), pp. 1–5; *Dusenbury MSS*, No. 19 5a; Fuson, pp. 77–8; Moore, pp. 187–9; Peacock, vol. II, pp. 584–7; Smith (Reed), pp. 162–3.

Alternative titles   It would seem that no definitive title exists for the song, so we have chosen 'The Sailor's Return' which is the oldest British title. Laws calls it 'Pretty Fair Maid'. Other titles involve word combinations such as 'young and single sailor', 'lady or maiden in the garden', 'broken ring or locket', 'brisk young, or welcome sailor', and so on.

A. 'The Brisk Young Sailor', sung by Maggie McPhee.

B. 'In a Garden a Lady Walking', sung by Charlotte Higgins.

C. 'Seven Long Years', sung by Caroline Hughes.

A.

1   A lady in her garden walking,
    When a nice young sailor boy went passing by;
    He steppit up to her, just to view her,
    I say, my lady, would you fancy I?

2   I once had a love, but it was for a sailor,
    But it's seven long years since he's went away;
    And other seven I'll wait upon him,
    Till he comes back again, and marry me.

3   O, do you see those high, high castles?
    They're decorated by lilies white;
    I'll give you gold and I'll give you silver,
    If you say you'll be mine tonight.

4   O, yes I see those high, high castles,
    They're decorated by lilies white;
    I'll not take your gold, or I'll not take your silver,
    Or I will not be yours tonight.

5   He put his hand all into his pocket,
    His fingers they were now long and small;
    He took out a ring that was betwixt them,
    And when she saw it, now down she fell.

6   Rise up, rise up, my fair young lady,
    Rise up, rise up, O you're none the worse;
    For I am your sailor and I'm your Willie,
    And I've come back again to marry you.

7   O, yes I see those high high castles,
    All decorated by lilies white;
    I'll take your gold and I'll take your silver,
    And I will now be yours tonight.

1   In a garden a lady walking,
    A nice young sailor came passing by;
    He steppèd up to her, with chance to woo her,
    Saying, 'Lady, will you marry I?'

2   O no, kind sir, I'm not to marry
    A nobleman of high degree;
    For I have a true love and he's a sailor
    He sails upon the deep blue sea.

3   . . . .

    . . . .

    Perhaps he's married, perhaps he's drownded
    Perhaps he sails the ocean blue.

[131]

4   Well, if he's married I wish him pleasure,
     If he's drownded I wish him rest;
     But if he's out on the ocean sailing,
     He'll come back and he'll marry me.

5   O, do you see yon high, high castle
     All decorated with flowers white?
     I'll give you gold, dear, I'll give you silver,
     If you'll be mine just for tonight.

6   O, what do I care for your high, high castle?
     What do I care for your lilies white?
     What do I care for your gold or silver
     If my own dear Bill was here tonight?

7   He put his hands into his pocket,
     His fingers being long and small;
     He pulled out a ring which they'd broke between them,
     When she saw that she droppèd down.

C.

moderate, somewhat free   m I

O, sev-en long year you have-a been my sailor,

O, sev-en long year he been gone from me;

For 'tis if you're my young and my sin-gle sail-or,

Just show me the ring O that we broke be-tween.

1   O, seven long year you have-a been my sailor,
     O, seven long year he been gone from me;
     For 'tis if you're my young and my single sailor,
     Just show me the ring O that we broke between.

2   Well, (she) put his hand all into his pocket,   (he)
      Showing her the ring what they broke between;
      O surely,* surely, you're my own dear true love
      And the Lord'll send you O back home safe now.

*   pronounced 'sure-lie', with great emphasis.

28   MACDONALD'S RETURN TO GLENCOE
(Laws N 39)

Ford, Greig and Ord all collected singularly identical versions of this song. Our text is so confused that the story has almost disappeared. Laws gives the following résumé:

> The narrator meets a fair damsel in Glencoe and makes love to her, but she rejects him, saying she is loyal to MacDonald, the pride of Glencoe, who went to war ten years before. When he suggests that her lover may have forgotten her, she denies the possibility and says she'll remain single if she never sees him again. The speaker then produces the glove she has given him as a love-token and reveals himself as MacDonald.

Only the first two stanzas of our version maintain anything of the original story and, even so, our heroine has usurped the MacDonald title of the original line 'that once graced MacDonald the pride of Glencoe'. In more complete Scots texts, the love-token is produced in the penultimate stanza thus:

> Now proving her constant, I pulled out a glove,
> Which in parting she gave me as a token of love.

The revelatory function of the token is absent from our text. Instead, we have the exchange of a guinea and a pin, followed by a couplet expressing sentiments usually uttered by the heroine but here put in the mouth of the narrator. In the fourth and fifth stanzas, however, these sentiments are repeated, this time by the heroine, almost in the form of a refrain. The two lines with which both these stanzas begin appear to belong to a completely different song.

BIBLIOGRAPHY

Laws N 39.

British   Ford (2), vol. II, pp. 64–6; Greig, No. 55; *Henry Collection*, No. 655; *JFSS*, vol. II, p. 171; also vol. V, pp. 100–3; Ord, pp. 65–6.

Broadsides   British Museum, LR 271 a 2, vol. V, p. 42.
North American   Creighton (2), pp. 77–8; Huntington, pp. 113–16; Leach, pp. 310–11; Peacock, vol. II, pp. 579–80.

Alternative titles   Donald's Return to Glencoe; The Pride of Glencoe; Donald and Glencoe (etc.).

'The Lass o' Glencoe', sung by John MacDonald.

fairly slow, freely   m I

For as   I went a-   walk-   ing   one   eve-ning   in   June,

All   the   birds   in   the   bush- es   were   sing-ing   in   tune;

When   I   saw   a   fair   maid- en,   an   an- gel   ap-   peared,

'Twas the   fair- est   of   maid- ens that two   eyes   ev-   er   seen.

1   For as I went a-walking one evening in June,
     All the birds in the bushes were singing in tune;
     When I saw a fair maiden, an angel appeared,
     'Twas the fairest of maidens that two eyes ever seen.

2   For I asked her her name, ay, and where she came from;
    O, she answered, 'Kind sir, I daur not tell.'
    But the ribbons o' tartan all around her did flow,
    She was Flora MacDonald from the Pass o' Glencoe.

3   Now, I gave her a guinea and she gied me a pin,
    Just a token of friendship that we'd meet again;
    But if I never meet her, it's single I'll go,
    And I'll mourn for the maiden that I met on Glencoe.

4   Now, he may be a hero or he may be a king,
    Who has left his affection in some foreign land;
    But if I never see him, it's single I'll go,
    And I'll mourn for my stranger that I met on Glencoe.

5   Now, the big ship was ready o'er the ocean to go,
    Ay, to some foreign country and some foreign port;
    But if I never see him, it's single I'll go,
    And I'll mourn for my stranger that I met on Glencoe.

29 THE LASS O' GLENCOE

The second stanza of this song appears to have been borrowed from 'MacDonald's Return to Glencoe' (our No. 28), while the fifth stanza belongs to 'Portmore', or 'My Heart's in the Highlands', the song which inspired Burns's 'Farewell to the Highlands'. The remaining stanzas are probably the work of Mrs McPhee.

BIBLIOGRAPHY

British Christie, vol. II, pp. 180–1 ('Portmore'); Dick, pp. 453–4 (note on 'Farewell to the Highlands'); *JEFDSS*, vol. III, p. 245 (tune only).

'The Lass o' Glencoe', sung by Maggie McPhee.

1   Here's to the lassie o' bonnie Glencoe,
       I'll never forget her wherever I go;
       I painted her picture, it was lovely I know –
       But I still like my lassie o' bonnie Glencoe.

2   Her dress it was tartan of yellow and green,
       Wi' a bonnie blue ribbon to match her blue e'en;
       I asked her to marry, her answer was 'No',
       But I still like my lassie fae bonnie Glencoe.

3   It was in the heather I first met my lass,
       Wi' the bonnie green brackens that grow through the grass,
       Where the snake he does slither in the grass lyin' low,
       I still like my lassie fae bonnie Glencoe.

4   I'll tak' with me now, O, a lock o' her hair,
       Tae mak' me remember the lass I left there;
       Wherever I wander, wherever I go,
       I still like my lassie fae bonnie Glencoe.

5   My heart's in the Highlands, my heart is no' here,
       My heart's in the Highlands, a-chasin' the deer;
       All chasin' the wild deer and followin' the roe,
       My heart's in the Highlands of bonnie Glencoe.

This is probably one of the most frequently reported songs in the British Isles and, undoubtedly, one of the least printed. Texts show considerable regional variation, though the refrains remain consistent and most versions retain the stanza which begins 'When I was single I wore a black shawl'. This would seem to indicate a relationship with 'The Joyful Maid and Sorrowful Wife', a song in which a wife's loss of youth and freedom are symbolically represented through juxtaposed items from her premarital and postmarital wardrobe.

In North America there is a large group of songs with roughly the same theme, usually beginning in the following manner:

> When I was single, went dressed all so fine,
> Now I am married, go raggedy all the time.
>   Lord, don't I wish I was a single girl again! (A)

A Glasgow children's street-song of the 1930s expresses similar sentiments in a similar way:

> When I was single, I used to go and dance,
> Now I am married, I cannae get the chance.
>   O it's a life, a weary weary life,
>   It's better to be single than to be a married wife. (B)

In all these single-*vs*-married songs, a social institution (marriage) is viewed as the source of the heroine's unhappiness. In 'Still I Love Him', however, there is a different emphasis. The institution still exists, the heroine still has much of which to complain, but she has by her side a flesh-and-blood companion – less than perfect, perhaps, but human and therefore capable of inspiring love in spite of the institution.

BIBLIOGRAPHY

British Kennedy, p. 460.

General 'The Joyful Maid and Sorrowful Wife': Cowell (unpaginated); *JFSS*, vol. VIII, pp. 148–50; *JEFDSS*, vol. III, pp. 51–2; also vol. IV, pp. 5–6; Kidson, pp. 156–7; Mason, p. 42; Ritchie (2), p. 33; Ritson (1), pp. 9–11.

Reference for song from which stanza (B) is quoted above: Buchan and Hall, p. 30.

References for songs from which stanza (A) is quoted above: Belden, pp. 437–9; Randolph, vol. III, pp. 69–70.

Alternative titles   Black Shawl; He Comes Doon Our Alley.

'Still I Love Him', sung by Charlotte Higgins.

1   For he comes to the wagon, he whistles me out,
       A light brown suit and his shirt hanging out.

Chorus: Still I love him – can't deny him,
           I'll go with him wherever he goes.

2   He bought me a muffler, both red white and blue,
       Because I wouldn't wear it he tore it in two. (chorus)

3   Before I was married I wore a black shawl,
       Now since I'm married I've sweet bugger-all. (chorus)

Like most identifiable combinations of floater-verses, this song has its kernel: the opening stanza of our A-text. The couplets which form the first halves of the second and third stanzas are relatively stable elements, as is verse 4.

The song does not appear to have survived in the New World, though one can find stanzas from it scattered throughout the huge corpus of love-lamentations like 'The Wagoner's Lad', 'Little Sparrow', 'Pretty Saro', 'Turtle Dove' and many others.

Sheila Hughes learned the song from her mother – so it is interesting to note the differences between the two texts. Caroline Hughes's tune, however, was far more inventive and varied.

BIBLIOGRAPHY

British   *Gardiner MSS*, H-355 and H-356; *Hamer*, p. 52; *Henry Collection*, No. 79; O'Lochlainn (1), p. 92; Purslow (3), p. 57; Reeves (1), p. 163; Sharp and Karpeles (2), vol. I, pp. 493–4.

Alternative titles   The Blackbird; My Love.

A. 'If I Was a Blackbird', sung by Sheila Hughes, to the same tune as the B-text.

B. 'If I Was a Blackbird', sung by Caroline Hughes. We give the melody as sung in the fourth verse, as this was the most stable.

A.

1   If I were a blackbird I would whistle and sing,
       I would follow the vessel my true love sailed in,
       All on the top rigging then I will build my nest,
       And I'd sleep the long night on his lily-white breast.

2   For he promised to take me to Donnyport Fair,
       To buy me red ribbons to tie on my hair;
       O, when I do meet him I will crowned him for joy,
       And the rest of my love, give to my sailor lad.

3   O, if I was a scholar, I would write him a letter,
       Line after line I would tell my sweetheart;
       When I got to the end, love, I would tell my sailor lad
       I love him and no one else.

4   O, my parents they slight me they would drive me away from my home,
Let them think what they like, dear, let 'em do what they can;
Let them think what they like, dear, let them do just what they can;
So long as breath's still in my body, I will still love that young man.

5   I cannot think the reason why women love men,
Nor I can't think the reason why men should love those,
Since a man's been my ruin, been my sadden downfall,
He's a-caused me to sleep under slimy cold walls.

B.

1   Now, I can't not think the reason why women loves men,
No, I can't not think the reason why men should love they;
But since a man has been my ruin, now I will send him downfall,
But he have caused me to lay between lime and cold stone.

2   Now, I once loved a sailor, he was a (britched) young man,   (brisk?)
My parents dislike me, turned him from the door;
And now he have left me and gone far away,
Long as breath's in my body, I'll still love that one.

3 Now, if I was a scholar, well I'd handle my pen,
   I would write my love a letter to return home again;
   And when I did meet him, I would crowned him with joy,
   And I'd kiss the fond lips of my bold Irish boy.

4 If I were a blackbird I would whistle and sing,
   I would follow the vessel my true love sailed in;
   On the top of the riggin' I would there build my nest,
   And I'd pillow my head on his lily-white breast.

32 THE YELLOW HANDKERCHIEF
(Laws O 37)

Commenting on a version of this song in the *Folk Song Journal*, Cecil Sharp describes the tune as 'a curious medley of "Green Bushes", "The Turtle Dove" and "Amble Town" ("The Oak and the Ash", etc.) tunes.' All the texts that we have seen are similarly compounded of lines and couplets from other songs. A stanza common to all of them (but lacking in ours) is:

  In the middle of the ocean
  There shall grow a myrtle tree
  If ever I proves false, my love,
  To the girl that loves me.

This verse is also found in 'The American Stranger' (Greig), a song which provides Mr Ridley's piece with its opening couplet.

BIBLIOGRAPHY

Laws O 37.

British *Gardiner MSS*, H-365; Greig, No. 59; *JFSS*, vol. V, pp. 174–5; Kennedy, p. 791; Purslow (3), p. 43.

Alternative titles Flash Company; Once I Loved Thomas; Bonnie Blue Handkerchief (etc.).

'I'm a Stranger in this Counteree', sung by Nelson Ridley.

1   I'm a stranger in this counteree, from America I came,
    O, there's no one they'll know me and can tell my name;
    There's a flower in my garden, all the beauties are gone,
    Can't you see what I am caming to by loving that one?

2   You take this yellow handkerchief by remembrance of me,
    And you'll never build your nest, my love, on top of any high tree;
    For the leaves they will wither and the roots will decay,
    That's the beauty all of a fair maid at any high degree.

3   I courted lovely Nancy by the age of sixteen,
    She was borned and brought up at a place called Ardene;
    There's a flower in my garden and the beauty's all gone,
    That's the beauty all of a fair maid, she will soon fade away.

33   BUSK, BUSK, BONNIE LASSIE

This piece does not appear in any of the major Scots collections. It is a kind of mirror-image of 'O No, No', a song of the 'Lisbon'/'Banks of the Nile' genre, in which a girl's plea that she should be allowed to accompany her lover to war is rejected on the grounds that her beauty would fade and her colour stain when exposed to the frost and rain of the highlands.

The first halves of stanzas 1 and 3 of 'O No, No' (quoted below) correspond to the first halves of our third and fourth stanzas:

1   O don't you see yon mountains sae gloomy and sae high?
    They've parted many a lover and they'll part you and I.
    But sae sair's that does grieve me, away I maun go,
    And ye canna come wi' me, lovie, O no, no.

3   O don't you see yon soldiers, how they march along?
    Their guns are all cocked and their swords are all drawn.
    But sae sair's (etc.)

In the second half of each of the above stanzas, the young man is obviously refusing the girl's plea while, in the corresponding stanzas of 'Busk Busk', he is trying to persuade her to accompany him.

The song is a great favourite with Scots Travellers.

BIBLIOGRAPHY

British   Buchan and Hall, p. 111; Greig, Nos 107 and 141; Ord, pp. 136–7.

Alternative title   Bonnie Glenshee.

'Busk, Busk, Bonnie Lassie', sung by Charlotte Higgins.

1   Busk, busk, bonnie lassie, and come alang wi' me,
    I will tak' ye tae Glenisla near bonnie Glenshee.

2   O, do you see yon shepherds as they all march along,
    Wi' their plaidies buckled roond them and their sheep they graze on?
    Busk, busk, bonnie lassie, and come alang wi me,
    I will tak' ye tae Glenisla near bonnie Glenshee.

3   O, do you see yon soldiers as they all march along,
    Wi' their guns on their shoulders and their broadswords hanging
        doon?
    Busk, busk, (etc.)

4   O, do you see yon high hills a' covered wi' snaw?
    They hae pairted mony a true love and they'll soon pairt us twa.
    Busk, busk, (etc.)

34   THE COURTING COAT

In English variants of this song, pit-boots (navvy-boots, a kettle-smock, or cattle-smock) take the place of the coat mentioned here. Reeves mentions a version 'noted by Mr Patrick Shuldam-Shaw in the Shetlands, of which the refrain is "Wi' my coortin' coat on".' More distant relatives are 'Jackie Tar' (Greig No. 73; Ord, pp. 324–5) and 'Wi' His Apron On' (Greig, Nos 40 and 148; Ord, p. 105).

BIBLIOGRAPHY

British   Kennedy, p. 397; Reeves (2), pp. 139–40.

Alternative titles   Pit (Navvy) Boots; The Bold English Navvy.

'The Courting Coat', sung by Wilhelmina MacAllister.

1   One night after supper I was shaving my beard,
     No better for courting could I be prepared;
     For the moon shining clearly it led me along,
     And I couldna bide awa' wi' my courting coat on.

2   There we did sport and it's there we did play,
     Counting the hours as the night passed away,
     Early next morning, she says to me, 'John,
     O, see what you've done wi' your courting coat on.'

3 O lassie, O lassie, O dinna grieve me,
 It wasna for courting that I come to thee;
 My spirits gaed wafting when I thought aboot yon
 And look what I've done wi' my courting coat on.

35 THE WALNUT GIRL

When John Lydgate (1370–1451) wrote 'The London Lykpeny', he started a fashion for poems and songs about London's street-vendors and their cries which was to last for more than four hundred years. Eighteenth- and early nineteenth-century songwriters turned out scores of popular love-lyrics extolling the beauties of young women engaged in selling lavender, oysters, water-cresses, pretty flowers, codlings, cockles and mussels, and even cat-meat. 'The Walnut Girl' is probably a late representative of the type.

'The Little Walnut Gel', sung by Nelson Ridley.

1

    Now, as I was a-walking one bright and summer's morning,
    I met a fair young creature, she was passing by my way;
    The basket stood before her and quickly I adore her,
    She were so pretty and handsome and her eyes was just like sloes.

Chorus: Ten-a-penny walnuts, my Nellie she were by,
             Fresh from Common Garden, please to came and try;
             Fresh from Common Garden and please to came and try,
             So who would buy my ten-a-penny walnut?

2

    Now, my love, I'm sick of single life, no longer can we tarry,
    From three weeks next Sunday, my love I'm going to marry;
    O, won't we be happy till wedlock breaks us here?
    But to tell the truth, I fell in love with that little walnut gel.

Chorus: Ten-a-penny walnut, my Nellie she will try, (etc.)

EROTIC SONGS

36 ALL FOURS

The most striking aspect of this song is its popularity among southern English singers as opposed to its scarcity in printed collections. Almost all the English informants, whether Traveller or *gorgio*, encountered by the editors had either a full text, a fragment, or knowledge of the existence of the piece.

The game of All Fours is listed in Hoyles *Rules of Games* as an ancient one. It is still played in Britain though it is not as popular as it was at the turn of the century. It is one of a large family of card games in which the ace is high and the jack low. The object is to win High, Low, Jack and (therefore) the Game. Although All Fours went to the United States under various titles (Seven-up, Old Sledge, High-Low-Jack, Pitch), the song does not appear to have followed it unless there, too, it has managed to maintain an underground existence.

BIBLIOGRAPHY

British *Gardiner MSS*, H-73 and H-1278; Kennedy, pp. 402–3; Purslow (2), p. 35; Reeves (1), p. 43; Sharp and Karpeles (2), vol. II, pp. 247–61.
Alternative titles The Game of All Fours; The Game of Cards.

A. 'All Fours', sung by Caroline Hughes. We have given a full notation of this song to demonstrate how complicated is the task of notating Mrs Hughes's melodies. It was difficult to decide whether this tune is in Mixolydian with a frequently *raised* VII degree or in Ionian with a frequently *lowered* VII degree, as the singer often rendered this note as a quarter-tone. We settled for Ionian and starred the indeterminate VII interval, also the IV degrees which were in between F and F $\sharp$.

It is interesting to note the points at which the long, held notes occur (especially in verse 3). And it is not by accident that 2/4 bars with triple quarter-notes are introduced in the fifth and sixth verses.

B. 'One-Two-and-Three', sung by Levi Smith.

A.

Verse 3

Well, we walked and we talked 'long to- geth-er,

Till we come to an old —— el- der tree.

Now she sat down and I sat down be- side her,

Then we start play- in' says High Low the Game.

Verse 4

Well, she chucked the cards out and pulled out the pack, love.

She chucked the Jack, O, and I chucked the Queen.

She chucked the Jack, love, and I chucked the Queen, then.

That's how I come, now, Jack High Low the Game.

Verse 5

Now he said, 'Will we play a bit long-er?

Now I feels wea-ry and ti-red as well.

I say, young girl, I'll al- low that you beat me

If you will play the game o- ver a- gain.'

Verse 6

O now will you be this way to- mor- row?

Tell me if you'll be on this high-way a- gain?

Yes, I will pro- mise you I'll be this way to- mor-row —

Then we will play the game o- ver a- gain.

1   O, as I were a-walking from Broadway to Glasgow,
     O, a fair purty damsel came walking my way;
     O, quickly I made to that fair purty damsel
     Quickly now she took hold of my hand.

2   I said, 'Where are you going, my fair purty damsel?
     Where are you going so early this way?
     For I am a-going my way home to Glasgow.
     Can I now make you and walk 'long with you?'

3   Well, we walked and we talked 'long together,
     Till we come to an old elder tree.
     Now she sat down and I sat down beside her,
     Then we start playin' says High Low the Game.

4   Well, she chucked the cards out and pulled out the pack, love.
     She chucked the Jack, O, and I chucked the Queen.
     She chucked the Jack, love, and I chucked the Queen, then.
     That's how I come, now, Jack High Low the Game.

5 Now, he said, 'Will we play a bit longer?
  Now I feels weary and tired as well.
  I say, young girl, I'll allow that you beat me
  If you will play the game over again.'

6 O now will you be this way tomorrow?
  Tell me if you'll be on this highway again?
  Yes, I will promise you I'll be this way tomorrow –
  Then we will play the game over again.

B.

moderate, slightly free   a M (with inflected IV and VII)

O, as I was a- walk- ing one bright sum-mer's morn-ing,

O, as I went out walk-ing all on the high- way;

O, but who should I meet but a fair pret- ty crea-ture

She was walk- in' and chat-ter- in' all on the high- way.

6 - for verse 2   13- for verse 3

Till we come to some sha-dy green tree;(etc.) Sir, I'm go-ing to a place they call Wind-sor

14

1 O, as I was a-walking one bright summer's morning,
  O, as I went out walking all on the highway;
  O, but who should I meet but a fair pretty creature
  She was walkin' and chatterin' all on the highway.

2   For we both walked, we both talked, a few miles together
Till we come to some shady green tree;
For she sat down first, for I sat myself beside her,
For the game that we played was the One-Two-and-Three.

3   For she saddled up her horse and she bid me good morning;
For she saddled up her horse and she bid me farewell;
She says, 'I says, kind sir, I'm going to a place they call Windsor
For that old little sweet town, that's where I was born.'

4   For she saddled up her horse and she bid me good morning;
For she saddled up her horse and she bid me farewell;
She says, 'I says, kind sir, I'll be this way tomorrow.'
And the game that we played was the One-Two-and-Three.

37   THE JOLLY BARBER LAD

The English and Scots traditional repertories are rich in euphemistic songs
and scores of trades and occupations have contributed their terminologies
and their tools to the vocabularies of sexual symbolism. While the barber is
a comparative late-comer to the scene he is, apparently, no stranger at the
campfires of Scots travelling people.

The song is probably of music-hall origin and possibly no older than
1905, the year in which the word 'skivvy' became a popular slang synonym
for a maid-servant. On the other hand, the 'crown' mentioned in the fifth
stanza had become a rare item of currency as early as 1870, so the song may
be earlier than that. It is, however, unlikely to be older than 1816, the year
in which the gold sovereign (fifth stanza) was first minted.

'The Jolly Barber Lad', sung by John MacDonald.

moderate, with enjoyment

p I/Ly

Now, there was a jol- ly bar–ber lad, lived down in A- ber- deen;

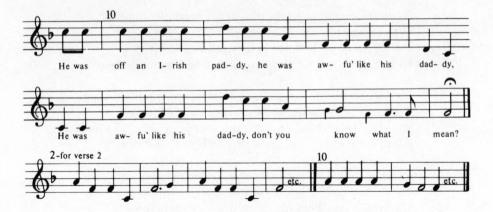

Note: MacDonald went straight from line 1 to line 3 when he sang the first verse.

1   Now, there was a jolly barber lad, lived down in Aberdeen;
. . . .
He was off an Irish paddy, he was awfu' like his daddy,
He was awfu' like his daddy, don't you know what I mean?

2   There was a lady fair, she lived in Easter Square,
She sent for this young barber for to come and curl her hair;
Wi' his curlin' tongs and scissors, his soap-brush and his razor,
He went to shave the lady, don't you know what I mean?

3   He went up to the doorway and he boldly rang the bell;
He was answered by a skivvy, for she knew her business well.
Is your mistress at her leisure, for I have come to shave her,
I have come to shave her, don't you know what I mean?

4   If that's the jolly barber lad, just send him up to me,
I've always been united and united I will be;
For my husband he's a yeoman, and I might as well have no man,
He's just like a lady when he goes to bed with me.

5   Noo, after all was over, and after all was done,
She handed this young barber lad a sovereign and a crown;
Now, he always goes to shave her, but he never takes a razor,
He never takes a razor, don't you know what I mean?

38   THE MOLECATCHER

As with the preceding song, it is only during the last few years that this immensely popular piece has succeeded in finding its way into print. Before publishing it in 1904, Baring-Gould felt himself obliged to supply a completely re-written text and five years later Vaughan Williams contributed three tunes to the *Journal* with the comment 'the words are unsuitable for this journal'.

A Hampshire version collected by Gardiner ends with the following stanza:

> So, now the young farmer must live at the last,
> For he spent all his money at the sign of the cross;
> He spent all his money, I cannot tell how,
> I dare him hang up at the sign of the plough.

Reeves, in a footnote to the song, makes the comment that 'at the sign of the Cross is probably a euphemism for "in support of a bastard (i.e. cross-bred) children", just as "the sign of the Plough" implies fornication,' If such a euphemism exists it has escaped the notice of British lexicographers. The euphemistic French phrase *logé à l'Hôtel du Croissant* would appear to have no English equivalent, and in any case the reference there is to a cuckold and our discomfited young farmer is definitely not one of that unhappy company.

Mr Ridley's text, though reduced to a mere skeleton, retains the most essential elements of the plot.

BIBLIOGRAPHY

British   Baring-Gould and Sheppard (2), pp. 90–1; *Gardiner MSS*, Hp-218 and Hp-1017; *JFSS*, vol. IV, p. 87; Kennedy, p. 463; Purslow (1), p. 61; Reeves (1), p. 191.

'The Molecatcher', sung by Nelson Ridley.

1   It's somewhere in Sussex, not far from The Plough,
      There lives a molecatcher I can't tell you how;
      He goes a-molecatching from morning till night,
      Till some jolly young farmer come and play with his wife.

2   Now, it's upstairs he went there was (no park could be)
      The molecatcher followed him closely behind;
      And when he got into the middle of his fun,
      The molecatcher grabbed hold of the tail of the young farmer's coat.

3   Ay ay!* What have you got at?
      He says, 'I've got you in my moletrap.'
      He looked to the farmer, he laughed to his wife,
      He's the finest old mole I ever caught in my life.

*   Spoken with great gusto.

39 FEATHERIN' OOT AND IN

The formula on which this song relies is a simple but effective one. The first three lines of each of the five stanzas deal with prosaic, domestic matters such as buying a pair of shoes, a gown, a plaid, or in introducing members of the narrator's family. The last line of each stanza promises to explain the motivation behind the purchases and the earning power of the singer and her female relatives. The promise is fulfilled by the chorus, which graphically describes all the ins and outs of the matter without actually naming the action or its source.

The song appears to have escaped the notice of collectors, though the second stanza is paralleled by one found in a fragment in Herd's MSS, entitled 'Still Cauld, Ay Cauld':

> He bought to me a pair of shoon
> And a' to ha'd the cauld frae me,
> He bad me dance till they were done,
> And that wad keep the cauld frae me.

BIBLIOGRAPHY

British Hecht, p. 144.

'Featherin' Oot and In', sung by Maggie McPhee.

moderate, slyly

m I (with inflected VII)

For they ca' my faith-er 'Drunk-en Tom', My mith-er's 'Gleid Gra-cie';

And for my-sel' I'm a clev- er quean, Be- cause I have a

Chorus:

Fine gyang feath-er-in' oot and oot and ae, Feath-er-in oot an ad-die;

O, fol the doo, a fal the day, O, fol the doo a- dad-die.

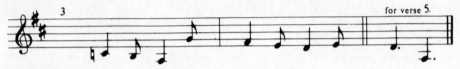

Note: Mrs McPhee half spoke, half sang this song. As a result, a number of the pitches were difficult to determine.

1 For they ca' my faither 'Drunken Tom',
  My mither's 'Gleid Gracie';
  And for myself' I'm a clever quean,
  Because I have a

Chorus: Fine gyang featherin' oot and oot and ae,
  Featherin' oot an addie;
  O, fol the doo, a fal the day,
  O, fol the doo a-daddie.

2 O, I bocht to her a pair o' sheen
  And O, but they were bonnie;
  But she made me dance till they were deen
  Because I had a (chorus)

3 He bocht to her a braw new goon
  And O, but it was bonnie;
  But he tried wi' her to mak a loon
  Because she had a (chorus)

4 I bocht to her a bonnie plaid,
  And O, but it was bonnie;
  But he wanted me to gang to bed
  Because I had a (chorus)

5 My mither is an auld bitch,
  And so is my granny.
  They earn mony's a paper pound
  Because they have a (chorus)

40   RING DANG DOO

Though common enough in the United States and the West Indies, this piece is rarely found in the repertories of English and Scots traditional singers. The use of the word 'pussy' as a euphemism for the female pudenda has been current in France since Rabelais and in Britain since the mid-seventeenth century.

BIBLIOGRAPHY

North American   Brand, pp. 80–1; Cray, pp. 60–1.

'Rackyman Doo', sung by Caroline Hughes.

1   Now, as I was a-walking all up the street,
     Who should I meet but a nice young fellow?
     I said, 'Hello, and how do you do?
     Would you like to have a game on my rackyman doo?'

2   O, the rackyman doo, pray what is that?
     It's very soft, like a pussy cat;
     With hairs all 'round and split in two,
     And that's what you call my bangyman doo.

3   O, the bangyman doo, pray what is that?
     It's something smooth and very soft;
     With hairs all 'round and split in two,
     And that's what you calls playing on the bangyman doo.

4   She took him down her father's cellar;
     She gave him wine and whiskey too.
     Well, I've gived you wine and whiskey, too —
     Would you please to have a game on my bangyman doo?

5   (repeat verse 3)

41   AYE SHE LIKIT THE AE NICHT

This song corresponds roughly in form and, to some extent, in character,
to 'Let Me in This Ae Nicht'. The similarity is particularly marked in the
refrain and in the two stanzas which follow:

Chorus: O let me in this ae nicht,
          This ae ae ae nicht,
          O let me in this ae nicht
          And I'll ne'er come back again, jo.

          Cast up your door unto the weet,
          Cast aff your shoon frae aff your feet,
          Syne to my chamber ye may creep
          But ye mauna do 't again, jo.

          But ere a' was done and a' was said,
          Out fell the bottom of the bed,
          The lassie lost her maidenhead
          And her mither heard the din, jo.

Hecht, in his commentary on the Herd manuscripts, has observed that 'this
and many similar songs are related to black-letter ballads of the type

"John's Earnest Request" (*Roxburghe*) tracing back to "O Who is At My Windo, Who, Who?"'. The request motif is absent from 'Aye She Likit the Ae Nicht', which should perhaps be considered as a sequel to the older song rather than as a version of it.

BIBLIOGRAPHY

British (sources for 'Let Me in This Ae Nicht') *Caledonian*, pp. 32–5; Glen, No. 311; Hecht, pp. 149–52; Herd, vol. II, pp. 167–9; *Museum*, vol. IV, No. 311; *Roxburghe*, vol. VI, part xvi, pp. 202–15; Thomson, vol. II, p. 2.

'Aye She Likit the Ae Nicht', sung by Maggie McPhee.

Chorus: Aye, she likit the ae nicht,
The ae, ae, ae nicht, – (it's)
Aye, she likit the ae nicht,
It's lassie, let me in!

1 When he got into bed,
He knockit the bottom boards over her head,
He jumped in and a' he said was
'Lassie, let me in, O.' (chorus)

2 When we got into bed,
He rolled the blankets over her head,
Then he give her the hairy peg
O, lassie, let me in, O. (chorus)

3 When he got into bed,
He rolled down the blankets and fund her leg,
Then he gied her his hairy peg,
O, lassie, let me in, O. (chorus)

4 For my door is almost green,
It will never sheen or shine;
Slip you up in your stockin' soles,
And (I'll) come slippin' in. (chorus)   (ye'll?)

5 But when he come doon the stair,
The auld wife she was standin' there;
She lifted her claes and said, 'O here,
O, laddie, put it in,' and (chorus)

Note: Each chorus ends with the fourth line of the verse which precedes it. The
chorus is sung more freely than the verse, almost in semi-recitative style,
especially bars 3–5 (incl.) which were delivered with such deliberation and
relish as to slow down the pace considerably.

42 MY FAITHER WAS HUNG FOR SHEEP-STEALING

The large family of songs of which this is an immodest member has,
according to Cray, a common ancestor in 'Old Hewson, The Cobbler'.
Hewson, a cobbler-turned-soldier in Cromwell's army, later became a
prominent political figure in the Commonwealth and was frequently the
object of calumny and satire in political songs and ballads of the early
Restoration period. In Chappell there is an air entitled 'My Name is Old
Hewson the Cobbler' with the information that, as early as 1731, it was

introduced into *The Jovial Crew* and *The Grub Street Opera*. Dick mentions having seen a copy of the verses of 'Old Hewson' in *The Vocal Miscellany* (Dublin, 1738). The editors of this book have been less fortunate, as none of the miscellanies, drolleries, garlands and broadsides in the British Museum have yielded up the verses in question.

'Old Hewson' notwithstanding, the pattern established in the opening stanza of Mrs McPhee's song is one common to a number of old songs. 'My Daddy's a Delver of Dykes' (Thomson, 1733) has for its theme a young woman lamenting her lack of suitors. Its opening lines are:

> My Daddy's a Delver of Dykes,
> My Minny can card and spin,
> And I'm a bonnie young lass
> And the siller comes linkin' in.

The Herd collection (1776) has another version entitled 'Slighted Nancy', and *The Thrush* has an English set of the verses:

> My father's a hedger and ditcher,
> My mother does nothing but spin
> I once was a pretty young maid
> But the money comes slowly in.

In *The Sword Dancer's Interlude* (Bishoprick Garland, 1834), the 'Bessie' gives an account of his forebears:

> My father he was hanged,
> My mother was drowned in a well;
> And now I'se left alone
> All by my own sel'.

Dixon and Bell quote a somewhat different version 'as now performed at Christmas in the county of Durham [1846]':

> My mother was burned for a witch,
> My father was hanged on a tree;
> And it's because I'm a fool
> There's nobody meddle wi' me.

A First World War version goes:

> My sister she works in a laundry,
> My father he fiddles for gin;
> My mother she takes in washing,
> My God, how the money rolls in. (Sandburg)

The 'Dick Darby/Denby/Darling the Cobbler' members of this song-family are found in three main forms: (1) as a set of verses describing the shoemaker's craft; (2) as a piece in which craft stanzas alternate with stanzas cataloguing the various occupations of a single family group and (3) as a set of verses consisting entirely of variations on the family occupation theme. For more detailed discussion of this song and its New World connections, see Cray's note.

BIBLIOGRAPHY

British   Chappell (2), vol. II, pp. 450–1; Dick, pp. 414–15 (note); Dixon and Bell, p. 398; Ford (2), vol. I, pp. 229–30; Greig, No. 18; Herd, vol. II, pp. 81–3; Kennedy, p. 502; Ritchie (2), pp. 103–4; Sharp (Cuthbert), no page number; Sola Pinto and Rodway, pp. 438–9; Thomson, vol. I, pp. 69–70; *The Thrush*, pp. 145–6; Williams, pp. 226–7.

North American   Brown, vol. II, pp. 456–7; Cray, pp. 23–4 and 222–6; Flanders, Ballard, Brown and Barry, pp. 223–4; Flanders and Olney, pp. 176–7; Gardner and Chickering, pp. 435–6; Lomax (3), pp. 134–5; Randolph, vol. I, pp. 385–6; Sandburg, p. 381.

Alternative titles   My Father's a Lawyer in England; My Sister She Works in a Laundry; (My God,) How the Money Rolls In; There's Naebody Comes to Marry Me (etc.).

'My Faither Was Hung for Sheep-Stealing', sung by Maggie McPhee.

Note: Chorus and verse are sung to the same tune.

1   My faither was hung for sheep-stealin',
        And my mither was burned for a witch;
        And my sister's a bawdy-hoose keeper,
        And mysel' I'm a son-of-a-bitch.

Chorus: Come twine-a-me ine-a-me idle,
              Come twine-a-me ine-a-me ay,
              Come twine-a-me ine-a-me idle,
              To me birse to my rossety-ends.

2   For I hae a root like a cuddy
          And ballocks like mountains o' brass;
          I could buck a' the whores in damnation
          And rattle my things at their arse. (chorus)

3   For I am a cobbler in Dublin,
          And I live at the back of the muck;
          I earn five shillin's every morning
          For learnin' young ladies tae buck. (chorus)

4   For I am a hedger and ditcher
          I'm up to the airse amang snaw,
          And the de'il took a-hold o' my pintle
          And he swore that he'd never let go. (chorus)

CASUAL ENCOUNTERS

43   ROSEMARY LANE
(Laws K 43)

In the eighteenth and early nineteenth centuries, the London thoroughfare known as Rosemary Lane (now called Royal Mint Street) consisted mostly of cheap lodging-houses and shady second-hand shops. The heroine of the song to which the street has given its title is generally described as a servant in such a house, though in some versions the scene of the action has been moved bodily to Drury Lane.

   The song shares a story and some of its stanzas with several other pieces, the most well-known of which is 'Bell-Bottom Trousers'. The third stanza of our text has been borrowed from the north-country song 'The Oak and the Ash', a broadside version of which, under the title of 'The Northern Lasse's Lamentation', was published between 1672 and 1695.

BIBLIOGRAPHY

Laws K 43.

British   Buchan and Hall, p. 83: *Hammond MSS*, D-153 and D-514; Hugill, pp. 498–501; *JFSS*, vol. VI, pp. 1–3; *JEFDSS*, vol. VI, p. 18; Purslow (2), p. 42; Purslow (3), p. 99; Reeves (1), p. 223; Reeves (2), pp. 181–3; *Rymour*, vol. II, p. 188; Sharp and Karpeles (2), vol. I, pp. 671–9.

Broadsides   *British Museum*, No. 1876 e 2, p. 66 (Jackson of Birmingham).

North American   Cray, pp. 32–3 and 160–2; *Fowke MSS* (under the title of 'Home Dearest, Home').

Alternative titles   When First I Went to Service; He Called For a Candle; The Sailor Boy; Never Trust a Sailor; Servant of Rosemary Lane (etc.).

'Once When I Was a Servant', sung by John MacDonald.

moderate, in rhythm

For it's once when I was a ser- vant in a house in A-ber- deen,

I was well be- loved by my mas- ter and his men;

O, till once there came a sai- lor tae oor hoose tae dine,

And that was the be- gin-nining o' my (doin', O)

1 For it's once when I was a servant in a house in Aberdeen,
 I was well beloved by my master and his men;
 O, till once there came a sailor tae oor hoose tae dine,
 And that was the beginning o' my (doin', O).   (downfall?)

2 He called for a candle to show him light to bed,
 He called for a napkin to tie all round his head;
 He called for a napkin, that's what he used to do,
 Saying, 'Pretty fair maid, will you come to bed wi' me?'

3 O home, dearie, home, and it's home you ought to be,
 Home, dearie, home to your home in Kilbirnie*
 Where the ash and the oak and the bonnie elm tree,
 They're aye growin' green in your own counteree.

4 Now, if it be's a boy, call him Johnnie after me;
 And if it be's a girl, you can nurse her on your knee.
 When the nine months is over and the time is going past,
 Sure I'll leave ye where I found you for to blow the candle out.

* Near the Mull of Kintyre.

44   SEVENTEEN COME SUNDAY
(Laws O 17)

Burns collected a version of this song from a girl in Nithdale and, after some re-writing, sent it to the editor of the *Museum*, where it appeared under the title of 'A Waukrife Minnie'. Most of the versions reported from Scotland during the last few years show signs of the narrative becoming overwhelmed by a nonsense chorus. This is undoubtedly due to the fact that the song has become a popular children's piece, which serves to accompany a game. In England, on the other hand, particularly in the southern counties, the song still retains its older form: a song of courtship, with a short nonsense refrain.

BIBLIOGRAPHY

Laws O 17.

British   Baring-Gould and Sheppard (2), pp. 150–1; Butterworth, pp. 16–17; Dick, No. 187; Ford (2), vol. I, pp. 102–5; *Gardiner MSS*, H-1203 and H-1351; *Henry Collection*, Nos 152 and 793; *JFSS*, vol. I, pp. 92–3; also vol. II, pp. 9–10 and 269–71; also vol. IV, pp. 291–3; also vol. VI, p. 7; Kidson and Moffat (2), pp. 2–3; *Museum*, vol. III, No. 288; Purslow (3), p. 104; Reeves (1), pp. 238–9; Seeger and MacColl, p. 7; Sharp (2), vol. I, pp. 104–6; Sharp and Karpeles (2), vol. I, pp. 422–9.

Broadsides   *British Museum*, LR 271 a 2, vol. VI, p. 112 (Such); also vol. II, p. 73 (Bebbington).

North American   Botkin (1), pp. 69–70; Brown, vol. III, pp. 21–3 and 339–41; Creighton (2), p. 44; Creighton (3), p. 32; Hubbard, p. 147; Moore, p. 213; Peacock, vol. I, p. 284.

Alternative titles   My Pretty Little Miss (Maid); That Blue-Eyed Girl; One Sunday Morning; My Rolling Eye; Haliky Daliky (etc.).

'Flash Gals and Airy Too', sung by Caroline Hughes.

1 O yes, as I was a-walking, O my love,
   So early in the morning;
   O, I met with a fair and a purty girl,
   She said, 'Morning, darling, do you love my roo dum day?'

Refrain: Fol di diddle die doe,
          Flash gals and airy too.

2 O, she got her horse and saddle ready,
   Down through the copses she did ride;
   O, she met her true love down on his walk,
   He said, 'Hello, darling, do you love me?' YES, MY DEAR.* (refrain)

3 O, will you have a man, my fair purty maid,
   Will you have a man, my honey?
   O, she answered me quite civilly:
   'I'm seventeen come Sunday, with my roo dum day.' (refrain)

* These three words were spoken.

45 THE LADY AND THE SOLDIER
(Laws P 14)

It has been suggested that this song has taken root in areas where the nightingale is a common bird, but this is not borne out by the facts. The song is widespread throughout North America and has even been collected in Texas – not nightingale country.

At first glance, it appears that the double-entendre refers directly to the bird itself and its alleged habit of singing only at night. The nightingale, however, sings both by day *and* night but is heard at its best when other birds have fallen silent. The bird has an honoured place in erotic symbolism, in romance literature, in song and, of course, in bird-lore and superstitious legend. In our song, however, it does not have the same significance that it has, for instance, in *The Decameron*. It does not even play the major role that it has in 'The Sweet Nightingale', a lyrical piece frequently confused with 'The Lady and the Soldier'. In our song the nightingale is merely part of a burden line and the word-play is centred on the fiddle – the bow, the strings, the tuning, and so on.

A large number of North American texts end with a stanza warning young girls not to trust soldiers who will 'leave you to rock the cradle while the nightingale sings'. Other versions end with the lusty soldier rollicking off to the tavern to round off his adventure.

BIBLIOGRAPHY

Laws P 14.

British *FMJ*, vol. II, p. 288; *Hammond MSS*, D-138; *JFSS*, vol. VIII, pp. 194–6; Kennedy, pp. 414–15; Purslow (2), p. 60; Sharp and Karpeles (2), vol. I, pp. 645–9.

North American Brown, vol. II, pp. 24–5; Cox (3), pp. 80–2; *Dusenbury MSS*, No. 77; Eddy, pp. 230–1; Karpeles (2), pp. 232–3; Moore, pp. 211–12; Niles, pp. 22–3; Peacock, vol. II, pp. 594–5.

General Belden, p. 239 (a good note).

Alternative titles The Nightingale (Sings); The Bold Grenadier; One Morning in May; As I Was a-Walking; The Wild Rippling Water (etc.).

A. 'The Lady and the Soldier', sung by Caroline Hughes.

B. (untitled), sung by Nelson Ridley (two renditions).

A.

moderate, cheerfully

m I (with inflected IV)

O, as I were a- walk- ing one morn-ing in May,

A fair pur- ty cou- ple I chanced for to meet;

And one she were a fair maid, she were dressed all in blue,

And the oth- er he's a sol- dier, he's a jol- ly dra- goon.

1   O, as I were a-walking one morning in May,
A fair purty couple I chanced for to meet;
And one she were a fair maid, she were dressed all in blue,
And the other he's a soldier, he's a jolly dragoon.

2   Now where are you going, my fair purty maid,
O where are you going so early this way?
I am going down to yonder shady tree,
For to set and watch the flowers grow and hear the nightingales sing.

3   O, may I come 'long with you, my fair purty maid?
May I come 'long with you so early your way?

. . . .
. . . .

4   Now, we both walked on together to some old shady tree,
O, he throwed off his knapsack and he pulled out his flute;
He played her such music caused the valleys to ring,
And 'tis thus, my lovely fair maid, how a nightingale sing.

5   'O now,' said the soldier, ''tis time to give o'er.'
'O no,' said the fair maid, 'play me up one tune more.
I would rather hear your fiddle play by the touch of its string
Than set and watch the flowers grow and hear the nightingale sing.

6   'O now,' said the fair maid, 'will you marry me?'
'O no,' said the soldier, 'it won't never be,
For I've got a little wife at home in my own counteree,
She's the cleverest little woman that your eyes ever see.'

7   'O now,' said the fair maid, 'O what shall I do?
My apron strings won't tie now, my gown won't pull to.'
And if ever I return again, it shall be in the spring,
O, to set and watch the flowers grow, hear the nightingale sing.
    And if ever I return again, it shall be in the spring,
    O, to set and watch the flowers grow, hear the nightingale sing.

B.

As I was a- walk- ing one morn-ing in May,

I met a young cou- ple, they was walk- ing my way;

One was a sol- dier, he look- ed so gay,

And one was a wo- man with her ap- ron strings long

THE LADY AND THE SOLDIER

I. *Recorded 19 June 1973*

1   As I was a-walking one morning in May,
    I met a young couple, they was walking my way;
    One was a soldier, he lookèd so gay,
    And one was a woman with her apron strings long.

2   Now, the maid to the soldier, will you marry me?
    'O no,' said the soldier, 'I won't marry you.
    I have a little girl at home in my own land can be,
    Where I long to see the flowers grow, to hear the nightingales sing.'

3   .   .   .   .
    .   .   .   .
    If ever I return again it will be all in the spring,
    When I long to see the flowers grow, to hear the nightingales sing.

II. *Recorded 24 August 1973*

1   As I was a-walking one morning in May,
    I met a young couple was passing my way;
    One was a soldier he lookèd so gay,
    And one was a woman with her apron strings long.

2   'O now,' said the soldier, 'to now marry me;'
    'O no,' say the fair maid, 'I won't marry you.
    I have a little boy at home in my own land can be,
    Where I long to see the flowers grow, hear the nightingales sing.'

3   I'd love to hear your music by the touch of your bow;
    He played the finest tune, caused the valleys to ring;
    Then if ever I return again, that will be all in the spring,
    When I long to see the flowers grow, to hear the nightingales sing.

The air of this song appears originally to have been called 'The Hessian March'. It was first noted down in 1815 by William Christie of Monquhitter, from a Buchan farmer who said that he had heard it played in the Duke of Cumberland's army en route from Aberdeen to Culloden. Gavin Greig discusses the history of the song and quotes four sets of verses built around a common refrain and sharing an identical melody. In all other respects, they must be considered as four distinctly different songs, different from each other and from the one presented here.

BIBLIOGRAPHY

British   Buchan and Hall, pp. 80–1; Greig, No. 10; *Lyric Gems* (1857); Ord, pp. 347–8; Rogers, p. 271 and 339; *Scottish Studies*, vol. XVIII, pp. 11–12.

Alternative titles   I Wish I Were Where Gadie Rins; The Back o' Bennachie.

'Where Gadie Rins', sung by Maggie McPhee.

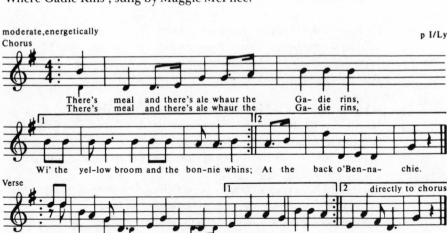

Chorus: There's meal and there's ale whaur the Gadie rins,
                 Wi' the yellow broom and the bonnie whins;
                 There's meal and there's ale whaur the Gadie rins,
                 At the back o' Bennachie.

2   O, I took my lassie on my knee,
         Her kilt was short and I could see;

I put my hand upon her knee
At the back o' Bennachie. (chorus)

3   O, she says to him, 'O that's nae fair!
We've slept thegither and you dinna care;
And the things that ye did ye'll dae nae mair,
At the back o' Bennachie.' (chorus)

4   She says to him, 'Noo, I'll gang hame,
And I'll tell my mither what ye've done;
And if it's a loon, it's Jock's the name
At the back o' Bennachie.' (chorus)

5   He says to her, 'Put on your kilt,
You're a gey braw dame, and you're gey weel built;
In nine months' time ye'll hae nae kilt
At the back o' Bennachie.' (chorus)

6   O, when her mither comes to ken,
I hae to fly noo frae my hame,
And sleep in the heather up the glen
At the back o' Bennachie. (chorus)

7   O, here's to the lassie o' Bennachie,
I'll never gane for her to see;
I'll bide wi' my mither until I dee
At the back o' Bennachie.

47   THE OVERGATE

In spite of its popularity, this rollicking account of a lost weekend in Dundee doesn't appear to have found its way into print. We have heard versions in which the text has been amplified by floater-verses from well-known bothy songs. It is, of course, quite possible that 'The Overgate' is itself an original bothy creation written at the time when urban music-hall song was exerting its greatest influence. Conversely, it may have begun its career as one of those music-hall pieces modelled on a corn-kister.

'The Overgate', sung by John MacDonald.

THE OVERGATE

1   For as I went doon the Overgate
    I spied a bonnie wee lass,
    She winked to me wi' the tail o' her e'e
    As I went rollin' past.

Refrain: Wi' my toorin ee all fal laddie
                Toorin addie wi' my all fa lee.

2   For I taen her tae a rest'rant
    A wee bit doon the burn;
    I gien her pies and porter
    I gien her beer and rum,
    She set doon and ate as much
    As wad an elephant for the next three years to come. (refrain)

3   She invited me to her hoose, noo,
       To hae a jolly nicht;
       And there were a big fat bobby,
       He catched me by the hair,
       He gien me yen o' they whirly-jigs
       And he sent me doon the stair. (refrain)

4   For I says, 'I lost my waistcoat,
       My watch and chain and purse.'
       O, she says, 'I've lost my maidenheid
       And that's a damn sight worse.' (refrain)

5   But when I go hame to Auchtermuchty
       I wonder what they'll say?
       The breakin' o' a five-pun' note
       Wi' the lassie in Dundee. (refrain)

6   For that day at Dundee Market
       It was a big decline,
       The day at Dundee market
       'll never leave my mind. (refrain)

48   THE OYSTER GIRL
(Laws Q 13)

A nineteenth-century broadside appears to have sired this infrequently reported piece. The five references given under its title in Dean-Smith are misleading, since they all properly belong to 'Eggs in Her Basket' (our No. 49).

BIBLIOGRAPHY

Laws Q 13.

British   Greig, No. 96; *Henry Collection*, No. 725; Kennedy, p. 519; Sharp and Karpeles (2), vol. II, pp. 115–16.

Broadsides   *British Museum*, LR 271 a 2, vol. II, p. 209 (Hodges); also vol. VI, p. 54 (Such); *British Museum*, 1875 D-16 (W. Selmerdine).

North American   see Laws.

Alternative titles   The Girl and the Oysters; The Basket of Oysters.

'The Oyster Girl', sung by Nelson Ridley.

1 As I was a-walking through London Town as well,
  Love, being quite a stranger I wandered up and down;
  Man, when I did finish the toury then quickly you shall hear
  That was where do you think I found myself, in the corner of a square.

2 'O landlord, O landlord, O landlord,' said (me),   (he)
  Said, 'Have you got a private room for the oyster girl and me?
  So as we can sit down and so merrily's we'll be,
  If you'll bargain with a basket of oysters.'

3 'O oysters, O oysters, O oysters!' said (he),   (she)
  I've got the finest little oyster gel that ever you did see;
  We sell 'em two-a-penny and three I'll give to you,
  If you'll bargain with a basket of oysters.

4   'O landlord, O landlord, O landlord,' said (me),   (he)
        Said, 'Have you seen that oyster gel came in the room with me?
        She have picked me of my pockets of all my money,
        And she's left me with a basket of oysters.'

49   EGGS IN HER BASKET

The second line of the opening stanza printed below belongs to 'The Oyster Girl', a song with which 'Eggs in Her Basket' is often confused. The remaining stanzas consist of a random selection of odd lines and couplets which so dislocate the plot as to render it unintelligible. The story should be as follows: Two sailors out walking encounter a young woman carrying a basket. They offer to carry it and she accepts, with the warning that the basket contains eggs and must be handled with care. The sailors 'being brisk with liquor' outwalk the young woman and arrive at an inn where they call upon the cook or landlord to fry some bacon along with the stolen eggs. When the basket is uncovered it is found to contain not eggs but an infant child. The sailors, made desperate by this discovery, offer the sum of fifty or a hundred pounds to anyone who will undertake to nurse the child. A young woman (the child's mother), her face concealed by a shawl, steps forward and accepts the money and the child. At this point in English versions of the song, the mother reveals her true identity and informs one of the sailors that he is the child's father. In Scots versions, which generally run to sixteen or seventeen stanzas, this revelation is postponed until the sailors have undertaken and returned from a sea-voyage. Both versions end with arrangements being made for a wedding 'and our sailors all to it were invited, / And many more that I do not know.'

BIBLIOGRAPHY

British   *FMJ*, vol. II, p. 284; *Gardiner MSS*, Hp-52; Greig, No. 100; *JFSS*, vol. I, pp. 46–7; also vol. II, pp. 102–3; *JEFDSS*, vol. VI, p. 16; Ord, pp. 144–5; Purslow (1), pp. 27–8; Reeves (1), pp. 99–100; Reeves (2), p. 73; Sharp and Karpeles (2), vol. II, pp. 111–12.

Alternative titles   The Foundling Baby; The Basket of Eggs.

'The Sailor's Child', sung by Nelson Ridley.

1   As I walked out then one May mid-morning,
     I found a gay gold watch and my money gone;
     Till I came unto them some fair maid walking,
     I said, 'My (name) see you came with me.'   (dame?)

2   And then young Nancy, she started weeping,
     She caused the sailors to weep and cry;
     O landlord, landlord, you fry some bacon,
     Because I've got some eggs to fry.

3   O fair maid, fair maid, I'll carry your basket,
     In the room of eggs it's a sailor's child;
     Here is fifty pounds, now, I will lay down
     If anyone will take this child.

4   They walked along and they talked together,
     Till they came unto some halfway house;
     Here is fifty pound now I will lay down,
     If anyone will take this child.

50   THE BIRD IN THE BUSH

It is only during the last half-century that unbowdlerised versions of this beautiful song have begun to appear in print. When Dean Christie's book was published in 1881, it contained a tune to the song with the rider: 'The editor in his young days has often heard this last strain sung to "There Were Two Pretty Maidens a-Wooing as They Went" which is altogether unsuitable for this work.' Kidson, who published a solitary stanza in 1891, was equally disapproving: 'It could be wished that the succeeding verses to the first (the only one which I have printed) were equally meritorious and more suitable for this work.' Baring-Gould, also, appears to have been shocked by the song, so much so that he had the text re-written for the first edition of *Songs of the West*. For the second edition he was content to present 'a modified text'. Cecil Sharp collected a version in Oxfordshire in 1923 (the last song he collected), but followed Kidson's example by publishing only one stanza. It was not until 1958 that a complete and unmodified traditional text appeared when Reeves published the Baring-Gould/William Stokes version.

    All of these texts have stanzas in common with an early nineteenth-century broadside text of a song entitled 'Three Maids a-Milking Would

Go'. This text has none of the extravagant literary conceits characteristic of so many broadsides and Reeves is probably correct in surmising that it was 'transferred to broadside literature from oral tradition'. On the other hand, it is not impossible that the theme and even some of the lines of the traditional lyric were quarried from 'There Was Three Birds', a convivial song published in *Merry Drollery* (1661).

Apart from Christie's reference, no Scots version has been reported and the only version from the north of England is the one collected by Kidson in the Leeds district almost a hundred years ago. With the exception of a solitary stanza, grafted on to a southern American version of 'The Sprig of Thyme', the song does not appear to have been reported from North America.

The incomplete fourth stanza given here is not present in any of the other versions we have seen and is undoubtedly an intrusion from another song.

BIBLIOGRAPHY

British   Baring-Gould and Sheppard (2), pp. 184–5; Christie, vol. II, pp. 256–7; Farmer (1), vol. I, pp. 140–1; *Hammond MSS*, D-68 and D-266; *JFSS*, vol. IV, pp. 93–4; also vol. VIII, p. 22; *JEFDSS*, vol. IX, pp. 75–6; Kennedy, p. 422; Kidson, p. 73; Purslow (2), p. 2; Reeves (1), pp. 259–60; Reeves (2), pp. 208–10; Sharp and Karpeles (2), vol. I, pp. 450–6; Sola Pinto and Rodway, p. 369; Williams, p. 229.

Broadsides   *British Museum*, 11602 gg p.31 (Williamson of Newcastle).

North American   Cray, pp. 231–3.

Alternative titles   The Blackbird in the Bush; There Was Three Birds; Three Maidens (Maids) a-Milking (a-Wooing) Did Go, (etc.).

'The Bird in the Lily-Bush', sung by Caroline Hughes.

1   O, I met with some young man I know,
    O, I met with some young man I know;
    Now, I askèd that young man if he have got any skill,
    For to catch me a small bird or two.

2   O yes, I've some very nice skills,
    O yes, I've some very nice skills;
    If you'll come along with me down to yonders lily-bush,
    I will catch you a small bird or two.

3   Straightaway that young man and me went,
    Straightaway to that lily-green bush;
    O, we wrapped up the bush as the birdie did fly out
    He fled a little above my white knee.

4   .   .   .   .
    .   .   .   .
    O, tonight I'll take my pay, and tomorrow I will spend it
    And go home by the light of the moon.

[183]

HESITANT LOVERS

51   CAROLINE OF EDINBURGH TOWN
(Laws P 27)

Laws has observed that 'this ballad begins not in the fifth act of the play but in the first and proceeds chronologically through half-a-dozen episodes.' Those half-dozen episodes are generally dealt with in ten or eleven somewhat pedestrian stanzas. John MacDonald's broken-down text scarcely does justice to the story, which is as follows: Caroline, against the wishes of her parents, accompanies her Highland suitor to London and is there married to him. Later, her husband goes to sea, abandoning Caroline, who finally drowns herself in the sea.

Laws described it as a British ballad 'exceptionally popular in America', a judgment borne out by the large number of published versions of it to be found there. Greig considered it to be 'a favourite ballad of the folk-singer'. This may well have been so though it appears to have been published but rarely in Britain.

BIBLIOGRAPHY

Laws P 27.

British   Greig, Nos 70 and 72; *Hammond MSS*, Dt-191 and Dt-707; Ord, pp. 186–7; Purslow (4), pp. 14–15; *Rymour*, vol. I, pp. 181–2.

North American   Creighton (3), pp. 99–100; Huntington, pp. 137–41; Moore, pp. 172–4.

'Caroline of Edinburgh Town', sung by John MacDonald.

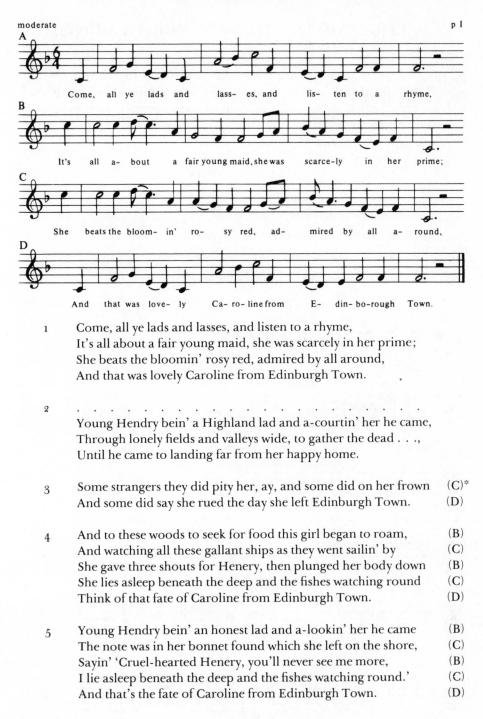

1   Come, all ye lads and lasses, and listen to a rhyme,
    It's all about a fair young maid, she was scarcely in her prime;
    She beats the bloomin' rosy red, admired by all around,
    And that was lovely Caroline from Edinburgh Town.

2   . . . .
    Young Hendry bein' a Highland lad and a-courtin' her he came,
    Through lonely fields and valleys wide, to gather the dead . . .,
    Until he came to landing far from her happy home.

3   Some strangers they did pity her, ay, and some did on her frown   (C)*
    And some did say she rued the day she left Edinburgh Town.   (D)

4   And to these woods to seek for food this girl began to roam,   (B)
    And watching all these gallant ships as they went sailin' by   (C)
    She gave three shouts for Henery, then plunged her body down   (B)
    She lies asleep beneath the deep and the fishes watching round   (C)
    Think of that fate of Caroline from Edinburgh Town.   (D)

5   Young Hendry bein' an honest lad and a-lookin' her he came   (B)
    The note was in her bonnet found which she left on the shore,   (C)
    Sayin' 'Cruel-hearted Henery, you'll never see me more,   (B)
    I lie asleep beneath the deep and the fishes watching round.'   (C)
    And that's the fate of Caroline from Edinburgh Town.   (D)

* The letters in parenthesis indicate which line of music is used.

52 THE MAID OF THE SWEET BROWN KNOWE

(Laws P 7)

In spite of an interesting story and the handsome melodies generally associated with it, this attractive song does not appear to have achieved widespread circulation either in Ireland (where it originated) or in Britain. On the other side of the Atlantic, it has been reported from Newfoundland, Ontario, Minnesota and Michigan.

BIBLIOGRAPHY

Laws P 7.

British   *Henry Collection*, No. 688; O'Lochlainn (1), pp. 38–9.

North American   Fowke, pp. 90–1; Leach, pp. 128–9.

Alternative titles   The Foot (Maid) of the Mountain Brow.

'The Sweet Brown Knowe', sung by Big Willie McPhee.

brisk   m I

A Verse 1 only

For it's   all a-bout a young   man and a maid, and I'm   gaun tae tell you   how,

Sure, they   fell up- on   a-   court-ing   at the   foot of the Sweet Brown   Knowe.

B Verses 2–5

O, come   on, my pret-ty   Ka-thl- een, come   on   a- lang with   me,

Sure, we'll   both run off to-   geth- er   and   mar-ried we will   be;

We'll   wed waur hands with   wed- lock bands, I'm   speak-ing to you   now,

Sure, I'll   do my best, what- ev-er   I can, for the Maid of the Sweet Brown Knowe.

1 . . . .
. . . .
For it's all about a young man and a maid and I'm gaun tae tell you how,
Sure, they fell upon a-courting at the foot of the Sweet Brown Knowe.

2 O, come on, my pretty Kathleen, come on along with me,
Sure, we'll both run off together and married we will be;
We'll wed waur hands with wedlock bands, I'm speaking to you now,
Sure, I'll do my best, whatever I can, for the Maid of the Sweet Brown
    Knowe.

3 O, look you down in yonder valley, where my crops they gently grow;
Down in yonder valley where my men are at the plough;
Down in yonder valley where my men are at the plough;
Sure, they're at their daily labour for the Maid of the Sweet Brown Knowe.

4 'Then, if they're at their daily labour then, kind sir, that is not for me.
I've heard of your behaviour, I've heard of it,' said she.
'There is an inn (for you, Colin) I've heard the   (where you call in)
    people say,
That you rap and you call and you pay for all and come home at the break
    of day'.

5 Then, if I rap and I call and I pay for all, the money is all my own.
I will never spend your fortune, for I hear you have none;
But you raved and you spoke and my poor heart's broke as you spoke to me
    just now,
And I'll leave you where I found you – at the foot of the Sweet Brown Knowe.

53 THE BRAES OF STRATHBLANE

Stirlingshire and Aberdeenshire, where it is known as 'The Braes of
Strathdon', both lay claim to this song. Ford commented '. . . it has often
been printed in broad-sheet form and ballad-hawkers continue to find
ready sale for it at feeing markets in Glasgow and the west of Scotland.' The
printed texts which still exist are indeed remarkably similar to each other.

BIBLIOGRAPHY

British   Ford (2), vol. I, pp. 76–7; Greig, No. 18; Kidson, pp. 90–1; Ord, p. 125;
Rymour, vol. I, pp. 116–17.

Broadsides Madden Collection, M 16-524 (John Ross, Newcastle); M 18-893 (Harkness).

North American   Hubbard, pp. 102–3; Peacock, vol. II, pp. 499–500.

Alternative titles   The Braes (Beach) of Strachblane (Strablane).

'The Braes of Strathblane', sung by Christina MacAllister.

1   As I went a-walking one evening in May,
    Down by a green meadow I careless did stray;
    I spied a young lassie, she was standing her lane,
    And bleaching her claes on the braes o' Strathblane.

2   I steppit up to her, as I seemed to pass:
    You are bleaching your claes, my handsome young lass;
    It's a twelve-month and better since I had in my mind
    To make you my own bride, if you would incline.

3   O, it's haud your tongue, laddie, and dinna say so.
    . . . .
    It's my father and mither, displeased they would be,
    If I were to marry a young rover like thee.

4   O, it's haud your tongue, lassie, and dinna say so;
You don't know the pain it's I undergo;
But the clouds they hang heavy, I'm afraid we'll have rain,
And I'll court another fair maid on the braes o' Strathblane.

5   O, it's come you back, laddie, you have fair won my heart.
Here is my hand, lover, we never will part.
Here is my hand, lover, to the day that we dee –
And it's a' good may attend us wherever we be.

6   O, it's lassie, dear lassie, I have altered my mind,
Since the last words I spoke you, it's quite out of time.
But the clouds they hang heavy, I'm afraid we'll have rain.
And we both shook hands and parted on the braes o' Strathblane.

7   O, fair maids and maidens, take a warning by me,
For it's never slight a young man for his poverty.
For the slighting of the young man I'm afraid I'll get nane,
And I'll wander alone on the braes o' Strathblane.

UNFAITHFUL LOVERS

54   THE SEEDS OF LOVE
(Sprig of Thyme)

This is perhaps the most common love-song in the traditional repertoire. The use of flower and herb symbols as a substitute for various emotional states and stages in a love relationship – thyme for virginity, rue for loss of virginity, the rose for passion, willow for regret, and so on – has long been a feature of English and Scots love-poetry. The song known as 'Seeds of Love'/'Sprig of Thyme', which uses these symbols, has a distinctive form. It is possible that the two titles at one time represented two different songs but, as many collectors have remarked after having thrown up their hands in despair at trying to separate the two, they have become inextricably intertwined.

Another piece which uses flower symbols as part of its structure is 'The Gardener' (Child 219). This exquisite ballad, of which Child gives only two satisfactory texts and one small fragment, consists entirely of a dialogue between a gardener and a young maid. The gardener offers the girl various flowers (each with its own erotic significance) as apparel if she will yield to him. The girl replies, using wintry weather symbols. The relationship between 'The Gardener' and 'Seeds of Love' appears at first sight to be a tenuous one, but in Child's Additions and Corrections there are three texts which combine elements of the ballad with those of the lyric song.

1   The first of these texts begins with a girl lamenting the infidelity of her lover, a squire's son. The gardener then enters, offering various flowers. This presence of two men in the plot is unusual, but occurs in an Ohio text of 'The Seeds of Love' (Eddy). This text has a chorus:

> It's brave sailing here, my dear,
> >And better sailing there,
> Brave sailing in my love's arms
> >O, give I were there!

2   The second of the texts is entitled 'Dead Maid's Land'. In it a girl is offered the choice of a number of flowers – the lily, the violet and the pink, etc. – and she refuses them. She is then offered the lily, the jonquil, the gilly-flower, the marigold, the stock. These too she refuses and accepts instead a rose with which she pricks herself and dies. This motif of a sharp thorn hidden in the red rose is found in many 'Seeds of Love' texts. 'Dead Maid's Land' concludes with a magnificent stanza:

> A gardener stood at the gate,
> With cypress in his hand;
> And he did say, 'Let no fair may
> Come into Dead Maid's Land.'

This is a transitional piece; the flowers are still offered as apparel but the weather symbols have disappeared. Furthermore the gardener is no longer part of the action but merely an observer. The flower language is now the core of the song.

3   The third text is a six-verse fragment from Motherwell's MSS. It opens with the 'It's braw sailing here' stanza (quoted above). Stanzas 3–6 are standard 'Seeds of Love' material, involving the gardener, the primrose, the rose and the willow. It is the second stanza which is unique as Scotland does not seem to have produced any other purely Scots texts of 'Seeds of Love':

> It's braw drinking beer
> And it's braw drinking wine,
> And it's braw courting a bonnie lass
> When she is in her prime.

This stanza is fairly common in English and North American versions, which are all from the woman's point of view:

> It's good to be drinking the beer,
> It's good to be drinking the wine,
> But it's better far to be on the bonnie laddie's knee
> That's stolen this heart of mine. (Bruce and Stokoe)

The ballad treatment, 'The Gardener', rarely appears outside of Scotland. England and North America have, instead, the lyric form. Would it be feasible to suggest that 'The Seeds of Love' is an adaptation of the first half of the older narrative, lopped off and sent south and west? Certainly, the existence of so many motifs and so much poetry held in common by the song and the ballad would appear to suggest a connection between the two.

BIBLIOGRAPHY

British   Baring-Gould and Sharp, pp. 36–7; Baring-Gould and Sheppard (2), pp. 14–15; Broadwood and Maitland, pp. 58–9; Bruce and Stokoe, pp. 90–1; Butterworth, pp. 6–7; Campbell, vol. I, pp. 40–1; Chappell (2), vol. II, pp. 520–3; Child, No. 219 (see also Additions and Corrections, vol. V, pp. 258–60); Dixon and Bell, pp. 440–1; *Gardiner MSS*, H-263 and H-515; Greig, No. 67; Hamer, p. 14; Hammond, pp. 10–11; Harland, pp. 273–5; *JFSS*, vol. I, pp. 86–9 and 209–11; also vol. II, pp. 23–5 and 288–9; also vol. III, pp. 77–8; also vol. V, p. 93; also vol. VIII, pp. 19–21; *JEFDSS*, vol. VIII, p. 202; also vol. IX, pp. 190–1; Joyce (2), No. 381; Kennedy, p. 367; Kidson, p. 69; Kidson and Moffat (2), pp. 116–17; Kidson and Neal, p. 58; Merrick, p. 34; Purslow (2), p. 84; Reeves (1), pp. 229–38; Reeves (2), pp. 194–6; Sharp (1), pp. 10–11 and 216–22; Sharp (2), vol. I, pp. 42–7; Sharp and Karpeles (2), vol. I, pp. 577–88; Sharp and Marson, pp. 2–4; Stokoe and Reay, pp. 80–1; Williams, pp. 85–7.

Broadsides   *British Museum*, LR 271 a 2, vol. III, p. 221 (Catnach).

North American   (starred items give many further references) *Belden (*Publications of the Modern Language Association*, no. 33, 1918), pp. 363–6; *Cox (2), pp. 415–16; Creighton (4), pp. 53–4; Creighton and Senior (1), pp. 40–1; Eddy, pp. 87–9; Owens, pp. 196–7; *Randolph, vol. I, pp. 357–8; Thomas, p. 102; Thomas and Leeder, p. 27.

Alternative titles   These are too many to list, but they use words like 'thyme', 'rue', 'garden', 'seeds', 'willow tree', 'clean garden', 'gardener', 'gardener's son', 'red rosebud' (etc.).

'The Running, Running Rue', sung by Caroline Hughes.

moderate, somewhat monotonous   p I

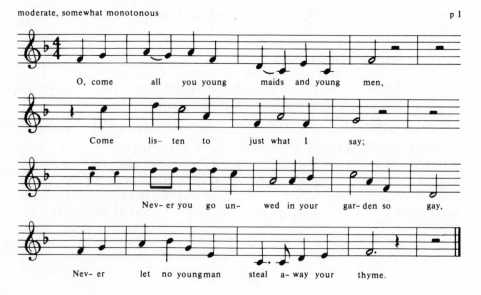

1 O, come all you young maids and young men,
Come listen to just what I say;
Never you go unwed* in your garden so gay,
Never let no young man steal away your thyme.

2 O, it's love, I've got plenty of thyme,
I've got thyme in my garden for you;
I'm just like a bit of grass that's been tread down underfoot,
Give me time and I will rise and grow again.

3 O, that running, running, running, running rue,
He runs all too soon for me;
It's I will cut down that running, running rue
And I'll plant up the jolly (old) tree.   (oak?)

4 O that purty (William) tree will freely grow,   (willow?)
He will freely now grow any higher;
While he twist and he twine to a true lover's knot,
And a rose wrapped round my sweet briar.

5 I walkèd my garden all down,
And I walkèd my garden along;
Wherein all in the midst of my purty flowers grown,
There's not one sprig of thyme could I find.

6 Now, my jolly old gardener stood by,
And I askèd him to choose for me;
And he choosèd me the violets, sweet lilies and the pinks,
Out of them I refusèd all three.

7 O stand up, O stand up, my purty oak,
And 'tis you, O you'll now fade away;
For I will be so true to that young man there
As the stars shine so bright in the sky.

* At another time she sang 'Never you go wed', possibly a transliteration for '"I would have you weed" your garden so gay'.

There is a large group of love-lamentations which have enough verses in common to be called a 'family'. They are all based upon a man's infidelity to his avowed lover and have been collected widely in England, Scotland and (to a lesser extent) the United States. Essentially, they share a body of floater-verses and each member of the family deals with this common stock in a different manner, with one or two verses acting as a nucleus with complementary verses clustered about. The main song types are as follows (the titling is not definitive).

1   'Deep in Love' – a collection of lyric verses in which the girl may or may not be pregnant. The verses may be put in any order, and the kernel verse contains the phrase 'Must I go bound or am I free?', surrounded by images of the prickly bush and flowing water.

2   'The Butcher Boy' (our No. 73) – a narrative song in which the girl (not pregnant) hangs herself, leaving warnings and regrets. The nucleus-stanza nearly always sets the scene in a town:

> In (——) Town there did dwell
> A butcher (railroad) boy, I loved him well (etc.).

3   'Love Has Brought Me to Despair' – a narrative piece in which a maiden is overheard complaining that her false lover has caused her downfall. She often gives her family background (one of riches and comfort). She goes to the meadow, gathers her apron full of flowers (as our B-text, Stanza 1), makes a bed of them and lies down to die (reminiscent of Ophelia?). The 'blind worm' motif appears often in this song and flowers abound throughout. The turtle-dove and 'I wish I wish' motifs are also very common.

4   'Waly Waly' (occasionally called 'The Water is Wide' in English versions) – a generalised love-lyric, mostly found in Scotland. The girl is pregnant and the kernel stanza is familiar:

> Waly waly, love is bonnie,
> A little time while it is new (etc.).

5   'The Tavern in the Town' ('Let Him Go, Let Him Tarry') – a rather light-hearted form somewhat similar to 'The Butcher Boy'. The girl is rarely pregnant and does not usually hang herself. The alehouse verse is vital to this type.

6   'Careless Love' – a non-narrative sequence of lyric verses, found chiefly in the United States, but based on a southern English piece entitled

'You've Been Careless, Love'. The girl is pregnant and the apron motif is rarely missing.

7 'Died for Love' – a sequence of floater-verses with no predetermined order. The girl is pregnant. The song often begins with:

> A bold young farmer (sailor) courted me,
> He stole away my liberty (etc.).

The most common stanza is to be found in the chorus of our A-text.

In view of the difficulties of sorting out and classifying our two versions we used the following criteria:

(a) Is the song lyric or narrative?
(b) What are the kernel stanzas?
(c) Is the girl a maid, a mother-in-waiting, or a mother?
(d) Does the girl kill herself?

Both our texts are non-narrative. They have two stanzas in common, those containing the apron and alehouse motifs. Our B-text begins and ends like 'Love Has Brought Me To Despair' but contains few of the distinctive or constant features of that song. Neither of our texts mention the trade of the lover (as in No. 2 above), nor the lineage of the girl (as in No. 3), nor details of the happier days of courtship (as in No. 4). Our A-text, in the first couplet of stanza 4, contains material which was probably wrought out of the more common treatment:

> I wish my baby it was born
> And set upon its daddy's knee,
> And I myself was dead and gone
> And green grass growing over me.

Considering that there are so many verses available in this large group, it is surprising that the songs have kept their identity at all. 'Died for Love' texts are always brief – they do not tell a love-story, they only emit a short, sharp cry of pain.

BIBLIOGRAPHY

British Buchan (Norman), p. 61; Buchan and Hall, p. 93; *JFSS*, vol. I, pp. 252–3; also vol. II, p. 155; also vol. III, pp. 188–9; *JEFDSS*, vol. III, pp. 192–3; also vol. V, pp. 16–17; also vol. VI, p. 103; Kidson, pp. 44–6; Kidson and Moffat (2), pp. 36–7; Sharp (1), pp. 51–3; Sharp and Karpeles (2), vol. I, pp. 597–605.

North American Hubbard, p. 65; Sharp and Karpeles (1), vol. II, p. 268.

General (1) 'Deep in Love' – *Henry Collection*, No. 218; Purslow (2), p. 23; Reeves (1), p. 89; *Roxburghe*, vol. VI, part xxix, p. 791.

(2) 'Love Has Brought Me to Despair' – Laws P 25; *JFSS*, vol. V, pp. 188–9.

(3) 'Waly Waly' – *Museum*, vol. II, No. 158.

(4) General notes, plus further texts: *JFSS*, vol. V, pp. 181–7; also vol. VII, pp. 69–75; *JEFDSS*, vol. VII, pp. 161–71.

Alternative titles   I Wish, I Wish (My Baby It Was Born); A Bold Young Farmer (Brisk Young Sailor) Courted Me; Must I Go Bound? Will Ye Gang, Love? (etc.).

A. 'I Wish I Wish', sung by Charlotte Higgins.

B. (untitled), sung by Caroline Hughes.

A.

1   It's when my apron it was new,
 It was a bricht and bonny blue;
 But noo my apron's to my knee,
 He cares nae mair what becomes o' me.

Chorus: O, I wish, I wish, but I wish in vain:
  I wish I were a maid again;
  But a maid again I ne'er will be,
  Till the apple grows on an orange tree.

2   When I was young and in my bloom,
       A false young man came a-courting me;
       But now he's left me all alone
       Nursing a baby on my knee. (chorus)

3   O, there is an alehouse in this town,
       Where my true love goes and he sits down;
       He takes a dark girl on his knee,
       He tells her what he once told me. (chorus)

4   O, I wish my father ne'er had whistled;
       I wish my mother never had sung;
       And for myself was dead and gone,
       And the green grass growing over me. (chorus)

B.

moderate, recitative style   m I (with inflected IV)

1   O for that dear girl, she roamed those meadows.
       She were picking these flowers by one, two or three;
       She picked, she plucked until she gained
       Until she gathered her apron full.

2   O, when I were single, I wear my apron strings long;
     My love passed me by and say nothing;
     But now my belly it's up to my chin,
     My love he pass by and frowns on me.

3   A grief, a grief, I'll tell you for why:
     Because that girl she's got more gold than me;
     Well, gold shall glitter, her beauty will fade,
     That's why it puts back a poor girl like me.

4   On yonders hill, there stands an alehouse,
     Where my true love goes and sets himself down,
     He takes another strange girl on his knee
     And kisses her and frowns on me.

5   A grief, a grief, I'll tell you for why:
     Because that girl she's got more gold than me;
     Well, gold shall glitter, her beauty will flee,
     That's why she'll become a poor girl like me.

6   On yonders hill there's blind beetles crawl,
     As blind as blind could be;
     I wish to God that I'd been one of those
     Before I gained my love's company.

56   THE BLACKSMITH

Though this is a fairly common song in southern England, little appears to have been written about it. Certain of its stanzas are found in other songs. Our fourth and fifth stanzas (A-text), for instance, form the opening of a broadside entitled 'A Dialogue between a Town Spark and his Miss':

She: Did you not promise me when you lay by me
        That you would marry me, can you deny me?
He: If I did promise thee, 'twas but to try thee
        Call up your witnesses, else I defie thee.

(D'Urfey, 1719)

The same stanza occurs in 'The Deluded Lasse's Lamentation of the False Youth's Unkindness to his Beloved Mistress' (c. 1672) the first verse of which appeared in *The Westminster Drollery* (1671) in a playhouse song under the title of 'The Careless Swain'. Both these old pieces are dialogue songs, but neither of them have any other verses in common with the song given here, though they do have occasional similar rhymes.

BIBLIOGRAPHY

British　Butterworth, p. 4–5; D'Urfey, vol. II, p. 193; *Euing*, No. 70; *JFSS*, vol. IV, pp. 279–80; also vol. VIII, pp. 17–18 and 206–8; Kennedy, p. 346; Purslow (1), p. 62; *Roxburghe*, vol. IV, part i, pp. 23–5; Sharp and Karpeles (2), vol. I, pp. 613–17.

Broadsides　Madden Collection, M 8–811 (Pitts); also M 23–98 (Ring Hurd, Shaftesbury); also M 23–194 (W. Collard of Bristol).

Alternative titles　The Shoemaker; A Blacksmith Courted Me; With the Hammers in My Hand (etc.).

A. 'The Blacksmith', sung by Caroline Hughes.

B. 'The Blacksmith', sung by Nelson Ridley.

A.

THE BLACKSMITH

1   A blacksmith courted me, and I loved him dearly,
A blacksmith courted me, and I loved him dearly;
Just to think how I love that man when he's so false-hearted.

2   I courted you nine months, nine months and better,
I courted you nine months, and not no other;
And why should you slighted me, just to wed some other?

3   There is nine long months has gone, as I proved a child was,
That nine long months as gone, as I proved the child was,
Now (you're) behind, and I'm a ruined girl forever.   (left)

(5) 4   Now, Willy is your name, you can't deny me,
'Tis Willy is your name, you can't deny me;
I have proved that child by you, and not no other.

(4) 5   Can you bring your witness, love, now I won't deny you.
It's witness I've got none but (my) Almighty   (God)
And it's with my love I'm going to do my duty.

6   My love's across those fields, gathering roses,
My love's across those fields, gathering fine roses;
I'm afraid the sun will rise now and spoil his beauty.

B.

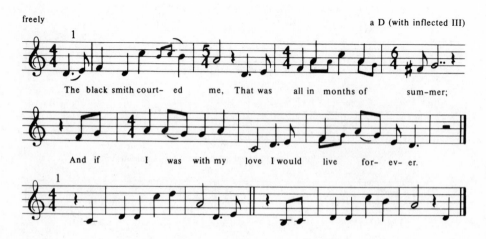

1 The blacksmith courted me,
  That was all in months of summer;
  And if I was with my love
  I would live forever.

2 The blacksmith courted me,
  That was nine long months or better;
  And if I was with my love,
  I would live for ever.

3 That's when he striked his bill,
  We thought of a mighty clever;
  And if I was with my love,
  Gathering the primroses.

57 THE CUCKOO

The cuckoo is one of the most common birds in British and western European folklore and song. A brief survey of its habits will perhaps make clear the reason for this.

1 The cuckoo is one of the first birds to appear in the spring and, as such, it is generally regarded as heralding the agricultural year. Various parts of England have a 'cuckoo's day' which may be at any time from early April to late June and numerous superstitions regarding sowing and reaping, courtship and marriage, luck and misfortune, are based on the first appearance of the bird. The cuckoo is also regarded as a prognosticator of the harvest.

2 The bird, often prompted to sing by the coming of wet weather, is looked upon as a rain-prophet, even as far east as India; this is probably the bird's most universal folk role.

3 The cuckoo is known for the monotony of its song. Indeed there are few names for the bird in western Europe that do not reflect onomatopoeically the call itself.

4 The cuckoo is a difficult bird to catch – upon hearing its call you may walk in that direction only to discover upon reaching the spot that the bird is calling from a different place altogether.

5 The young of the cuckoo are proverbially stupid and this

reputation has given rise to the application of 'cuckold' to a deceived husband, and 'gowk' (the Scots name for cuckoo) to a foolish person.

6 The cuckoo is unpredictable in the sense that weather is unpredictable. One knows that the sun will follow rain, but one cannot say exactly when.

7 The cuckoo is predictable in the sense that it always arrives in spring and leaves in midsummer, when the going is good. As the folk poet puts it:

> The cuckoo comes in April
> Sings a song in May;
> Then in June another tune
> And then he flies away.

The habit for which the bird is most widely known is that of leaving its eggs in the nests of other birds, whose own fledglings are then crowded out or whose flesh is fed by the foster-parents to the intruder.

> The Cuckoo is a lazy bird,
> She never builds a nest,
> She makes herself busy
> By singing to the rest.
>
> She never hatches her own young
> And that we all know,
> But leaves it for some other bird
> While she cries, 'Cuckoo!' (Williams)

The opportunistic habits of the bird find artistic parallels in the songs – the pregnant girl, abandoned to fend for herself, watches the free, unfettered flight of her lover who, it would appear, has not chosen her nest because it was dearest but because it was nearest, even as the cuckoo is not finicky when egg-laying time comes round.

The contradictions in the above sketch of the cuckoo's habits – of a bird wise enough to predict weather, harvest (etc.) and yet stupid in the nest; of a bird both predictable and unconstant – are reflected in the various verses of the song. Just as the bird is inconsistent in its behaviour, so is life, and love, and men. The message of the song (which is always sung from the girl's point of view) is roughly the same: the call of the cuckoo (man) is charming, but deceptive and monotonous ('they'll all tell you the same thing', 'they only want one thing'). The bird comes in the spring of the year, when all things burgeon, descending on the virgin year even as the man descends upon the girl at her most impressionable time of life. Both cuckoo and man leave after the planting and before the harvest. Neither have any logical reason for acting as they do, but then that is part of their charm – while I, poor maid-mother, must hear the tune long after June is gone. (Incidentally, the female cuckoo does not sing.)

'The Cuckoo' is a convenient title for a group of songs which always contain a stanza similar to our fifth verse. Thereafter the song may take to itself a number of floater-verses among which the following motifs appear most often:

> . . . the flowering tree with rotten roots

> . . . meeting is a pleasure, parting a grief
> an unconstant lover is worse than a thief

> . . . the grave he will rot you (as our stanza 3)

Only rarely does the young girl curse her lover or wish him bad fortune. She is more bewildered than angry and, in most of the versions, expresses a determination to find another love quickly. Of all our five stanzas, only the fourth is not common to this song.

BIBLIOGRAPHY

British   Baring-Gould and Sheppard (1), pp. 2–5; Barrett, p. 81; Butterworth, pp. 12–13; Ford (1), p. 30; Halliwell (1), p. 195; Halliwell (2), p. 99; *Hammond MSS*, S–33; *Henry Collection*, Nos 479 and 709; *JFSS*, vol. III, pp. 90–1; also vol. VI, p. 14*; Kennedy, p. 348; Northall, pp. 267–71; Opie (1), p. 139; Purslow (3), p. 32; Reeves (1), pp. 79–85; Sharp (1), pp. 24–5; Sharp (2), vol. I, pp. 48–9; Sharp and Karpeles (2), vol. I, pp. 623–30; Williams, p. 165.

Broadsides   British Museum, LR 271 a 2, vol. VII, pp. 188–9.

North American   Arnold, p. 45; Belden, pp. 473–6*; Brewster, pp. 346–7; Brown, vol. III, pp. 271–4; Carey, pp. 101–2; Cox (2), pp. 425–6*; Karpeles (1), pp. 122–4; Karpeles (2), pp. 245 and 333; Randolph, vol. I, pp. 237–9*; Sharp and Karpeles (1), vol. II, pp. 177–83*.

General   Starred items above give copious further references. Folklore about the cuckoo may be found in: Ingersoll, pp. 223–5; Swainson, pp. 109–22; Swann, pp. 223–5.

Alternative titles   The Forsaken (or Unconstant) Lover; Young Girls, Take Warning; A-Walking and a-Talking; On Top of Old Smoky; or almost any title containing the word 'Cuckoo'.

'The Cuckoo', sung by Caroline Hughes.

THE CUCKOO

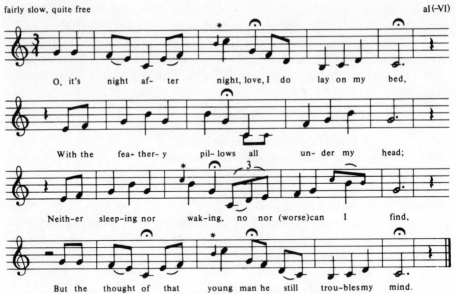

fairly slow, quite free

al (-VI)

O, it's night af-ter night, love, I do lay on my bed,

With the fea-ther-y pil-lows all un-der my head;

Neith-er sleep-ing nor wak-ing, no nor (worse)can I find,

But the thought of that young man he still trou-bles my mind.

*Note: At these points the singer often hit a B instead of a C because the song was pitched slightly too high. It is a matter of speculation how she would have sung the melody had the pitching been suitable.

1 O, it's night after night, love, I do lay on my bed,
   With the feathery pillows all under my head;
   Neither sleeping nor waking, no nor (worse) can I find,   (rest?)
   But the thought of that young man, he still troubles my mind.

2 Now, I will rise then and meet him as the evening draws nigh;
   I will meet him in the evening, as the evening draws nigh;
   And if you think you love a little girl, your mind for to ease,
   O, can't you love the old one, till the young one (came on)?   (can
                                                              please?)

3 It's like the flowers all in your garden when the beauty's all gone,
   Can't you see what I'm come to by a-loving that one?
   Now, the grave he will rot you, he will rot you all away,
   Not one young man out of twenty can a young maiden trust.

4 Now, I'll take my week's wages, to the alehouse I'll go,
   O, and there I'll set drinking till my money's all gone;
   Here's my wife and little family at home, starving too —
   And me in this alehouse, a-spending all that I earn.

5 Now, the cuckoo, she's called a merry bird, for she sings as she flies,
   O, she brings us good tidings and she tells we no lies;
   She sucks all small birds' eggs for to keep her voice clear,
   And every time she hollers 'cuckoo!', don't the summer draw nigh?

This odd little song is made up entirely of floater-verses. Unlike many pieces which are magnets for such verses, this song seems to have no kernel-stanza. Each of its verses may be found in a number of widely distributed and varied pieces. For instance:

Stanza 1 turns up in an English Song 'Flash Company' (Purslow (3), p. 43 – see also 'Yellow Handkerchief', our No. 32) and is fairly common in American songs such as 'I'm Troubled' (Lomax (3), p. 208) and 'I'm Sad and I'm Lonely' (Sandburg, pp. 243–5).

Stanza 3, also found in 'Flash Company', can be found in our version of 'The Cuckoo' (No. 57).

Stanza 4 is one of the most ubiquitous of the floater-verses and can be found in 'Rosemary Lane' (our No. 43) and 'The Banks of Red Roses' (our No. 72).

Stanza 5 is a commonplace in the American song 'On Top of Old Smoky' (of which there is an interesting English analogue in *JEFDSS* (vol. VI, p. 208) entitled 'The Americans That Stole My Love Away'.

Greenleaf gives a text which is strikingly similar to ours. See also the note to No. 32 in this collection, as it is conceivable that this song is a reduced version of 'The Yellow Handkerchief'.

BIBLIOGRAPHY

North American   Greenleaf and Mansfield, p. 121.

Alternative title   The Lass That Loved a Sailor.

'The False-Hearted Lover', sung by Caroline Hughes.

1 Once I had a colour,
   It were just like a rose;
   But now I'm as pale as
   The lily that do grow.

2 O, there's me and my baby,
   Now contented we'll be;
   Well, I will try and forget you
   As you forgot me.

3 Like the flowers all in the garden
   When the beauty's all gone;
   Can't you see just what I'm come to
   By a-loving that one?

4 Now, all you young ladies,
   You take warning by me;
   Never let a young man
   Get one inch above your knee.

5 He will kiss you and he'll coax you,
   And he'll call you his love;
   And a false heart, deceitful,
   Will bid you farewell.

6 Well, there's love on the ocean,
   And there's love on dry land;
   Long as breath's in my body
   I'll still love that one.

59   BLUE-EYED LOVER

This is another of those unstable 'love has brought me to despair' texts. The first two stanzas are from 'Fond Affection' (see Brown, vol. II, pp. 398–408). Stanzas 4 and 5 are compounded from the second stanza and chorus of 'In a Cottage By the Sea' (see Brown, vol. II, pp. 347–8), a song which – according to Randolph – was written by C. A. White and published in Boston in 1868.

BIBLIOGRAPHY (for both of the songs mentioned in above note)

British   Greig, No. 169; Ord, pp. 181–2.

North American   Belden, pp. 209–10; Ford (Ira), p. 334; Henry (1), pp. 250–3; Leach, p. 300; Neeley, pp. 225–6; Peacock, vol. II, p. 453; Randolph, vol. IV, pp. 160–1; Sharp and Karpeles (1), vol. II, p. 109; Spaeth, pp. 44–5.

'The Blue-Eyed Lover', sung by Caroline Hughes.

1   O, once I had a blue-eyed lover,
    Once he thought this world of me;
    Until one day he found some other,
    Then his love was not on me.

2   You take this ring from off your finger
     And that locket from round my neck;
     You'll give it to the one you fancy
     Give it to the one you love.

3   O, once I was on my bed of hap'ness,
     Now I'm on my bed of sad;
     But when you meet my blue-eyed baby
     Then you'll want me back again.

4   O, can't I see those hills and valley
     Can't I see those mountains stand?
     Can't I see the sea a-tossing
     Where my thyme it used to roam.

5   Well, all alone, O all alone,
     By the seasides he left me;
     Many happy hour with thee I've spent,
     All this time I'm left a widow
     At the cottage near the sea. (repeat this verse)

60   FALSE, FALSE HAE YE BEEN TO ME, MY LOVE

It is difficult to tie this fragment down to a specific title as it shares the last of its three stanzas with the following songs:

'The Belt Wi' Colours Three'
'As I Cam Doun by Yon Castle Wa'
'The False Young Man'
'Deep in Love'
'Love Has Brought Me To Despair'

The motif of striving against the stream is found in 'Deep in Love' and our first verse is quite common in texts of 'The False Young Man'.

All of these songs have two things in common:

(a) A lover is accused of infidelity by his deserted mistress.

(b) There is always one or more stanzas in which an impossible natural phenomenon is invoked (such as the sun rising in the west); or a symbolic gift is given (such as a belt made up of three colours, representing shame, sorrow and misery); or there is a curse of impossible magnitude wished by the girl upon her false love and his new bride ('may the meadows

through which you ride become sharp pins'); or an impossible solution is
offered to any young girl who dares not trust another man:

> I will never believe a man any more
> Let his hair be white, black or brown,
> Save he were on the top of a high gallows tree,
> And swearing he wished to come down.

This idea of the *impossible* runs through all these songs, as does another
common feature of the entire group: the presence of an observer who
comments on the meeting of the lovers or who overhears either a
conversation or a long lamentation. He occasionally offers advice to the
sufferer.

Although our song has many features in common with the above-
mentioned pieces, it still appears to us to be unique, so we have given it Mrs
MacAllister's title.

BIBLIOGRAPHY

General   References for the songs mentioned above: 'As I Cam Doun by Yon
Castle Wa' – *Museum*, vol. IV, No. 326. 'The Belt Wi' Colours Three' – Christie, vol.
II, pp. 226–7; Ord, p. 194. 'Deep in Love' – see note to our No. 55. 'Love Has
Brought Me to Despair' – note to our No. 55. 'The False Young Man' – Brown, vol.
II, pp. 283–4; Christie, vol. I, pp. 198–9; Hughes, vol. I, pp. 1–3; Ord, pp. 173–4;
Purslow (3), p. 109.

'False, False Hae Ye Been to Me, My Love', sung by Christina MacAllister.

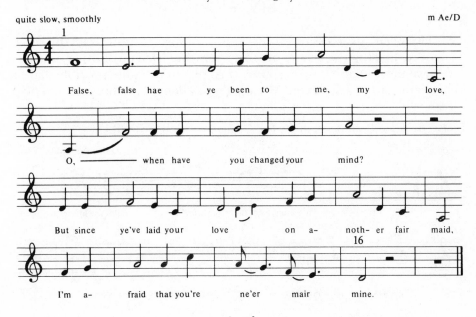

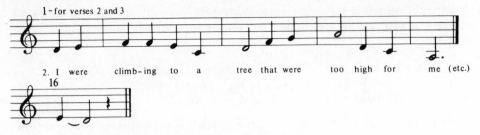

1

False, false hae ye been to me, my love,
O, when have you changed your mind?
But since ye've laid your love on another fair maid,
I'm afraid that you're ne'er mair mine.

2

I were climbing to a tree that were too high for me,
Asking fruit where there weren't any grew;
I been lifting warm water oot aneath cold clay,
And against the streams I were rowing.

3

But I mean to climb up some higher tree,
To harry a white (snowflake's) nest,
And down shall I fall, ay, without any fear,
To the arms that loves me the best.

61   MY LOVE LAYS COLD BENEATH
MY FEET

We have been unsuccessful in uncovering any information about this song.
There are in it fugitive echoes of other songs, but what those other songs *are*
we have been unable to determine. It is, of course, quite possible that its
enigmatic nature arises from Mrs Hughes's talent for combining odd lines
from half-a-dozen different songs.

'My Love Lays Cold Beneath My Feet', sung by Caroline Hughes.

If my love will give me com-fort then I will give him joys,

O, strange thoughts that come knock-ing at my door.

verse 2

Good morn-ing to you, my fair pur-ty dam - sel. How come you here so ear-ly My

love's lay-ing so cold be-neath my feet. For the (etc.)

verse 3

That was-n't what you pro-mised me, you nev-er know no oth-er, My love lay so

cold be-neath my feet; You pro-mised that you'd mar-ry me and nev-er O no oth-er

But don't my love lay so cold be-low my feet.

1 We was a-sitting by the fire of a cold winter's night,
We was telling purty tales that we dreamed the other night;
If my love will give me comfort then I will give him joys,
O, strange thoughts that come knocking at my door.

2 Good morning to you, my fair purty damsel, how come you here so
  early?
My love's laying so cold beneath my feet;
For the night is coming very dull, the morning's coming very bright,
Strange faces I'm going to meet the day.

3   That wasn't what you promised me, you never know no other,
       My love lay so cold below my feet;
       You promised that you'd marry me and never, O, no other,
       But don't my love lay so cold below my feet.

62   GREEN GROWS THE LAUREL

The refrain stanza of this somewhat trite and often confused lyric succeeds in combining a stable motif-structure with constantly changing verbal images inside that structure. The opening line is sometimes given as 'Green grows the laurel and so does the rue', two plant names with (as Belden has remarked) opposite symbolical significance. On occasion, however, the word *rue* is replaced by *yew* and the language of the flowers becomes distinctly incoherent. The most radically changed first line that we have encountered is in a version of the song reported by Cox from West Virginia: 'Green grows the wild island and so does the rose.'

    The second and third lines of the refrain stanza remain, on the whole, fairly consistent. It is in the fourth line that changes occur most frequently. For example:

      . . . Change the green laurel for violets so blue.
      . . . Change the green willow for orange and blue.
      . . . Change the green laurels for the bonnets of blue.
      . . . Change the green laurels for the red, white and blue.
      . . . Change the green laurels for the origin blue.

The variation in refrain endings has produced a correspondingly large crop of interpretations. Lucy Broadwood has suggested that 'the orange and the blue probably means the wedding-dress'. Anne Gilchrist, commenting on the 'bonnets of blue' ending, observed that 'the bonnet of blue refers to the Young Pretender – the blue bonnet being worn by those attracted to the Stewart cause'. She does not pursue the connection but goes on to suggest that 'this song of "The Orange and Blue" may have carried a political significance at the period of the '98 rebellion'. She draws attention also to the fact that '"The Green Laurel Tree" is used to symbolise Irish liberty in "MacInnon's Dream"' and that '"The Orange and Blue" is used in the Orange song "The Protestant Boys" to symbolise a union of Irish and English Protestants'.

    In explanation of the 'origin blue' ending, Vance Randolph, quoting an unspecified source, has written that '*origin* is a corruption of *marjoram*, a bluish plant somewhat resembling thyme'. The other name for marjoram is, of course, oregano.

Our two versions have similar refrains but tell different stories. Our A-text, which Mrs Higgins learned as a girl in Stromness, Orkney, is the most commonly reported type and matches fairly closely Greig's first text, which was 'picked up from the singing of some fishergirls in Shetland'.

BIBLIOGRAPHY

British   Gillington, pp. 8–9; Greig, Nos 70 and 72; *Henry Collection*, No. 165; *JFSS*, vol. I, p. 246; also vol. V, pp. 70–1; Kennedy, p. 358; Ord, p. 182; Sharp and Karpeles (2), p. 637.

Broadsides   British Museum, 11621 i 12, p. 54 (Stephenson of Gateshead).

North American   Belden, pp. 490–1; Brown, vol. II, pp. 366–7; also vol. III, pp. 328–9; Chappell (Louis), p. 136; Creighton (4), pp. 40–1; Cox (2), pp. 417–18; Flanders and Brown, pp. 113–14; Fowke, pp. 110–11; Gardner and Chickering, pp. 101–2; *JAF*, vol. 77, No. 306, pp. 348–50 (Notes and Queries); Lomax (3), pp. 332–3; Moore, pp. 200–1; Peacock, vol. II, pp. 454–7; Randolph, vol. I, pp. 272–5; Sharp and Karpeles (1), vol. II, p. 211.

Alternative titles   The Green Laurels; The Bonnets So Blue; The Orange and Blue; Red White and Blue; I Wrote My Love a Letter; Can't You Love Who You Please? (etc.).

A. 'Green Grows the Laurel', sung by Charlotte Higgins.

B. 'Green Grows the Laurel', sung by Caroline Hughes.

A.

slow but in tempo   p I (with inflected IV)

I once had a sweet–heart, now I've got none,

He's gone and he's left me to weep and to mourn,

But I'll find a– noth– er one bet– ter than he,

We'll share the green lau– rel and vio– lets of blue.

*Occasionally these bars of rest are omitted.

1   I once had a sweetheart, now I've got none,
     He's gone and he's left me to weep and to mourn;
     But I'll find another one better than he,
     We'll share the green laurel and violets of blue.

Chorus: Green grows the laurel, sweet is the dew,
          Sorry was I when I parted with you;
          By our next meeting I hope you'll prove true,
          We'll share those green laurels and violets of blue.

2   He wrote me a letter in sweet, rosy lines;
     I wrote him another, all twisted and twined;
     Saying, 'Keep your love-letters and I will keep mine.
     You write to your sweetheart and I'll write to mine.' (chorus)

3   He passes my window both early and late
     And the looks that he gives me, it makes my heart break;
     And the looks that he gives me, ten-thousand times o'er,
     Saying, 'There is the girl I once did adore.' (chorus)

B.

very slow, very free

p I

Green grows the   lau–rels   and   cold blows the   dew,

How   sor– ry was   I when I   (first met with)   you.

Note: The above single strain is repeated for the second half of the quatrain. It is literally a composite tune, as when Mrs Hughes sings the song she uses four or five structurally different melodic patterns. The pattern above seems to be the average of these. Sometimes Mrs Hughes sings the verse free, with long waits at the cadences, other times almost in rhythm.

1   Green grows the laurels and cold blows the dew,
How sorry was I when I (first met with) you;   (parted from?)
But when we did meet we would have a sweet kiss,
And we changed the green laurels for the violets of blue.

2   Once I was a schoolgirl with my pencil and slate,
But see what I've come to by stopping out late;
My parents misliked me, they turned me 'way from the door,
And I told them that I'd ramble like I used to before.

3   . . . .
. . . .
Then I picked up my baby and walked round the door,
Then I told them that I'd ramble like I rambled before.

4   Then it's green grow the laurel, yes, and cold blow the dew,
How sorry was I when I first met with you;
It's like the lilies in the garden, when their beauty's all gone,
They will go away and they'll leave you, like my true love left me.

63   I WENT TO MASS ON SUNDAY

This appears to be a modern adaptation of 'The Lover's Lament', a song in which a young woman, or occasionally·a young man, reproaches an unconstant lover. The second and third stanzas are common to most versions of the song and the opening line of the final stanza echoes 'I Wish I Was in London/Dublin', a line found in a number of American songs ('Handsome Molly', 'Bowling Green', etc.). Mrs Kelby learned the song from a North of Ireland Traveller in the early 1950s.

BIBLIOGRAPHY

British   Henry Collection, Nos 615 and 625; *JFSS*, vol. VIII, pp. 16–17; Kennedy, p. 355; Sharp and Karpeles (2), p. 254.

North American   Brown, vol. II, pp. 279–83; Peacock, vol. II, pp. 465–6; Randolph, vol. IV, pp. 232–4.

Alternative titles   Black-eyed Mary; Dark-Eyed Molly; Sweet Bann Water; The Forsaken Lovers; Meeting is a Pleasure; In Courtship There Lies Pleasure (etc.).

'I Went to Mass on Sunday', sung by Ruby Kelby.

fairly slow, somewhat free   m I

There   is a tree grows at   li-ber-ty, And   dressed all round with   green;

But   at   the   top there   is a rose That   eve- ry- one has   seen.

1 –for verses 2, 3 and 4

1 - for verse 5

1   There is a tree grows at liberty,
      And dressed all round with green;
      But at the top there is a rose
      That everyone has seen.

2   I went to Mass one Sunday,
      My lover passed me by;
      O, I knew his mind had altered
      By the rovin' o' his eye.

3   I knew his mind had altered
      To a girl of high degree,
      But her gold and beauty would fade away
      Like the rose that's on the tree.

4   He said that he would marry me
      If I would turn my coat;
      But before I'd change my religion
      I'll die like Queen Mary Scot.

5   I wish I was in old Ireland
      Lyin' on the grass,
      With a prayer-book upon my lap
      And upon my breast a cross.

64   THE BONNIE IRISH BOY
(Laws P 26)

In some English and most North American versions of this song, the girl's search for her departed lover takes her to Boston, London, or some other foreign part where she learns that he has married another girl. Dying of a broken heart, she asks that her remains be buried in Ireland. In most Scots versions of the song she does not actually travel abroad but merely expresses her intentions of doing so.

BIBLIOGRAPHY

Laws P 26.

British   Greig, No. 48; *Henry Collection*, No. 168; *JFSS*, vol. I, p. 17; Kidson, pp. 152–3; Ord, pp. 162–3.

Broadsides   *Madden Collection*, M 18-619 (John Harkness of Preston); also M 24-218 (Haly of Cork).

North American   *Fowke MSS*; Hubbard, p. 136; Peacock, vol. II, pp. 560–3.

Alternative titles   Bonnie Young Irish Boy (etc.).

'The Bonnie Irish Boy', sung by Charlotte Higgins. Musically, this song is usually found in quatrain form, so we have notated the full four lines even though Mrs Higgins's first stanza has only three. As she usually reduced the melody to its third and fourth lines, we have put the verse into couplets, other than where a three- or four-line verse is obvious.

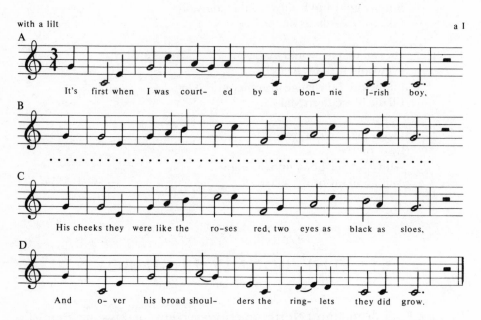

with a lilt   a l

A

It's first when I was court– ed   by a   bon– nie   I–rish   boy,

B

C

His cheeks they were like the   ro–ses   red, two eyes as   black as   sloes,

D

And   o– ver   his broad shoul– ders the   ring– lets they did grow.

Note: In verse I, Mrs Higgins goes without hesitation from line A to line C.

1   It's first when I was courted by a bonnie Irish boy,

     His cheeks they were like the roses red, two eyes as black as sloes,
     And over his broad shoulders the ringlets they did grow.

2   He courted me for his own true love, his heart's delight and joy,
     But he breaks the hearts of all fair maids wherever that he goes.

3   But now he's gone and he's left me to wander all alone,
     But I'll bundle up my clothing, in search of him I'll go.

4   . . . .
I'll wander east, and I'll wander west and I'll wander all alone,
And when I'm tired and wearied I'll just sit doon and cry,
And I'll think of all the joys I spent with my bonnie bold Irish boy.

5   There's one request I'm going to ask before I'm dead and gone,
You'll carry my bones to Ireland and there you'll lay them down.

6   You'll write upon a small stone to the passers who pass by:
'I die brokenhearted for the love of an Irish boy.'

65   THE GIRL I LEFT BEHIND
(Laws P 1-B)

Laws gives this song an A and B classification:

A . . . in which a young man of rambling ways leaves his sweetheart after promising to be faithful to her. He goes to Glasgow and, after spending some time there in congenial female company, he proceeds to another town where he marries another girl. His parents and the jilted girl die broken-hearted and the young man is left prey to remorse and regret.

B . . . in which a girl promises her departing lover that she will remain true to him while he is away. Later, however, in Glasgow, he receives a letter informing him that she has married another man. The rejected lover laments the fact that he didn't marry her when he had the chance. In some versions he marries, albeit regretfully, another girl.

It is to this second category that Mrs Hughes's text belongs and though her version is much abbreviated it manages to convey the basic elements of the story.

BIBLIOGRAPHY

Laws P 1-B.

British   Greig, Nos 83 and 157; *Henry Collection*, No. 188; *JFSS*, vol. VIII, pp. 262–3; Ord, pp. 45–7.

Broadsides   *British Museum*, LR 271 a 2, vol. V, p. 161.

North American   Creighton (2), pp. 106–7; Moore, pp. 202–5; Sharp and Karpeles (1), vol. II, pp. 62–5.

Alternative titles   Lover's Lament; All Frollicking I'll Give O'er; I'll Ne'er Forget the Parting; Jenny Ferguson.

'The Girl I Left Behind', sung by Caroline Hughes.

moderate, smoothly   a Ae/D (with inflected VII)

I was brought up with some good old pa-rents, Like an-y young squire, you see;

But since I've took up to ram-bl- ing, That's been the ruin of me.

1   I was brought up with some good old parents,
       Like any young squire, you see;
       But since I've took up to rambling,
       That's been the ruin of me.

2   As I walked over old George's Square,
       The post-boy I met there;
       And he handed to me a letter, love,
       For to give me to understand.

3   So rambling I will give over,
       (Good company I will deserve);   (Bad company I will shun?)
       For the girl that I left in old Dublin Town
       She's got wed to another man.

4   So rambling I will give over.
       Good company I will deserve.
       No more will I go rambling
       For the girl as I left behind.

66   GREEN BUSHES

(Laws P 2)

There has been some disagreement among scholars regarding the age and genesis of this song. Two stanzas of it were sung in J. B. Buckstone's play *The Green Bushes* (1845) and, as a result, it proved so popular that the complete song was later published as 'A Popular Irish ballad sung by Mrs. Fitzwilliams'.

Kidson's remark that 'there had long been sung both in England and in Ireland a ballad bearing this title' is disappointingly vague. In neither of the two Irish sources, Petrie and Joyce, are there texts provided and, in view of the uncertainty in identifying traditional songs solely from the title, they cannot be considered as conclusive proof of Kidson's claim that the song had 'long been sung' in Ireland. The only additional information given in *Traditional Tunes* is that 'Mrs. Holt of Alderhill, Meanwood . . . remembers it being sung in Stockport about 1838.' This is a mere seven years before the production of Mr Buckstone's play.

Baring-Gould too, believed that the words of the song were 'substantially old', and described them as 'a softening down of an earlier ballad which has its analogue in Scotland'. By way of illustration, he quotes the final two chorus lines of 'Low Down in the Broom', and if there *is* a relationship between the two songs it is an extremely tenuous one. In spite of this, however, Cecil Sharp inclined to Baring-Gould's point of view. Anne Gilchrist, on the other hand, has argued that the words of the song have much in common with those of an earlier stage song entitled 'A Dialogue in Imitation of Mr. H. Purcell – Between a Town Spark and a Country Lass' (Cary's *Musical Century*, 1740).

In discussing the various tunes of 'Green Bushes', Lucy Broadwood has observed that they fall into two main types: *major*, to which our B-text is sung and *modal* (a term which in early twentieth-century musical terminology may mean anything from minor in feeling to any mode but Ionian or Aeolian). Our A-text belongs to the *modal* classification.

BIBLIOGRAPHY

Laws P 2.

British   Baring-Gould and Sheppard (2), pp. 86–7; Broadwood and Maitland, pp. 170–1; Hamer, pp. 42–3; *Hammond MSS,* D-202 and D-559; *Henry Collection*, No. 143; *JFSS*, vol. V, pp. 177–8; also vol. VIII, p. 209; Joyce (1), pp. 24–5; Kennedy, p. 356; Kidson, pp. 47–8; Kidson and Moffat (2), pp. 40–1; Ord, p. 147; Petrie, Nos 222, 223, 368, 603, 674 and 771; Purslow (2), p. 38; Sharp (2), vol. I, p. 58; Sharp and Karpeles (2), vol. I, pp. 593–6.

Broadsides British Museum, LR 271 a 2, vol. II, p. 194 (Hodges and Pitts); also vol. VI, p. 144 (Such).

North American Creighton and Senior (1), pp. 20–1; Karpeles (2), p. 244.

Alternative title Down by Those Green Bushes.

A. 'Green Bushes', sung by Caroline Hughes.

B. 'Green Bushes', sung by Charlotte Higgins.

fairly slow, somewhat free   m D

Down by the bon-nie bush-es where I thinks to meet you,

He was like some lit-tle school-boy play-ing 'bout with his ball;

There's no false-heart-ed young girl, she'll nev-er serve me so no more,

I'll for-sake my own true-love and mar-ry to thee.

7 - for verse 4

1   Down by the bonnie bushes where I thinks to meet you,
     He was like some little schoolboy playing 'bout with his ball;
     There's no false-hearted young girl, she'll never serve me so no more,
     I'll forsake my own true love and marry to thee.

2   I don't want your beaver, not the beads that you wear,
     I don't want your flounces, not the feathers you wear;*
     I don't want your money nor the pride that you wear,
     O, forsake your own true lover and come along with me.

3   O, let we be going from under these trees,
    O, let's we be for going from under these trees;
    O, yonder's my true love, I see he now a-coming,
    Down by the green bushes where he seems to meet me.

4   O, when he got down there, O he found I was gone;
    He was like some little schoolboy wanderin' 'bout with his ball;
    There's no false-hearted young girl, she'll never serve me so no more,
    I'll forsake my own true love and get married to you.

*   Mrs Hughes's daughter gave the following as the first couplet in verse 2:
    I don't want your beavers, nor fine-station hose,
    I'm not such a fool as to marry for clothes.

B.

1   As I was a-walking one morning in May,
    Down by the green bushes I chanced for to stray;
    I met a fair damsel and charming was she,
    Down by the green bushes where she chanced to meet me.

2   O, why are you loitering, my pretty maid?
'I wait for my true love, kind sir,' she did say.
If I be your true love, O will you agree
To leave your own sweetheart and tarry with me?

3   I will give you fine beavers and fine silken gowns,
I will give you fine petticoats flounced to the ground.
I will give you nice beavers and fine silken gowns
If you leave your own true love and marry with me.

4   Come, let us be going, kind sir, if you please;
Come, let us be going from under those trees;
There's my sweetheart a-calling down yonder I see
Down by the green bushes where he vowed to meet me.

67   TOO YOUNG
(Laws P 18)

In singing this song, Mrs Hughes gave the first two stanzas a five-line form and three lines to each of the subsequent stanzas. This change in stanzaic structure has had surprisingly little effect on the plot used in this version. The story, of course, lacks its customary dénouement in which the young man, having seduced the very young girl, then tells her that he cannot marry her because she is no longer a virgin.

The earliest printed version we have been able to find is in *A Choice Garland* (c. 1790). That song concludes with the young woman mourning her lost lover. A Scots version published in the *Museum* (1792) matches its English predecessor stanza for stanza until the final couplet, when the young man relents and decides to marry the girl after all.

Albyn's Anthology gives a version part of which was written by James Hogg, the Ettrick Shepherd; in this text the seduction motif has completely disappeared. All subsequently reported Scots sets are similarly altered. In England, the song survives in two distinctly separate forms: (1) a lyrical piece with an attenuated narrative line and (2) a version which follows fairly closely the plot of the early *Garland* text.

BIBLIOGRAPHY

Laws P 18.

British   Campbell, vol. I, pp. 26–7; Christie, vol. I, pp. 256–7; Farmer (1), vol. II, pp. 249–50; *Gardiner MSS*, H-589 and H-781; Greig, Nos 131 and 135; *JFSS*, vol. III, pp. 296–7; also vol. IV, pp. 281–2; *Museum*, vol. IV, No. 397; Ord, pp. 170–1;

Purslow (3), p. 6; Reeves (1), pp. 41–2; Reeves (2), pp. 106–7; Sharp (1), pp. 100–1; Sharp and Karpeles (2), vol. I, pp. 656–62.

North American   Karpeles (2), pp. 208–9.

Alternative titles   (The Willing Maid) A Day (Year) Too Young; Seven Years Ower Young; Abroad As I Was Walking; As I Went Oot Ae May Morning; As I Was a-Walking; Down by the Greenwood Side.

'As I Was a-Walking Down Wackford Street', sung by Caroline Hughes.

Note: for verses 3–6, the following melody is used:

5– for verses 5 and 6

1   As I was a-walking up fair Wackford Street,
    I met a poor girl a-singing a song;
    And I popped the question to her,
    And the answer it was 'too young, too young',
    And the answer it was 'too young'.

2   The younger, my dear, the better for me
    (To be an old man's slave)   (More fitter for a bride?)
    And after a month I've got you,
    I can say I married a wife, a maid,
    I can say I married a wife, a maid.

3* And after the first nine months was up,

. . . .
. . . .

And you can say you proved a child by me
You can say you proved a child by me.

4* And what am I to wrap it in?
You'll wrap it in your petticoat
And you'll diddle it on your knee.

5 That's not the promise you made to me
When I was only sixteen years of age,
When I was only sixteen years of age.

6 You promised to me you'd marry me,
And make to me your lawful bride, your bride,
Make me your lawful bride.

* In verses 3–6 (incl.) Mrs Hughes proceeded without hesitation from line 1 to line 4, thus changing a five-line form to a three-line one.

68   THE BANKS OF SWEET PRIMROSES

There are few songs more popular with southern English country singers than this gentle narrative. A botanist might dispute the possibility of finding a bank of *Primula veris* in bloom on a midsummer's morning, but country singers appear to have a tolerant view of such inconsistencies.

It is, of course, remotely possible that the primroses in the song have symbolical significance. Reeves, and others, have pointed out that the plant is 'traditionally associated with wantonness, as in Ophelia's advice to Laertes and the porter's speech in *MacBeth*'. In *Cymbeline*, however, Shakespeare uses the primrose as a death symbol, as does Robert Herrick in 'The Mad Maid's Song'. Spencer, on the other hand, sees it as a symbol of constancy, 'the primrose true' (*Prothalamion*). In medieval literature the plant is generally associated with youth and innocence.

Mr Ridley's use of the middle-English word 'primarose' (albeit lacking the *r*) is common among southern English country singers and corresponds to the medieval Latin *Prima rosa* – earliest rose.

BIBLIOGRAPHY

British Baring-Gould and Hitchcock, pp. 16–17; Barrett, p. 80; *Gardiner MSS*, Hp–51; *JFSS*, vol. I, p. 21; also vol. IV, pp. 124–6; *JEFDSS*, vol. VII, p. 151; Kidson and Moffat (2), pp. 56–7; Moeran (*Six Folk Songs From Norfolk,* London, 1924), p. 12; Purslow (2), p. 5; Reeves (2), pp. 202–3; Sharp (2), vol. I, pp. 80–1; Sharp and Karpeles (2), vol. I, pp. 609–12; Sharp and Marson, pp. 8–9.

Broadsides British Museum, 1875 b 19 p. 134 (Paul of Spitalfields).

North American Creighton and Senior (2), pp. 127–8.

Alternative titles As I Walked Out; (Sweet) Primroses.

A. 'The Sweet Pimeroses', sung by Nelson Ridley.

B. 'Three Long Steps', sung by Caroline Hughes, whose tune was so similar to Mr Ridley's that we do not print it.

A.

This is on- ly you that's caused my mind to roam.

1   Now, as I walked out one May midsummer's morning,
      Down in the woods for to take fresh air;
      There it's who should I spy was a fair pretty creature,
      As she took a stroll to my heart's (dislike).   (desire)

2   Stand off, stand off, you are not deceitful,
      You have been a false and a wicked youth;
      It is only you that's caused my mind to wander,
      This is only you that's caused my mind to roam.

3   I will go back in some lonesome valley,
      Where no man, no mortal will never find me;
      That's pretty little small bird he changed his noting,
      He changed his voices from tree to tree.

4   Will you take me back in some lonesome valley,
      Where no man, no mortal will never find me,
      And as I was (pervoiding) amongst the sweet pimeroses
      That was only you that caused my mind to roam.

B.

1   O, 'tis three long steps I stepped up till her
      And the last three steps I heard a moanful groan;
      O, 'tis you what have causded my poor mind to wander
      If you'll give me comfort and all in vain.

2   O, go home, go home, you false damnceitful,
      O, to see what a curse, O, you been to me;
      O, 'tis you what has causded my dear mind to wander
      If you'll give me comfort in all in vain.

3   Well, the twelve o'clock the next day morning
      It was just before the old clock struck twelve,
      She come appearing up to me, O, just like any virgin –
      O, good morning dear, how come you this way?

4   O, I've come to tell you that I've been weepin',
I been weepin' on these cold stones all night,
O, 'tis you that have causded my poor mind to wander
If you'll give me comfort in all in vain.

5   O, go home, go home, you artful, seekful,
O, to see what a curse, O, you proved to me;
O, 'tis you that have causded my poor mind to wander
If you'll give me comfort in all in vain.

69   THE BONNIE GREEN TREE

The story of a young woman who, after first resisting the advances of a fine gentleman, is seduced and then abandoned by him, is common enough in Scots traditional song. The sentiments expressed in the third stanza of Mrs McPhee's song constitute an important element in such pieces as 'The Laird of the Denty Doon Bye' (our No. 21), 'The Laird o' Drum' (Child 236), 'The Broom of the Cowdenknowes' (Child 217) and others. The symbol of the 'bonnie green tree' appears to have been borrowed from 'The Waulkin' o' the Claes', a song in which our theme is given a more complex treatment (see Greig, No. 98).

BIBLIOGRAPHY

British Henry Collection, No. 794; O'Lochlainn (2), pp. 20–1; *Scottish Studies*, vol. V, pp. 100–6.

Alternative title   Under the Shade of a Bonny Green Tree.

'The Bonnie Green Tree', sung by Maggie McPhee.

1 O, a fine summer's evening, a braw summer's evening,
 A fine summer's evening as it happened for to be;
 When who did I spy but a fair young damsel
 Sitting under the shade of a bonnie green tree.

2 I stepped up to her, a' just for to view her,
 I says, 'My bonnie fair maid, your looks entices me;
 I would make you a lady of high riches and honour,
 If you'd shelter me under your bonnie green tree.'

3 O, I'm not a lady of high riches and honour,
 I'm only a poor girl as it happens for to be;
 And if I would marry you, your friends would frown on me,
 So I'll not shelter you under my bonnie green tree.

4 O, she sat now down and he sat down beside her,
 O that's the very place where he vowed to marry me;
 But when he approached me, he found me a virgin,
 Crying, 'Tomorrow we'll get married,' but a bride I'll never be.

5   O, come all you fair maids, O now take a warning,
     O, don't take any heed what any young man he does say,
     For when he gets the wills o' you, that's then he will leave you,
     It's then he will leave you as my love left me.

70   SHEEP-CROOK AND BLACK DOG

Kidson mentions 'a garland copy of this song printed in the year 1775 entitled "The Constant Shepherd and the Unconstant Shepherdess"'. Another version consisting of seven eight-line stanzas was published by Christie under the title of 'Clara and Corydon'. Lucy Broadwood collected a version in Sussex under the title 'Floro the Unkind Shepherdess'. More recently it has been reported from Nova Scotia, Newfoundland and the province of Ontario.

BIBLIOGRAPHY

British   Broadwood and Maitland, pp. 128–9; Christie, vol. II, pp. 90–1; *Henry Collection*, No. 30; *JFSS*, vol. I, pp. 90–1.

North American   Creighton (3), p. 82; *Fowke MSS* (under the title of 'My Flora and I'); Huntington, pp. 227–8; Karpeles (1), pp. 114–17; Karpeles (2), pp. 191–3; Peacock, vol. II, pp. 480–1.

Alternative titles   Floro, the Unkind Shepherdess (and varying combinations using the name Floro and Flora); The Young Shepherd; The Shepherd's Lament.

'Sheep-Crook and Black Dog', sung by Caroline Hughes.

SHEEP-CROOK AND BLACK DOG

moderate, steadily

p D (with inflected III and VII)

Verse 1

There's my black dog and sheep-crook, I will give it to you,
There's my bag and my bud-get, I will bid it a- dieu;
There's my sheep-crook and black dog, I will leave it be- hind,

Fine flo- ral, fine lau- rel, you've proved all un- kind.

Verses 2-4 (inclusive)

All to my dear Di- nah these words I did say,

'To- mor-row we'll be mar-ried, love, to- mor-row is the day.'

'Tis too soon, dear Wil- lie, my age is too young,

One day to our wed- ding is one day too soon.

1   There's my black dog and sheep-crook, I will give it to you,
    There's my bag and my budget, I will bid it adieu;
    There's my sheep-crook and black dog, I will leave it behind,
    Fine floral, fine laurel, you've proved all unkind.

2   All to my dear Dinah these words I did say,
    'Tomorrow we'll be married, love, tomorrow is the day.'
    'Tis too soon, dear Willie, my age is too young;
    One day to our wedding is one day too soon.

3   Now, I'll go into service if the day ain't too late,
        To wait on a fine lady it is my intent;
        And when into service a year or two bound,
        It's then we'll get married, and both settle down.

4   O, a little time after a letter was wrote,
        For to hear if my dear Dinah had changèd her mind;
        And she wrote that she lived such a contrary life,
        And she said that she'd never be a young shepherd's wife.

5   (repeat verse 1)

71   THE FATAL SNOWSTORM
(Laws P 20)

Peacock refers to this rather melodramatic piece as 'a tearjerker, a sort of half-baked hymn' and finds it merciful that the song is rare. This type of piece, however, which is designed to wring tears and pity from the audience and thankfulness that they are not in the shoes of the poor unfortunate is common in the folk repertory. Unlike the traditional ballads, these pieces are highly subjective and, at every turn, they moralise and (hopefully) instruct the young. The song, attributed to one John Embleton, was circulated widely as a broadside but never achieved the popularity of 'Mary of the Wild Moor' (Laws P 21), which has an even more melancholy theme.

Mrs Hughes's song differs from other versions in that the young mother dies at the workhouse door instead of in some un-named place. The singer's use of the first person plural in stanzas 5 and 8, to indicate mother and child presumably, is most unusual.

BIBLIOGRAPHY

Laws P 20.

British   *Gardiner MSS*, Hp-714 and Hp-1113; Hughes, vol. I, pp. 55–8; Kennedy, p. 354; Purslow (1), p. 33.

North American   *Fowke MSS* (under the title of 'Wintry Winds'); Hubbard, pp. 214–15; Peacock, vol. II, pp. 447–8.

Alternative titles   The Forsaken Mother and Child; Cruel Was My Father; The Fanaid Grove (etc.).

'It Was on a Cold and Winter's Night', sung by Caroline Hughes.

fairly fast, evenly

m I

It was on a cold and win-ter's night When it first came down to snow;

I took my in-no-cent babe in my arms, Not know-ing where to go.

1   It was on a cold and winter's night
       When it first came down to snow;
       I took my innocent babe all in my arms,
       Not knowing where to go.

2   How cruel was my father
       When he turned the door on me;
       And how cruel was my false-hearted mother
       When she knowed how things would be.*

3   Come hush-a-bye, my darling son,
       Don't you begin to cry,

       . . . .
       . . . .

4   O, but did your daddy know
       These things you're suffering from:
       He'd roll you in his arms this night
       And wrap you in flannel warm.

5   We both jogged on together
       Till we came to that union door,†

       . . . .
       . . . .

6   So, come all you trusting young women,
       Take warning what now I say:
       Don't trust yourself to no young man
       Till your heart he steals away.

7   They will kiss, they'll coax and cuddle you,
        And they'll call you to be their bride;
        Then they'll leave you like my first love left me
        In sorrow, grief and pain.

8   O, as we felt tired and sleepy
        We set ourselves down to rest;
        And we closed our eyes to the heavens above
        And we both laid there and died.

*   Later, Mrs Hughes sang this verse:
        How cruel was my father
        When he turned the door on me;
        And how cruel was that false-hearted man
        When he changed his love for gold.

†   Later, Mrs Hughes sang 'workhouse door'.

72   THE BANKS OF RED ROSES

As can be seen from the bibliography below, this piece is most commonly found in Ireland (where it has a different melody), less commonly in Scotland (nearly always found to the melody given here) and scarcely found at all in England and the United States. In all the printed texts to which we refer, 'The Banks of Red Roses' is a sweet and whimsical love-song expressing the viewpoint of the man. Some of these texts refer pointedly to the disapproval of the girl's parents but comment philosophically on the fact that 'she's pretty, but I can leave her alone and go court some other'. Other texts end happily at the altar.

     There are a number of significant differences between these printed sets and those now found commonly in oral tradition. First of all, the song is now generally sung from the *girl's* point of view. Secondly, a new melody of Scots derivation shares the scene with the more commonly printed Irish tune (see O'Lochlainn). But the most striking new feature of the song is the murder element and, though this is not found in any of the sources given below, it appears in almost every rendition of 'The Banks of Red Roses' that we have heard. The admonition given in the third stanza is not a common feature of the song and it is interesting to note that on a previous occasion Mr MacDonald gave the line as 'It's never let a country lad an inch abune your knee'.

BIBLIOGRAPHY

British   Buchan and Hall, p. 52; Cunningham, vol. II, p. 316; Glen, No. 7; *JFSS*, vol. II, p. 254; Joyce (2), No. 128; *Museum*, vol. I, No. 7; O'Lochlainn (1), p. 158; Reeves (2), p. 115.

Broadsides   MacNie of Stirling, 1825; *Madden Collection*, M 4–85 and M 4–86 (c. 1790).

North American   Doerflinger, pp. 315–16; Greenleaf and Mansfield, pp. 210–11; Peacock, vol. II, pp. 497–8.

Alternative titles   The Banks of the Dizzy; The German Flute; Beds of (Sweet) Roses (etc.).

'The Banks of Red Roses', sung by John MacDonald.

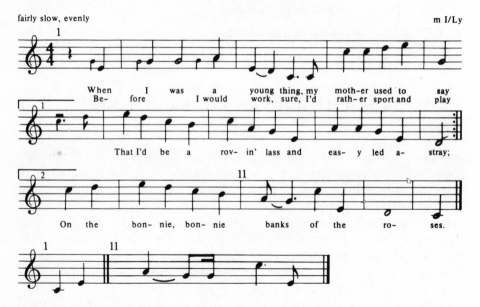

fairly slow, evenly

m I/Ly

1

When I was a young thing, my moth-er used to say
Be- fore I would work, sure, I'd rath-er sport and play

1

That I'd be a rov- in' lass and eas- y led a- stray;

2   11

On the bon- nie, bon- nie banks of the ro- ses.

1   11

Note: The chorus is sung to the same tune as the verse.

1   When I was a young thing, my mother used to say
       That I'd be a rovin' lass and easy led astray;
       Before I would work, sure, I'd rather sport and play
       On the bonnie, bonnie banks of the roses.

Chorus: On the banks of the roses, my love and I sat doon;
          He's ta'en oot his German flute to play his love a tune;
          In the middle o' the tune, noo, the bonnie lassie cried:
          'O, it's Johnnie, dear, O Johnnie, dinna leave me!'

2 For he's ta'en oot a wee penknife as sharp as ony lance,
  And he plunged it right in tae yon bonnie lassie's hairt;
  He plunged it right in tae yon bonnie lassie's hairt,
  And he left her lyin' low amang the roses. (chorus)

3 Noo, come a' ye traivellin' lasses, a warnin' take by me,
  It's never let a Gorgi lad an inch abune your knee;
  For if ye dae, ye'll be sure for to rue
  For he'll leave ye lyin' low amang the roses. (final chorus omitted)

73 THE BUTCHER BOY
(Laws P 24)

In its more complete form, this song often has several verses in common
with 'Died for Love' (our No. 55), a lyric song which has taken firm root in
England and parts of lowland Scotland. 'The Butcher Boy' is found most
commonly in North America, and appears in most American collections
not only with a consistent title (above), but with fairly standardised texts.
Most of these versions have seven to ten stanzas and fall roughly into the
following format:

Stanza 1: as in our text.
Stanza 2: as in 'Died for Love', A-text, verse 3.
Stanza 3: as in 'Died for Love', B-text, verse 3.
Stanza 4: in which the girl goes upstairs to make her bed, followed by
     her mother who asks 'What is your trouble?'
Stanza 5: in which is incorporated the last couplet of our stanza 2.
     This is part of a verse normally found in 'Sweet William'
     (our No. 25), although lacking in our two versions:

      Get me a chair, and I'll sit down
      With pen and ink I'll write it down.
      On every line she shed a tear,
      On every verse called 'Willie, dear!'

Stanza 6: as in our text, verse 3.
Stanza 7: as in our text, verse 4.
Stanza 8: as in our text, verse 5. The dove is usually mentioned here,
     but a new American element involving a fence around the
     grave is often introduced. An Ozark version has the
     following couplet:

> Around my grave build a five-rail fence
> To show the world that I didn't have any sense.

These stanzas, then, comprise the average North American story-line, on-to which are grafted various stanzas taken from the 'Died for Love' family (see note to No. 55), notably those beginning thus:

> . . . I wish I wish, but it's all in vain

> . . . Must I go bound while he goes free?

> . . . Once I wore my apron low

These stanzas enrich the narrative of 'The Butcher Boy' but, as Mrs Hughes's text demonstrates, are not vital.

As 'The Butcher Boy' has only infrequently been reported from England in this form, Belden (whose note, in our opinion, stands out as a model) has surmised that the song was crystallised in America and was later re-introduced to Britain. Perhaps this accounts for an English version's unlikely title of 'Jessie City', Jersey City being a common venue for the song in American variants, with Jefferson City, London City, New York City and Dublin as other locations.

In American versions the unfaithful lover is almost always a butcher boy, occasionally a railroad boy, whereas in the British related songs of this family he is more often a brisk young sailor, a bold young farmer, a false young man, or merely 'my true love'.

It is, of course, possible that our song was assembled from four other songs: 'Sheffield Park' (a Catnach broadside); 'The Squire's Daughter' (or 'Mary Acklin', Laws M 16); 'Died for Love' and 'Sweet William'. Cox gives an excellent breakdown of a text and assigns the various stanzas to these original pieces.

BIBLIOGRAPHY

Laws P 24.

British Gardiner MSS, H-274 and H-1010; *JFSS*, vol. II, pp. 159–60; also vol. VII, pp. 74–5; Kennedy, p. 360; Purslow (3), p. 105; Sharp and Karpeles (2), vol. I, pp. 606–8.

Broadsides *British Museum*, LR 271 a 2, vol. I, p. 15 (Pitts) and p. 229.

North American Belden, pp. 201–7; Brown, vol. II, pp. 271–9; Cox (2), pp. 430–2; Henry (2), pp. 173–4; Thompson, pp. 387–8.

Australian Edwards, pp. 180–1.

Alternative titles   The Blue-Eyed (Brown-Eyed) Boy; The Brisk Young Lover; A Maiden's Prayer; I Am a Rambling, Rowdy Boy (etc.).

'The Butcher Boy', sung by Caroline Hughes.

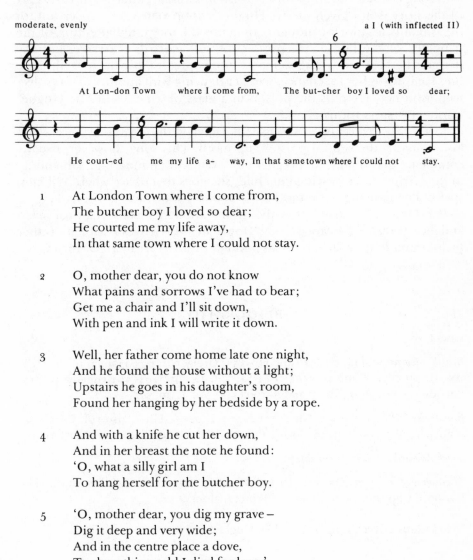

1   At London Town where I come from,
        The butcher boy I loved so dear;
        He courted me my life away,
        In that same town where I could not stay.

2   O, mother dear, you do not know
        What pains and sorrows I've had to bear;
        Get me a chair and I'll sit down,
        With pen and ink I will write it down.

3   Well, her father come home late one night,
        And he found the house without a light;
        Upstairs he goes in his daughter's room,
        Found her hanging by her bedside by a rope.

4   And with a knife he cut her down,
        And in her breast the note he found:
        'O, what a silly girl am I
        To hang herself for the butcher boy.

5   'O, mother dear, you dig my grave –
        Dig it deep and very wide;
        And in the centre place a dove,
        To show this world I died for love.'

74 OXFORD CITY
(Laws P 30)

This song is usually found with a consistent stanzaic pattern. The early part of the story is not given in Mrs Hughes's abbreviated text: A servant (or occasionally a sailor or ploughman) gains the interested attention of the daughter of the house. He presses his suit towards marriage, but she declares herself 'too young to marry, too young' to lose the joys of single life. He follows her to a dance, sees her dancing with another and resolves to poison her. He puts the poison in a glass of wine – and Mrs Hughes finishes the story for us.

It is easy to confuse this song with 'Down in the Groves', a piece which also contains the central poison-cup motif. This song, however, usually commences with Maria, pregnant by William, wandering, lamenting, in the groves. After bearing her child, she goes to a dance where William, spying her dancing with another, becomes jealous and poisons her. As in the 'Oxford Tragedy', they die in one another's arms in a protracted and heartbreaking death-scene. 'Down in the Groves', with its rather melodramatic approach, is not as popular or widespread as 'Oxford City'.

BIBLIOGRAPHY

Laws P 30.

British Gardiner MSS, Hp-340 and Hp-353; Greig, No. 137; Hamer, p. 36; *JFSS*, vol. II, pp. 157–8 and p. 200; *JEFDSS*, vol. IX, pp. 194–5; Kennedy, p. 715; Purslow (1), pp. 46–7; Sharp and Karpeles (2), vol. I, pp. 310–12.

Broadsides British Museum, LR 271 a 2, vol. I, p. 85 (Pitts); also vol. IV, p. 392 (Catnach); also vol. V, p. 26 (Such); also vol. VII, p. 158 (Livesey of Manchester).

North American Creighton (2), pp. 121–2.

Alternative titles In Oxford Town; Newport Street; In Midfordshire; The Poisoned Cup; Poison in a Glass of Wine; Jealousy.

'The Jealous Lover', sung by Caroline Hughes.

1   Three girls they went to service together,
     A lady invited them to tea;
     But how to 'stroy their own true lover,
     She put some poison in a glass of wine.

2   She drinked the wine and then she uttered:
     'Pray, young man, will you take me home?
     For the glass of wine that you've kindly give me,
     That will carry me to my grave.'

3   If that will carry you to your grave, dear,
     Hand it to me and I'll drink the same;
     In each other's arms we will die together,
     And there put an end to (all jealousy mind).   (a jealous mind)

4   Too young to court, too young to marry,
     Too young till you have a wedding day;
     But when you're married you're bound forever,
     When you're single you've sweet liberty.

75   THE WEXFORD GIRL
(Laws P 35)

According to Cox, the name of the villain in this song was John Mauge, who was hanged at Reading, Berkshire, in 1744. There is a Pepys ballad entitled 'The Bloody Miller', dated 1684, which is different in poetic structure and story detail, probably a different piece from ours. The Roxburghe ballad (c. 1700), 'The Berkshire Tragedy of the Wittam Miller', is probably a direct ancestor of 'The Wexford Girl'.

Since it first appeared in print, the song has been in a state of constant change. Laws gives a fascinating review of texts, showing how purposeful change on the part of broadsheet printers and writers has condensed the long, literary ballad into a short and fairly economical piece. He points out that 'the folk lean towards that economy which is the hallmark of traditional balladry', and notes that the deliberate chopping off of complicated or irrelevant material, as well as simplification of language, has enhanced the dramatic impact of the song. A comparison of the Roxburghe broadside with any of the American 'Oxford/Wexford Girl' texts demonstrates this admirably.

It is not only a matter of excising sections of the story (in this case about half of the old ballad has disappeared) but of re-phrasing the poetry. Caroline Hughes's text shows clearly how this comes about. Her lyric gives the impression of a précis, a re-telling of a story, the sense and basic features of which have been absorbed along with some, but not all, of the poetic imagery of the original piece. It is interesting to note that in her text the story is told in the third person, a feature rarely encountered in other versions, though occasionally (purely for dramatic effect) the third person may be used. Certain of Mrs Hughes's stanzas are not found in other versions and give the effect of having been introduced in order to fill out the story. Her first stanza, for example, is not in any other text we have seen and her last stanza appears to have been lifted from 'The Farmer's Boy'. Lucy Broadwood comments in a note to a southern English text (*JFSS*) that she had noted the same tune sung to both 'The Farmer's Boy' and 'The Wexford Girl', so it is easy to see how this final verse might have crept in. Mrs Hughes's melody, however, is not the same as the Broadwood air.

Small touches such as 'improving a child by thee' (a wonderful piece of word-play that really makes sense), or 'strivings of candlelight', give this text many of the characteristics of what Laws calls re-composition. This type of change characterises the ballad throughout its long history. Certain features identify the song:

1   A lover, who usually works in a flour mill or lives in town with a name that sounds like Oxford or Waterford.

2   The calling out of the girl for a walk.
3   Knocking the girl down with a stick or stake.
4   The girl begging for mercy.
5   The murder, with specific mention of blood.
6   Dragging the girl to the river by her hair.
7   The murderer's arrival home, the questioning and the reference to 'bleeding by the nose'.
8   Retiring to bed, usually with a candle.
9   Remorse and images of hellfire.
10 The discovery of the body.
11 The dénouement, in which the murderer foresees his punishment.

These features, though fairly constant, are dealt with in a variety of ways. The town may change from Wexford to Lexington, Town of Wickedness, Henley Ferry Town, Vago, etc. And the miller may become a 'millinder' or even a 'millionaire'. The moral strictures, too, find an equal variety of expression, ranging from the idiomatic 'Never let the devil get the upper hand of you', to the pious 'I hope my fate a warning will be to every young man'. Many of the stanzas are typical floaters and it is possible that the reworking process has involved borrowing ideas from older ballads. For example, 'Lie there, lie there, you Knoxville girl' echoes a line found in 'Lady Isabel and the Elf Knight' (Child 4): 'Lie there, lie there, you false young man'. Other stanzas in American texts echo verses from 'The Cruel Ship's Carpenter' (Laws P 36-A); from 'Jellon Grame' (Child 90); from 'Rosemary Lane' (our No. 43); and from the huge family of American murder-ballads which embraces pieces like 'Pretty Polly', 'Omi Wise', 'Pearl Bryan', 'Nell Cropsy', 'Fair Florella' and others. One version even suggests the theme of Dreiser's *American Tragedy*:

> I confess that I am guilty,
>   I tell the world the truth
> Farewell to lovely Anna!
>   I die for killing Ruth. (Brewster)

This wealth of material might bring into question Laws's statement that 'the typical folksinger is the transmitter of a received text. He rarely makes an effort to improve upon what he has learned or to invent anything new.' Several of the American texts actually take specific incidents and rework the poetry around them (see 'The Noel Girl', Randolph, vol. II, pp. 92–100). We would amend Laws's words to read 'the typical folksinger is the transmitter of a received story which he adapts to suit his own environment'.

BIBLIOGRAPHY

Laws P 35.

British Greig, Nos 137 and 179; Hamer, pp. 40–1; *Hammond MSS*, D-188; *JFSS*, vol. VII, pp. 23–4 and 44–5; Kennedy, p. 713; Petrie, No. 693; Purslow (3), p. 94; Rollins (2), vol. III, pp. 118–22; *Roxburghe*, vol. VIII, pp. 629–31; *Scottish Studies*, vol. XVI, pp. 150–1; Sharp and Karpeles (2), vol. I, pp. 294–7.

Broadsides *British Museum*, LR 271 a 2, vol. I, part 1, p. 229; also vol. IV, p. 384 (Catnach); also vol. VI, p. 209.

North American Creighton (2), pp. 194–5; Eddy, pp. 231–5; Greenleaf and Mansfield, p. 119; Henry (1), pp. 214–19; Peacock, vol. II, pp. 634–40.

Alternative titles The Oxford (Shreveport, Knoxville, Expert, Lexington, Waxford, Boston) Girl; (preceding places combined with the words City, Murder, Miller); The Murdered Girl; The Cruel (Bloody, Murdering) Miller; The Miller's Apprentice; My Confession; Hanged I Shall Be; Come All of You Who's Been in Love; The Wedding Day; Johnny MacDowell (etc.).

'The Prentice Boy', sung by Caroline Hughes.

moderate, fairly free — m D (with inflected III)

A ... 'pren-tice boy lived in Lon-don Town,(Well, he had such a joy- ful life),

If he spent one pound he spent ten, It were all for the want of a wife.

Note: Mrs Hughes' singing of this song compares to the above notation in the way that the full notation of 'All Fours' compares to a skeletal one. Her variations are extraordinary and the meter wavers constantly between 6/8 and 2/4. The above, therefore, is an 'average' notation, made up of the most common features present in each verse.

1   A 'prentice boy lived in London Town,
      (Well, he . . . for joys a while),*
      If he spent one pound he spent ten,
      It were all for the want of a wife.

2   Then Jackie went a-walking with his own true love,
And strange thoughts came into Jackie's mind;
For to murder his own true love
And for slighting her poor life.

3   She said, 'Jack my dear, don't murder me,
For I is not fit to die;
O Jackie dear, don't murder me,
'Cause I'm improving a child by thee.'

4   O, he puiled a stick out of the hedge,
He beat her across the head;
Blood came trinklin' from that innocent girl,
Come trinklin' all down her sides.

5   O, he catched hold of her curly locks,
And he dragged her to the ground;
He dragged her to some riverside
And her poor body lays there to drown.

6   O, he went along to his master's house,
At eight o'clock at night;
While they come down to let him in
(Strivings of) candlelight.   (Striking a?)

7   They asked him, they questioned him,
What stained his hands with blood?
The answer he 'plied back to they:
'It's the bleeding of my nose.'

8   Then he went up to get to bed,
No rest could ever Jackie take;
For belching flames of fire 'round him flew,
All for murdering his own true love.

9   It were just a few days after that
That poor innocent girl she were found;
She come floating by her mother's door
What did live in old London Town.

10   O, that young man he was took and tried,
And he was condemned to die;
   . . . .
   . . . .

11   He said, 'My mother died while I were young,
        Five children she left small:
        Have mercy upon me this day,
        For I'm the caretaker of them all.'

*   (Well, he had such a joyful life?)

76   CAMDEN TOWN

A young man seduces a young woman and, upon learning that she is pregnant, refuses to marry her claiming that she allowed herself to be led astray too easily. Thus far, the plot is much the same as 'Too Young' (our No. 67). Thenceforward the development takes us into a dénouement which seems to be a combination of the plots of 'The Wexford Girl' (our No. 75) and 'The Sailor's Tragedy' (Laws P 34-A). About half of the texts we have seen are similar to our two sets, in which the young man almost tenderly pushes his lover into the water. Wherever this gentle violence occurs, the young man declares his intention to move on to another place and find another girl, as in our A-text. The alternative story-line finds the girl so distraught that she kills herself whereupon the young man declares himself a villain and avows he will have a life of unhappiness thenceforward.

BIBLIOGRAPHY

British   *FMJ*, vol. I, 326–8; Hamer, p. 38; *Hammond MSS*, D-784 and D-405; Sharp and Karpeles (2), vol. I, pp. 300–3.

North American   Creighton (2), pp. 119–20.

Alternative titles   Floating Down the Tide; Molly and William; The Lily-White Hand; Abroad As I Was Walking (etc.).

A. 'My True Love's Got a Watery Grave', sung by William Hughes.

B. (untitled), sung by Nelson Ridley.

A.

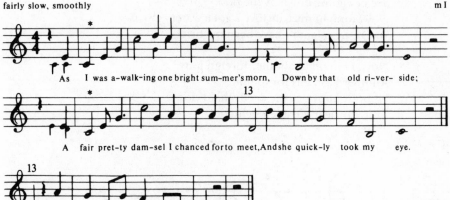

fairly slow, smoothly

m I

As I was a-walk-ing one bright sum-mer's morn, Down by that old ri-ver- side;

13

A fair pret-ty dam-sel I chanced for to meet, And she quick-ly took my eye.

13

*Lines 1 and 3 of verses 5 and 7 begin here without an upbeat.

1   As I was a-walking one bright summer's morn,
Down by that old riverside;
A fair pretty damsel I chanced for to meet,
And she quickly took my eye.

2   I asked that young girl to sit by my side
In terms for to make her my wife,

. . . .
. . . .

3   The night being gone and the morning being light,
This fair pretty damsel she did say:
'How do you think I could marry such a one
What lately did lead me astray?

4   'How can I go home to my father's house
Taking both shame and disgrace?
Before that I would, I would go and drown myself,
Or die in a lonesome place.'

5   I catchèd hold of her lily-white hand,
I kissed both cheek and chin;
I catchèd hold of her middle so small,
And I gently throwed her in.

6 You should see how she float, see how she go,
  See her going down by the tide;
  Now, tonight my true love's got a watery grave,
  When she ought to have been my bride.

7 Now, I am off to another foreign port
  Another flash girl for to find;
  Nobody knows of the deeds that I done
  (But) the dear girl I left behind.   (To?)

B.

rather free   m I

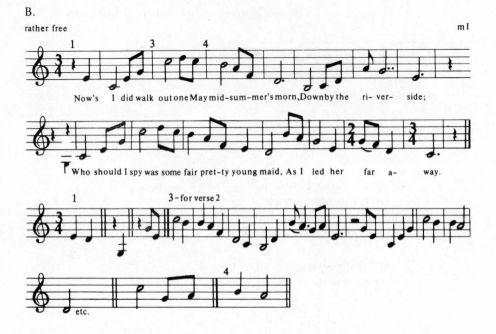

Now's I did walk out one May mid-sum-mer's morn, Down by the ri- ver- side;

Who should I spy was some fair pret-ty young maid, As I led her far a- way.

3 - for verse 2

etc.

1 Now's I did walk out one May midsummer's morn,
  Down by the riverside;
  Who should I spy was some fair pretty young maid,
  As I led her far away.

2 I took just hold of her lily-white hand,
  I kissed both cheeks and her chin;
  I led her down to the riverside,
  And I gently pushed her in.

3 To watch how she do float, to watch how she do go,
  She's floating away with the tide;
  In the room of her being a watery grave
  She had right to be my bride.

4 No, I could not go back to my mother's house,
  To make me shame and disgrace;
  Before I would go, I would drown myself,
  All in some lonesome place.

FAMILY OPPOSITION
TO LOVERS

77   ERIN'S LOVELY HOME
(Laws M 6)

The following three-verse fragment obscures the story of two ill-starred lovers, a young servant and his employer's daughter. Their plan to elope is discovered by the girl's father, who intercepts them as they board ship at Belfast. The young man is arrested, jailed in County Tyrone and is finally sentenced to be transported for seven years. His sweetheart swears that she will wait for him.

BIBLIOGRAPHY

Laws M 6.

British   *Gardiner MSS*, Hp-430 and Hp-947; Greig, No. 47; *Henry Collection*, No. 46; *JFSS*, vol. I, p. 117; vol. II, pp. 167–8 and 211; O'Lochlainn (1), p. 202; Ord, pp. 106–7; Purslow (4), p. 27; Sharp and Karpeles (2), vol. I, pp. 349–51; Sharp and Marson, p. 24.

North American   Creighton (3), pp. 64–5; *Fowke MSS*; Greenleaf and Mansfield, pp. 142–3; Huntington, pp. 198–201; Leach, pp. 48–9.

Alternative titles   Erin's Green Shore; Aran's Lovely Home; Seven Links in My Chain (etc.).

'Old Erin's Lovely Vale', sung by Nelson Ridley.

1   When I was young and in my prime and my age was twenty-one,
    Till I came onto some servant then I became a gentleman;*
    Till I came onto some servant then I became a gentleman,
    Then it's quickly they did banish me back to dear old Erin's land.

2   For the moon shone bright, the stars gave light, we was sitting all alone,
    Then I said unto my own true love, here's a carriage for to (pay);†
    But if I had had my liberty it's along with you I'd go,
    (But I'd never fret on them I loved) in old Erin's lovely isle.‡

3   Now cheer up, cheer up, my own true love, it will grieve my heart to go,
    (Whyever boat your dad will float) to a foreign land I'll go
    But if I had my liberty it's along with you I'd go,
    But I'd never fret for them I loved in old Erin's lovely isle.

*   Till I became a servant to a noble gentleman
†   She said, 'Prepare, my jewel, our passage for to pay'
‡   So never fret for those you left in (etc.)

78 MY FATHER'S SERVANT BOY
(Laws M 11)

John MacDonald said of this song: 'I've travelled all over Ireland; I've been in England, all over Scotland – and I never heard anyone who knew this song.' We might add that we have been equally unsuccessful in locating printed texts in the English and Scottish traditional collections.

BIBLIOGRAPHY

Laws M 11.

British   *Henry Collection*, No. 198.

Broadsides   *British Museum*, LR 271 a 2, vol. IV, p. 415 (Catnach); also vol. V, p. 122; *Madden Collection*, M 20–452 (Ward of Ledbury); also M 24–491 and 492, two slips from Cork City; also M 18-321 (A. Swindells, Manchester).

North American   See Laws.

Alternative titles   The Servant Boy; My Father's Servant Boy, Or, Answer to the Philadelphia Lass.

'My Father's Servant Boy', sung by John MacDonald.

moderate, smoothly   m I (with inflected VII)

For I was bred be-tween Glen-den-nie town And a   place ca'd Dun-   cal-   loy;

My   pa-rents tried   to   wed me All   till   a   gen-tle   man.

1   For I was bred between Glendennie town
     And a place ca'd Duncalloy;
     My parents tried to wed me
     All to a gentleman.

2   But the night before from them I stole
     All till a village near;
     It was there I met my own true love,
     My father's servant boy.

3   So we both rode down to Belfast town
       Where the Admiral's ship did lie;
       And in that ship we sailed away
       Bound for Amerikee.

4   But before we reached the other side
       Our money it ran down;
       Sometimes we were supported
       All by an Irish friend.

5   Well, a gentleman from Ireland
       Who gave us both some employ;
       And now I receive two pounds per week
       From my father's servant boy.

6   Now, my parents wrote me a letter
       And they sealed it with a crown,
       Saying if I return again
       Sure, I'd get five thousand pound.

7   But I wrote a-back an answer
       And I sealed it with a crown,
       Sayin' if they were worth one shilling
       That I was worth one pound.

8   Some lives and dies in wedlock's bands
       Sure, I'll crown my love with joy;
       And as long as I live, I'll never deceive
       My father's servant boy.

79   LOCKS AND BOLTS
(Laws M 13)

This is one of three Scots songs, all entitled 'The Lass of Bennachie' and all dealing with the same historical event. We will, however, use the Laws title above in the following discussion.

    There is evidence that the song is based on the courtship of a Miss Erskine, born 1747, daughter of the Laird of Pittodrie, who fell in love with Ensign William Knight in 1765 at Fort Augustus. In spite of family opposition to the match, the lovers were married in 1770 and their descendants are known as the Knight-Erskines. Greig has pointed out that historical records contradict the particular treatment of the events given in 'The Lass of Bennachie' but it is possible that the song has combined with, and borrowed from, other existing pieces.

The three songs which deal with the event are:

(1) 'The Lass o' Bennachie', a stilted and rather lengthy piece in which the girl is bound in prison by her father but upon gaining her freedom she follows her love to Germany and then returns home again with him. The style of the story is similar to that of 'Jack Munro' (Laws N 7) but it lacks the disguise motif.

(2) 'The Lass o' Bennachie', our song, in which the most prominent opening stanza is:

> 'Twas at the back o' Bennochie
> Where swiftly flies the swallow,
> 'Twas at the back o' Bennochie
> Where first I chose my marrow.

The story follows roughly the text given by Jock Higgins. This version does not state explicitly the difference in the social status of the lovers. It is by far the most popular of the three songs.

(3) 'The Lass o' Bennachie', a lyric song of five to six stanzas, beginning with the above-quoted stanza then proceeding to describe the girl, the parting and the love-vows.

All three of these forms can be found in both Greig and Ord. Only the second one, however, seems to have been freed from the stilted verse of the broadside.

No. 2 has borrowed stanzas from far and wide to make up the present, more or less standard, text. By 'standard', we mean in this case a fixed sequence of action and ideas rather than a consistent group of poetic images. Our verses 3–7 (A-text) constitute the core of most of the full versions. It is chiefly the openings and endings of texts which vary. For example the Scots texts nearly always begin with the above quoted stanza; American texts, however, generally begin with variants of the following two stanzas:

> I dreamed of my true love last night,
> My arms were all about her;
> And when I woke it was a dream
> I had to lie without her.

> Her yellow hair, like strands of gold,
> Came tumbling down the pillow,
> I swore I'd neither eat nor drink
> Nor sleep while I'm without her.

In *The Pepys Ballads* (under the title 'The Constant Wife') there is a two-part broadside (c. 1675). Verses 3–7 of our A-text form the core of Part I of this broadside. Its second part is a lyric description of a girl who has 'golden locks like threeds of gold'. The action in this early broadside proceeds as in the modern song but the language is different and has more in common with the United States texts.

Brown, in a note, mentions that 'Martin Parker, professional ballad-maker of the 17th-century, has a song entitled "The Lovers Joy and Griefe" [*Roxburghe*] with the refrain "but locks and bolts do hinder"'. It is possible that by that time this had become a stock phrase.

The most interesting vein of research on this song was opened up by Phillips Barry, in a note on 'Johnnie Scot' (Child 99), which has a story similar to that of 'Locks and Bolts'. For instance, Child's A-text of No. 99 contains the following lines:

> Here I am kept wi' bars and bolts
> Most grievous to behold (Stanza 15)

After opposing the family of his beloved, the hero 'has ta'en his true love by the hand', declaring:

> 'I'm seeking nane o' your gold,' he says,
> 'Nor of your silver clear;
> I only seek your daughter fair
> Whose love has cost her dear.'

This corresponds with a final couplet in Brown's 'Locks and Bolts' text:

> I never married her for gold or silver,
> Nor none of her father's treasure.

Child refers to a Breton text of the 'Johnnie Scot' story, in which the name of the hero is 'Les Aubrays'. His C-text gives the 'King of Aulsberry' as the name of his hero. In Barry's A- and B-texts of 'Johnnie Scot', the rescuer is 'Salvaree' or 'Salgaree'. In a Utah text of 'Locks', the girl leans out of her window and whispers, 'Syvane, Syvane would I be with you/But locks and bolts does hinder.' This could, of course, be a transliteration of 'In vain, in vain would I be with you' but in view of all the other features common to the two pieces a definite relationship between the old ballad and 'Locks and Bolts' cannot be ruled out.

BIBLIOGRAPHY

Laws M 13.

British Christie, vol. I, pp. 36–7; *Euing*, No. 41; Farmer (2), pp. 46–7; *Gardiner MSS*, Hp-1274 and Hp-1302; Greig, No. 8; *Henry Collection*, No. 668; *JFSS*, vol. V,

p. 114; *JEFDSS*, vol. IV, pp. 180–1; also vol. IX, pp. 192–3; Kennedy, p. 362; Ord, pp. 438–41; Purslow (4), p. 53; Rollins (2), vol. II, pp. 201–6: *Roxburghe*, vol. I, part ii, pp. 599–601; Sharp and Karpeles (2), vol. I, pp. 346–8.

Broadsides   *Madden Collection*, M 5-1289 (Dicey?).

North American   Creighton (3), pp. 54–6; Hubbard, pp. 137–8; Moore, pp. 209–10; Sharp and Karpeles (1), vol. II, pp. 17–19.

General   Barry, Eckstorm and Smyth, pp. 213–33; Child, No. 99.

Alternative titles   The Lass (Back, Foot) o' Bennachie; Bolts and Bars; Love Laughs at Locksmiths; I Dreamt of My True Love Last Night; Rainbow Willow; The Vain Dreamer (etc.).

A. 'The Lass o' Bennachie', sung by Jock Higgins.

B. 'At the Back o' Bennachie', sung by Maggie McPhee.

A.

1   For I fell in love wi' a bonnie lass
     At the herdin' o' her cattle;
     Her father had me beguiled
     And sent me off to battle.

2   It was over dyke, it was over dale,
     It's over dykes and valleys;
     When peace it came and as I come hame
     A-spiering for my dearie.

3 As I gaed doon to my uncle's house
  A-spiering for my dearie,
  For they told me not such a one was there,
  It made my heart grow weary.

4 For my true love, she heard my voice
  All out of her high window;
  It's 'Here I am, but I cannot come
  Till the locks and keys lie sundered.'

5 I stood awhile to amuse myself
  And being in angry passion,
  My passion flew and my sword I drew,
  I made locks and keys lie sundered.

6 I made locks and keys and double-dells
  I made locks and keys lie sundered;
  I took my love all by the hand
  And my broadsword in the other.

7 Her uncle and her uncle's men
  They cowardly followed after,
  I told them a' to return again
  Else try it in the battle.

8 For as I have been where the bullets flew
  And the cannons loudly rattle,
  For it's at the back o' Bennachie
  Where swiftly flew the swallow.

B.

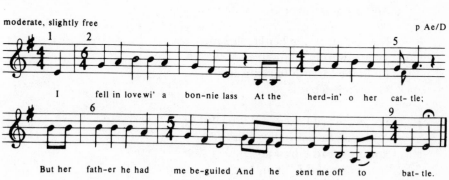

moderate, slightly free   p Ae/D

I fell in love wi' a bon-nie lass At the herd-in' o her cat-tle; But her fath-er he had me be-guiled And he sent me off to bat-tle.

1
I fell in love wi' a bonnie lass
At the herdin' o' her cattle;
But her father he had me beguiled
And he sent me off to battle.

2
It was over hills, it was over dales,
It was over lofty mountains;
It was over hills, it was over dales
It was there we fought our battle.

3
But peace it come and home I came,
O, askin' for my dearie;
But they told me not such a one was there,
Which made my heart to fury.

4
I stood awhile to amuse mysel',
My passion couldna stand me;
My sword I drew and the locks I slew,
I made locks and keys to sunder.

5
I made broken doors, I made double-dells,
I made locks and keys a-sinder,
I took my lovey by the hand
And my broadsword in the ither.

6
For her father and her father's men,
They cowardly followed after,
I told the cowards to retire again,
Or try it in a battle.

7
For my sword I drew and three I slew
And three lay mortally wounded;
For my sword I drew and three I slew
It was there I fought my battle.

[258]

8   It was at the back o' Bennachie,
     Where loudly (goes) the cannon;   (roars?)
     It was at the back o' Bennachie,
     It was there we fought wor battle.

80   ALL OVER THOSE HILLS

At first glance this appears to be merely another member of that large group of songs in which a young woman laments the loss of her lover. Mrs Hughes's song, however, has some unusual features. The tavern, for example, mentioned in stanza 1, is unusual first in that it is given a specific name and second in that the type of name is one incongruous in a love-lamentation. Furthermore, texts of the 'Love Has Brought Me To Despair' families (see note to our No. 55) lack the kind of positive action found in 'All Over Those Hills'. In the third stanza, for instance, images follow each other in a manner reminiscent of the rapid cross-cutting techniques used by modern film-makers, so that from a mood of resignation we are suddenly projected into one of violence and then, just as suddenly, into a mood of despair.

And what is the significance of the union (workhouse) reference in the final line? Has the possibility of death and destitution already been planted in an earlier but now absent stanza? Or has the phrase been borrowed from another song? It is, of course, possible that the entire text is made up of borrowed lines, couplets and whole stanzas arranged in a sequence that would seem logical to a singer steeped in the traditional repertory.

Another interesting possibility is that the song is made up of assonantal echoes of an entirely different song, viz. 'Locks and Bolts' (our No. 79). The opening line of our text is paraphrased in most of the 'Locks' texts as 'Out over hills, out over dales'. A recently-recorded version of an English text begins: 'It was over the hills . . .'.

Again, the second and third lines of our opening stanza:

(80)   A place called Hop and Bottle,
         Where my true love he got deluded from me,

find an echo in the most commonly reported Scots texts of 'Locks and Bolts':

(79)   Her father soon beguiled me
         And sent me off to battle.

Again compare the line 'Now I will walk on to the public house' (80) with 'I went to her uncle's house' (79). Or compare

(80)   And I'll look all through those windows
       O, who should I see but my Henry dear?

with

(79)   She put her head out of the window
       She said, 'My dear, you're welcome here.'

In the first and second lines of our third stanza, the narrator withdraws momentarily from the action, as does the main character in 'Locks and Bolts'. Furthermore, in both songs, this moment – given over to deliberation on the one hand and observation on the other – is followed by sudden violence:

(79)   I made broken doors of double-deal
       I made locks and bolts to sunder.

(80)   For the doors I'll smash and the windows I'll break
       And I'll leave the roof now in shadows.

A series of coincidences? Possibly. But it is equally possible that the maker of 'All Over Those Hills' (Mrs Hughes herself?) has borrowed something of the structure and mood as well as some of the verbal patterns from 'Locks and Bolts'.

'All Over Those Hills', sung by Caroline Hughes.

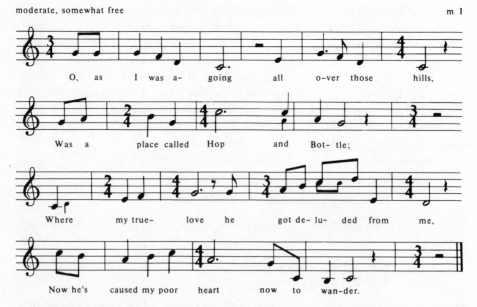

moderate, somewhat free   m I

O, as I was a- going all o-ver those hills,
Was a place called Hop and Bot- tle;
Where my true- love he got de- lu- ded from me,
Now he's caused my poor heart now to wan-der.

Note: This melody was almost impossible to notate. The above is reasonably exact if irregular in meter. A more regular form for general singing might be:

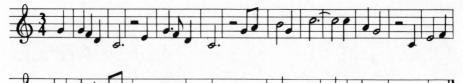

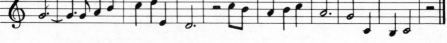

1   O, as I was a-going all over those hills,
     Was a place called Hop and Bottle;
     Where my true love he got deluded from me,
     Now he's caused my poor heart now to wander.

2   Now, I will walk on to the public house,
     And I'll look all through those windows;
     O, who should I see but my Henry dear,
     He was sitting by the side of his Ellen.

3   O, 'tis no more good, for I will go home,
     And I'll make my mind quite happy –
     For the doors I'll smash and the windows I'll break,
     And I'll leave the roof now in shadows.

4   .   .   .   .
     .   .   .   .
     But before I part from my Henry dear
     I would sooner leave him die in a union.

81   BOGIE'S BONNIE BELLE

This is probably the most popular bothy song sung in Scotland today. The fact that it is not included in the Ford, Greig or Ord collections leads us to suppose that it is of comparatively recent origin, possibly later than 1925 (the year in which Ord completed the compilation of *Bothy Songs and Ballads*). While the tune to which it is sung varies only slightly from singer to singer, the many texts already show a significant degree of variation.

BIBLIOGRAPHY

British   Kerr (1), Book I, p. 16.

'Bogie's Bonnie Belle', sung by John MacDonald.

BOGIE'S BONNIE BELLE

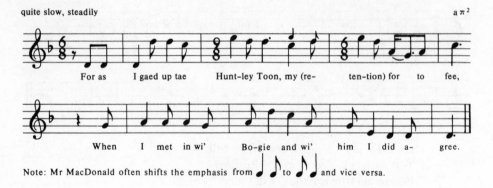

quite slow, steadily

a π²

For as I gaed up tae Hunt-ley Toon, my (re- ten-tion) for to fee,

When I met in wi' Bo-gie and wi' him I did a- gree.

Note: Mr MacDonald often shifts the emphasis from ♩♪ to ♪♩ and vice versa.

1   For as I gaed doon to Huntley toon, my (retention) for   (intention?)
      to fee,
   When I met in wi' Bogie and wi' him I did agree.

2   Noo, I had to work his foremost horse, I could either cart or ploo,
   I never ta'en a job in hand but a job I well could do.

3   Noo, Bogie had a daughter, and her name was Isabel,
   The fairest maid roond Cairney, she's kenned baith far and wide.

4   One night she gaed a-ramblin', she (re-choiced) me   (enticed, chose)
      for her guide,
   Doon by the banks o' Cairney to see the fishes glide.

5   Noo, when we were comin' hame at night, it was through yon grassy
      green,
   When we were comin' hame at night, we thocht that we were seen.

6   But three months bein' after that, ay, when Belle grew white and pale,
   And a' the roses left her cheeks and her voice got very low.

7   And six-a-months bein' after that, ay, when Belle gi'en birth tae a son:
   Auld Bogie he did send for me to see what would be done.

8   Noo, I promised for to marry Belle, ay, and Belle the same tae me;
   But Bogie said I was nae match, nor Belle a match for me.

9   So I'll tak' my wee son tae my breist, ay, and joys tae him I'll bring,
   I'll tak' my wee son on my knee and (dennies) here I'll sing.   (ditties?)

10   But Belle got married tae a man, ay, wha bides in Huntley toon,
   He makes tinny pans and ladles and hawks the country roond.

[262]

The events described in this song, a casual sexual encounter between two young people at a wedding party and the subsequent expulsion of one of them from college, have a curiously modern ring to them. They took place, according to Dean Christie, in the mid-eighteenth century. One hundred and fifty years later, Gavin Greig was able to report 'few folksongs are more popular in the northeast than "Alan MacLean"', an assertion which, to some extent, finds support in the different place-names which occur in the various texts. Christie quotes three separate broadsides, one of which has for its opening line: 'Young Alan MacLean was a free Baron's son.' A second describes him as a son of a minister of Cullen (a small town on the Banffshire coast between Portnockie and Portsoy). The third has it that he was the son of a minister in Caithness.

The popularity of the song appears to have waned considerably since Greig reported it in 1911. The editors of this collection have only encountered it three times in the last fifteen years.

BIBLIOGRAPHY

British   Christie, vol. II, pp. 184–5; Greig, No. 179; MacColl, pp. 76–7.

Alternative titles   The Aulton College Hall.

'The Minister's Son', sung by Charlotte Higgins.

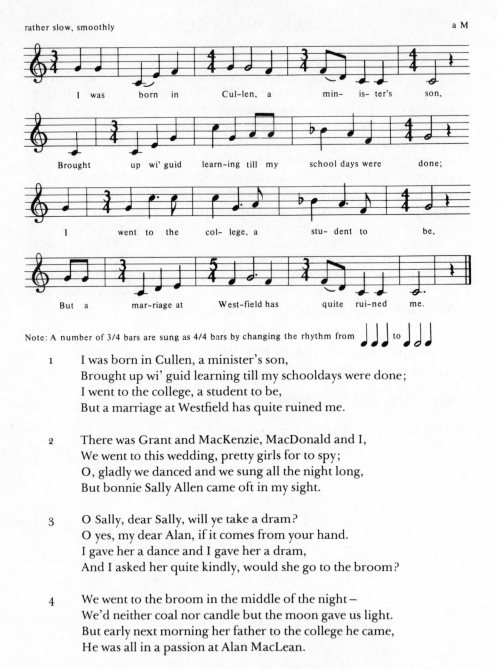

rather slow, smoothly

I was born in Cul- len, a min- is- ter's son,

Brought up wi' guid learn-ing till my school days were done;

I went to the col- lege, a stu- dent to be,

But a mar-riage at West-field has quite rui-ned me.

Note: A number of 3/4 bars are sung as 4/4 bars by changing the rhythm from ♩♩♩ to ♩♩♩

1   I was born in Cullen, a minister's son,
     Brought up wi' guid learning till my schooldays were done;
     I went to the college, a student to be,
     But a marriage at Westfield has quite ruined me.

2   There was Grant and MacKenzie, MacDonald and I,
     We went to this wedding, pretty girls for to spy;
     O, gladly we danced and we sung all the night long,
     But bonnie Sally Allen came oft in my sight.

3   O Sally, dear Sally, will ye take a dram?
     O yes, my dear Alan, if it comes from your hand.
     I gave her a dance and I gave her a dram,
     And I asked her quite kindly, would she go to the broom?

4   We went to the broom in the middle of the night –
     We'd neither coal nor candle but the moon gave us light.
     But early next morning her father to the college he came,
     He was all in a passion at Alan MacLean.

5   'If it's true,' said the Regent, 'as I doubt it's no lie,
     For this day from the Aulton College young Alan must fly.
     Tomorrow's the graduation, and Tuesday's the ball,
     So we'll have to banish Alan from the Aulton College Hall.'

6 My faither's a minister, he preaches in Tain;
 My mother died in the hielands, and I daurna gae hame;
 But the good ship, *Prince Charles Royal*, lies oot in the bay,
 Takin' on goods and passengers, she'll surely take me.

7 So farewell, Aulton College! Farewell, Aberdeen –
 Farewell to my Sally that lives doon by the green.
 If ever I return again, as some day that I will,
 I'll marry bonnie Sally in spite o' them all.
 And if ever I return again, as I know that I will,
 I'll drink a merry bottle by the Aulton College Hall.

Note: Mrs Higgins sang this song immediately following 'Van Dieman's Land', whose tune is identical to 'Alan MacLean'. It is possible that she did not mean to use that tune, as the words seem to fit awkwardly. She had to constantly make alterations in the metre. In verse 5, she halted before the 2nd line then seemed to find difficulty in putting the rest of the text to a melodic quatrain form. Or it is possible that she was accustomed to *reciting* the text?

SOLDIERS AND SAILORS

83 *THE RAINBOW*

An English ship sailing near the Spanish shore is engaged by a Spanish frigate. In the course of the battle the captain of the British ship is slain, whereupon a young woman (conveniently at hand) takes his place and overcomes the enemy. The battle over, the sailors drink a toast to her and to the gallant ship.

In some versions of the song the adversary is a French ship, while the victorious vessel is *The Union, The Britannia,* or *The Resolution.*

BIBLIOGRAPHY

British Christie, vol. II, pp. 176–7; *JFSS*, vol. III, pp. 180–3; Kidson, pp. 99–100; Sharp and Karpeles (2), vol. II, pp. 279–80.

North American MacKenzie, pp. 223–4.

Alternative titles As We Were a-Sailing; The Bold Damosel; Aboard *The Resolution; The Britannia* and *The Union.*

'*The Rainbow*', sung by Nelson Ridley.

They did not have a man, my boys, could fi-re off a gun,

That the blood from our scut- tling like wa-ter they did run.

2 - for verse 2   5 - for verse 2   14 - for verse 2

1   As I was a-walking down by the Spanish shore,
      Where the big guns they did rattle, then, and loud-lie cannons roared;
      They did not have a man, my boys, could fire off a gun,
      That the blood from our scuttling like water they did run.

2   By quarters, by quarters, this fair maid she required,
      Many will drink with your sweetheart and I will drink with mine;
      For here's to that fair maid that fell all on the main,
      They caught that big ship royal, callèd *Rainbow* by her name.

3   The little boy stood on her deck, the ship was sailing by,
      And little did that poor boy think, a-sailing with that maid;
      And little did that poor boy think, a-thinking of no harm,
      When they caught the big ship royal callèd *Rainbow* by her name.

4   Now, since we've gained this victory we will have a glass of wine,
      Many will drink with your sweetheart and I will drink with mine;
      For here is to that young man that 'luded me away,
      We caught the big ship royal callèd *Rainbow* by her name.

84   JAMIE FOYERS

'This typical bothy ballad' was, according to Ford, 'a prime favourite at the harvest homes, foys, and Handsel-Monday gatherings in the rural parts of Perthshire before and about the middle of the present century.'
    The military event which provided the subject-matter for the song was

the Siege of Burgos during the 1812 campaign of the Peninsular War. The Duke of Wellington's investment of Marshal Marmont's French forces and the retreat which followed it were not particularly bloody by modern standards – a mere 10,000 or so died. Wellington gained an earldom and a Perthshire militiaman gained an epitaph which is still sung round the campfires of travelling people during the berry-picking and potato-lifting seasons.

The translocation of Burgos to 'Blücher's castle' is interesting, particularly in view of the fact that Blücher's name crops up in other Napoleonic ballads. Here, he has been transformed from an enemy of Napoleon into an ally.

BIBLIOGRAPHY

British   Buchan (Norman), p. 111; Ford (2), vol. I, pp. 18–19; Greig, No. 134; Ord, pp. 294–5.

North American   Creighton (1), pp. 208–9; *Fowke MSS.*

Alternative title   Jimmy Folier.

'Young Jamie Foyers', sung by John MacDonald.

1   Far distant, far distant, lies Scotia the brave,
No tombstone memorial to hallow his grave;
His bones now lie scattered on the rude soil of Spain,
And it's young Jamie Foyers in the battle was slain.

2   From the Perthshire Militia tae serve in the line,
Then the brave Forty-Second we sailed, ay, to join;
From Wellington's army we did volunteer,
Ay, and young Jamie Foyers to lead us away.

3   But the night when we landed, ay, the bugle did sound.
O, the general give orders to form on the ground;
For to storm Blücher's castle before the break o' day,
And it's young Jamie Foyers to lead us away.

4   But a-scaling the ladder and climbin' the wall,
And a bullet from a French gun young Foyers did fall;
For he leaned his right arm all upon his left breast,
And it's young Jamie Foyers his comrades addressed:

5   'For it's you, Robert Pirie, that stands in command.
If the good Lord only sends you to old Scotland again,
Will you tell my old father, if his heart's still as warm,
That his son, Jamie Foyers, expired in your arms?

6   'Now, if but a few moments in Campsie I were,
My friends and acquaintance my sorrows would share.'
But as life's purple curtain was ebbing so fast,
That young Jamie Foyers soon drawed his last breath.

7   For his friends and acquaintance lament for the brave,
For it's Foyers that great hero who was laid in his grave;
For they take for a windin' sheet his own tartan plaid,
Ay, and mutterin' 'Poor Foyers!' march slowly away.

8   For his friends and acquaintance lament for the brave,
For it's Foyers the brave hero will never return.
For your war-drums may rattle and your bugles may sound,
But it's young Jamie Foyers will never return.

85 THE BONNIE BUNCH OF ROSES
(Laws J 5)

Anyone familiar with this very popular song might find our A-text somewhat startling. Not only has General Blücher (probably en route from 'The Grand Conversation with Napoleon') usurped Bonaparte's role as the narrator's father, but he has become the object of an apparently fruitless search by his distracted son. These departures from the original plot have succeeded in transforming a rather grand historical song into an inferior example of a Victorian tear-jerker.

BIBLIOGRAPHY

Laws J 5.

British Baring-Gould and Sheppard (2), pp. 54–5; Buchan and Hall, pp. 148–9; Christie, vol. II, pp. 232–3; *Gardiner MSS*, H-399; Greig, No. 94; Hughes, vol. II, pp. 92–100; *JFSS*, vol. II, p. 276; also vol. III, pp. 56–7; O'Lochlainn (1), pp. 32–3; Ord, pp. 301–2; Purslow (2), p. 7; Reeves (1) pp. 63–4; Seeger and MacColl, p. 91; Sharp and Karpeles (2), vol. II, pp. 325–7; Zimmerman, pp. 190–1.

North American Huntington, pp. 207–9; Peacock, vol. III, pp. 988–9.

Alternative title The Bunch of Roses, O.

A. 'Bold Blücher', sung by Nelson Ridley.

B. 'The Bonnie Bunch of Roses', sung by John MacDonald.

A.

free but not slow

m I (with inflected VII)

Did you know bold Blü- cher?

He was o- ver- pow- ered by the drift- ed snow;

Through Eng- land, Ire- land, Scot- a- land and Wales

He would take care of the bon- nie bunch of ro- ses.

2 - for verse 4

1   Did you know bold Blücher?
     He was overpowered by the drifted snow;
     Through England, Ireland, Scotaland and Wales
     He would take care of the bonnie bunch of roses.

2   You go and find your father,
     He's overpowered by the drifted snow;
     Then (mark) will follow after,
     I took care of the bonnie bunch of roses.

3   I cannot find my father,
     He must be overpowered by the drifted snow,
     I've searched England, Ireland, Scotaland and Wales,
     I've took care of the bonnie bunch of roses.

4   My father must be in great danger,
     For I cannot find him anywhere;
     For I've searched England, Ireland, Scotaland and Wales,
     I've took care of the bonnie bunch of roses.

B.

quite free

mI (with inflected VII)

On the mar-gin of the o- cean, it was ear-ly in the month of June,

When es- cor- ted by Na- po- le-on, when those birds did sweet-ly tune.

For it's moth-er dear, have mer- cy till onct I'm a-ble to com -mand,

I will raise a ter- ri-ble ar- a-my and con-quer the bon-nie bunch of ro-ses, O.

1   On the margin of the ocean, it was early in the month of June,
When escorted by Napoleon, when those birds did sweetly tune.
For it's mother dear, have mercy, till onct I'm able to command,
I will raise a terrible aramy and conquer the bonnie bunch of roses, O.

2   . . . .

. . . .

O son, dear son, have patience – on St Helena your father lies low,
*(You have been a halligation) concerning the bonnie bunch of roses,
O.

*   (All Moscow was a-blazing?)

86   McCAFFERY

A young man, McCaffery/McCafferty/McCassery, enlists in the Forty-Second Regiment (now known as The Black Watch), where he suffers victimisation at the hands of his captain. Confined to barracks for a trivial offence, his resentment builds up to the point where he determines to kill his persecutor. When the opportunity arises, he shoots his *colonel* by mistake. He is tried in a civil court (Liverpool Assizes is the most frequently cited venue), is found guilty and is finally hanged.

In spite of important narrative deficiencies in Mrs Hughes's text, her rendition of the song was greeted by her listeners with a good deal of respectful comment: 'That's a true song, that really happened. That poor unfortunate young man was hanged with nobody to speak up for him.' 'He was Irish and the officer had it in for him. Because he was Irish, he was always pickin' on him.' Billy Cole, a young Wiltshire Traveller, was more explicit: 'It was in the 1914 War, and he shot the colonel right through his heart. But he really meant to shoot the captain. And the only one to stick up for him was a girl, and a friend was she, and they hung him at Walton Gaol in Liverpool.'

The 1860s and 1880s are often given as dates for the events described but in point of fact the ballad's historicity is a matter of considerable uncertainty and doubt. Whether the story is indeed fact or fiction, it has given rise to a song which is widespread throughout Ireland and the British Isles. Two world wars have undoubtedly contributed to the ballad's dissemination and for tens of thousands of young men inducted into the Armed Forces 'McCaffery' has been a first introduction to traditional song.

BIBLIOGRAPHY

British   Seeger and MacColl, p. 73.

'McCaffery', sung by Caroline Hughes.

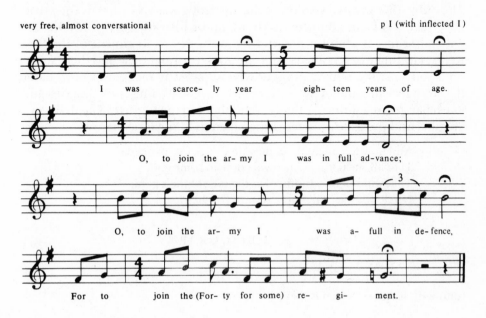

very free, almost conversational   p I (with inflected I)

I was scarce- ly year eigh- teen years of age.

O, to join the ar- my I was in full ad- vance;

O, to join the ar- my I was a- full in de- fence,

For to join the (For- ty for some) re- gi- ment.

1   I was scarcely year eighteen years of age,
O, to join the army I was in full advance;
O, to join the army I was a-full in defence,
For to join the (Forty for some) regiment.   (Forty-second)

2   Now, as I was put there all on guard one day
Three soldiers' children came out to play;
They gave me orders for to take their names –
Well, I took one's name there out of three.

3   I done the deeds, I shot his blood,
In old Liverpole his body lays.
O captain (mewater) I was content to kill
For I shot my colonel all against my will.

4   Well, I've got no mother to take my part,
I've got no father to break (my) heart.   (his)
I had one friend and a woman was she,
She would lay her life down for me again.

87   THE DESERTER FROM KENT

The only other printed version of this rare song was recorded in 1907 from a 75-year-old farm labourer, a Mr Kemp of Elstead, Surrey. Mr Kemp's ten-stanza text is about a deserter from the Ninth Regiment of the West Kents. Finding work as a harvester, he goes to an alehouse and there strikes up a conversation with a stranger who apparently recognises him. Later, the stranger encounters two soldiers who are searching for a deserter and, in exchange for a guinea, offers to lead them to the fugitive. The deserter is arrested and the following morning taken to Maidstone prison.

> And now to conclude on these few lines I've penned,
> That all sneaking fellows will come to some end.
> That will sell one another for the sake of their gain,
> No doubt they will find a reward for their pain.

BIBLIOGRAPHY

British *JFSS*, vol. V, pp. 154–5.

(untitled), sung by Nelson Ridley.

1   It's all of a deserter to you I will tell,
     He run away from the West Kents to go harvesting;
     He thought he'd been drinking with one of his pals,
     When away they did take him without more delay.

2   What (reachment), what reachment, now, do you belong?   (regiment)
     'None at all,' said the deserter, so bold and so brave;
     'None at all,'' said the deserter, so bold and so brave,
     'We will find one, then, for you,' this soldier did say.

3   One guinea I'll give you to show me this man –
     He's run away from the West Kents to go harvesting;
     One guinea I'll give you to show me this man,
     You will be well rewarded and sure of your pay.

4   They kept him in hold safe, it was all that night,
     They kept him in hold till it did turn daylight;
     Straightaway to The Roebuck they bundled him straight,
     And they sent for his regiment to take him away.

CRIME AND CRIMINALS

88   MACPHERSON'S FAREWELL

Tradition has it that James MacPherson was the son of a Highland gentleman and a 'beautiful gypsy woman'. During his lifetime, he achieved considerable notoriety as the leader of a gang of cattle-lifters operating in the province of Moray. On 7 November 1700, MacPherson, two men named Brown and a Gordon, were brought before the Sheriff of Banffshire, charged with being 'Egyptian rogues and vagabonds, of keeping the markets in their ordinary manner of thieving and purse-cutting, also being guilty of masterful *bangstrie* [violence against a person or property] and oppression'. Part of the evidence against them was that 'they spoke a peculiar gypsy language and spent their nights in dancing, singing and debauchery'.

MacPherson and Gordon were found guilty and sentenced to be hanged at the Market Cross next market day. It is said that MacPherson spent his last hours composing his famous rant, the song which inspired Burns's 'Farewell, Ye Dungeons Dark and Strong'. There is a persistent legend that the Banff authorities, anticipating a royal pardon for MacPherson, hanged him before the appointed time.

BIBLIOGRAPHY

British   Buchan (Norman), pp. 96–7; Dick (extended note), pp. 292–3; Herd, vol. I, pp. 99–101; MacColl, pp. 35–6; *Museum*, No. 114; Ord, p. 443; Seeger and MacColl, p. 89.

Alternative title   MacPherson's Lament.

'MacPherson', sung by Jock Higgins.

moderate   p π¹

Fare- well, ye dun-geons dark and strong, Fare- well, fare- well to thee;

Mac- Pher-son's time will nae be lang In yon-ders gal- lows tree.

Chorus:

Sae ran-ton- ly, sae wan- ton- ly, Sae daun-ton- ly gaed he-

14

For he played a tune and he danced a-roond Be- low the gal- lows tree.

14

1   Farewell, ye dungeons dark and strong,
Farewell, farewell to thee;
MacPherson's time will nae be lang
In yonders gallows tree.

Chorus: Sae rantonly, sae wantonly,
Sae dauntonly gaed he –
For he played a tune and he danced aroond
Below the gallows tree.

2   O, it was by a woman's treacherous hand
That I was condemned to dee;
Below a ledge o' a window she stood
A blanket she threw o'er me. (chorus)

3   O, the Laird o' Grant, that Hieland saint,
That first laid hands on me –
He placed the cause on Peter Broon
To let MacPherson dee. (chorus)

4   O, come tie these bands from off my hands
And gie to me my fiddle –
There's nae a man in a' Scotland
But brave's me at my word. (chorus)

5   O, there's some come here to see me hung
And some to buy my fiddle,
Before I would pairt wi' her
I'd brak her through the middle.

6*   I took my fiddle in both my hands
And broke her ower a stone;
There's nae anither will play on thee
When I am dead and gone.

7   O, it's little did my mither think
When first she cradled me,
That I would turn a rovin' boy
And die on a gallows tree. (chorus)

8   O, his reprieve was comin' o'er the brig o' Banff
To set MacPherson free
They put the clock a quarter afore
And they hung him tae the tree. (chorus)

*   The chorus melody is used for this verse.

89   THE HIGHWAYMAN OUTWITTED
(Laws L 2)

This is one of a group of witty songs in which a country person, an apparent simpleton, outwits a highwayman. Logan printed a lengthy text, rich in characterisation, much of it consisting of dialogue between the robber and the maid. The song has been most frequently reported from the south of England in recent times. The 'Chesfield' in our text is probably Chestfield, located in the urban district of Whitstable, Kent.

BIBLIOGRAPHY

Laws L 2.

British   Gardiner MSS, Hp-917 and Hp-1329; *Hammond MSS*, Sm-81; Holloway and Black, No. 46; *JFSS*, vol. I, pp. 236–7; also vol. II, pp. 21–2; *JEFDSS*, vol. IX, pp. 166–7; Kidson and Moffat (2), pp. 14–15; Leigh, pp. 267–9; Logan, pp. 133–6; Purslow (1), pp. 40–1; Sharp and Karpeles (2), vol. II, pp. 45–8; Williams, pp. 267–8.

Broadsides   British Museum, LR 271 a 2, vol. I, p. 102 (Pitts); also vol. VII, p. 31 (Cadman of Manchester); also vol. VII, p. 198.

North American   Hubbard, pp. 265–6; Peacock, vol. I, pp. 226–8.

Alternative titles   a series of combinations involving the words Highwayman, Farmer's Daughter, Merchant's Daughter; Maiden, etc., in a variety of venues, from Lincolnshire and Devonshire to Cheshire, Norfolk, Reigate and London; The Female Robber (etc.).

'The Rich Farmer of Chesfield', sung by Caroline Hughes.

1 O, there was a rich farmer of Chesfield,
 And to market his daughter did go;
 She was thinking that nothing would happen,
 For she'd been on the highway before.

2 She met with three daylighted robbers
 And three links they did hold to her breast;
 You'll deliver your clothes and your money,
 Or else you shall die in distress.

3 They stripped the poor damsel stark naked,
 And they gave her the bridle to hold;
 And there she stood shivering and shaking,
 Much perished to death by the cold.

4 She slipped her right foot in the stirrup,
 And she mounted her horse like a man;
 Over hedges and ditches she galloped:
 Come, catch me, bold rogues, if you can!

5 Well, she rode to the gates of her father,
 She shouted, her voice like a man:
 'Dear father, I've been in greater danger,
 But the rogues didn't do me no harm.'

6 She whipped the grey mare to the stable,
 And white sheets she spread on the floor;
 She counted her money twice over,
 She'd five-hundred bright pounds, if not more.

90 WHISKEY IN THE JAR
(Laws L 13-A and 13-B)

The hero of this ballad is a highwayman who, after having robbed a captain, is betrayed by his own sweetheart. Early next morning the captain and his troop of soldiers arrest the highwayman who is unable to resist owing to the fact that during the night his girl has discharged his pistols and re-loaded them with water. Occasionally texts are found in which the bold outlaw manages to escape from prison by striking the turnkey with his shackles. In addition to being deficient in narrative elements, Mrs McPhee's text has substituted couplets for the quatrains common to most versions. We have laid these out, for convenience, in short four-line stanzas.

BIBLIOGRAPHY

Laws L 13-A and 13-B.

British   *Henry Collection*, No. 792; Holloway and Black, No. 90; Joyce (2), No. 686; Kirkpatrick Sharpe, pp. 163–4; O'Lochlainn (1), pp. 24–5; Ord, pp. 368–9.

North American   Leach, pp. 288–9; Lomax (3), pp. 16–17.

Alternative titles   The Irish Robber; Captain Kelly; The Sporting Hero; Whiskey in the Bar; Peter Fleming; Gilgary Mountain (etc.).

'Whiskey in the Jar', sung by Maggie McPhee.

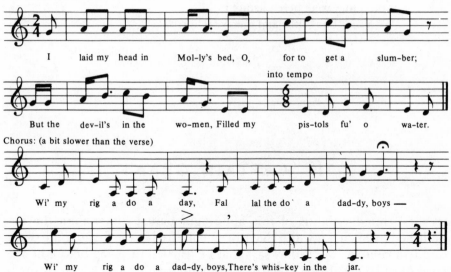

1   I laid my head in Molly's bed,
     O, for to get a slumber;
     But the devil's in the women,
     Filled my pistols fu' o' water.

Chorus: Wi' my rig a do a day,
          Fal lal the do a daddy, boys –
          Wi' my rig a do a daddy, boys,
          There's whiskey in the jar.

2   O, I laid my head in Molly's bed,
      O, for to get a slumber,
      When the strong guards surrounded me,
      And likewise was Captain Heaven. (chorus)

3   But I flew to me pistols
      And there I was mistaken,
      For I let a drop of water fall
      And a prisoner I was taken. (chorus)

4   But if my mother she was here the night
      O, wouldn't I be mistaken?
      She would take me in her arms
      And to Ireland I'd be taken. (chorus)

5   For I've a brother into Cork,
      I've another in Killarney;
      And if they were here the night
      Wouldn't I be blithe and merry? (chorus)

91   CAPTAIN GRANT

All the printed versions of this goodnight ballad (other than the one published by Such) appear to have been collected in the first decade of the twentieth century. Mr Ridley says that he learned the song before he was ten years old, i.e. before 1923. Apart from his opening line, which is usually associated with 'The Northamptonshire Poacher', his text makes no radical departures from the broadside text. The loss of three or four verses, however, makes the story less than clear.

Captain Grant, one of those bold heroes of the King's Highway, is in Edinburgh gaol awaiting trial for armed robbery. He escapes and hides in a wood. Eventually he is betrayed by a woman and imprisoned again. He prays that the Lord may have mercy on his soul and succour his wife and children.

W. P. Merrick quotes a Romani paraphrase of one of the stanzas (*JFSS*, vol. I).

BIBLIOGRAPHY

British   JFSS, vol. I, pp. 109–10; also vol. V, pp. 158–9; Sharp (1), pp. 204–6; Sharp and Karpeles (2), vol. II, pp. 169–70; Williams, p. 216.

'Bold Captain Grant', sung by Nelson Ridley.

1   Where I was bound apprentice was down in Northamptonshire,
        Where I did take my lodgings in the centry of a wood – ,
        With my two metal bullets and my bright shiny sword,
        And it's quickly they did banish me to Edinborough Town.

2   From Edinborough Town, my boys, I thought it myself good,
        Till I did take my lodgings in the centry of a wood;
        It was through that wicked woman had me surrounded as I were laying,
        'May the Lord have mercy on me!' cried bold Captain Grant.

3   Now, here's to my wife and my five children small,
      And since I've been drinking I have ruined them all;
      God save 'em and God keep 'em from sickness and from want,
      'May the Lord have mercy on me!' said bold Captain Grant.

92   THE BOSTON BURGLAR
(Laws L 16-B)

This popular American adaptation of the nineteenth-century English song 'Botany Bay' re-crossed the Atlantic in the early part of this century and has since been reported several times both from Scotland and Ireland.

BIBLIOGRAPHY

Laws L 16-B.

British Ashton (1), pp. 359–60; Barrett, pp. 90–1; Greig, No. 132; *Henry Collection*, Nos 202 and 691; *JFSS*, vol. V, pp. 85–6: O'Lochlainn (1), pp. 88–9; *Scottish Studies*, vol. VII, pp. 235–9; Sharp (2), vol. II, pp. 90–1; Sharp and Karpeles (2), vol. II, pp. 139–42.

North American Flanders, Ballard, Brown and Barry, pp. 253–4; Hubbard, pp. 249–51; Leach, pp. 254–5.

Australian Edwards, pp. 12–13.

Alternative title The Boston Smuggler.

'Boston City', sung by Charlotte Higgins.

1 I was born in the town of Boston, a town you all know well,
 Brought up by honest parents and the truth I'll now you tell;
 Brought up by honest parents and reared most tenderly,
 Till I became a rover at the age of twenty-three.

2 My (photograph) was taken and I was sent to jail, (character?)
 My parents did their very best to get me out on bail;
 To get me out on bail, they said, your trouble's all in vain,
 For seven long years you'll have to stay in the penitentiary.

3 The jury found me guilty, the clerk he wrote it down,
 God help my poor old father with his head there hanging down;
 My son, my son, what's this you've done? You're going to Charlies
   Town.
 God help my poor old mother as she sobbed for her son.

4 Now, every station I passed by, I could hear the people say,
 'There goes the Boston burglar boy, for some great crime he's done.'

 . . . .

 . . . .

5   But there's a girl in Boston town, a girl I know well,
       If ever I get my liberty, with her I mean to dwell.
       With her I mean to dwell, my boys, and shun bad company
       For the keeping of bad company, it was the ruin of me.

6   So, come all you Boston bad boys, a warning take by me,
       Never stop out late at night or keep bad company;
       For if you do, you're sure to rue and then you'll be like me:
       Doing seven long years in Boston in the penitentiary.

93   VAN DIEMAN'S LAND
(Laws L 18)

The transportation of convicts to the American plantations came to an end with the American Revolution and, for the next fourteen years, Britain's legislators debated the pros and cons of various projected penal settlements: the East and West Indies, the Falkland Islands, Gibraltar, Gambia, Senegal, South Africa, Nova Scotia, India, Madagascar, Tristan da Cunha, New Caledonia, Tunis and Algiers. In 1790, New South Wales was finally chosen as the site of the new settlement and before the turn of the century two further establishments were opened in Newcastle, Australia and in Van Dieman's Land (Tasmania).

Between 1793 and 1810, the number of transportees sailing from England and Ireland was just over 7,000. By 1814 the number had risen to over 1,000 a year. From 1816–25, the yearly average was 2,600, and during the next ten years the number rose to 5,000 a year. The total number of those transported from Great Britain and Ireland to the Australian settlements is unknown, but in the period 1831–40, 43,000 males and 7,700 females sailed from Britain in the notorious convict hulks. The total number of women and girls transported between 1797 and 1852 was 25,000.

During the half-century that the Tasmanian penal settlement existed, scores of transportation ballads issued from the broadside presses and a surprising number of them were absorbed into the traditional song repertoire. Variants of the song given here have been reported from Galway, Cork, County Mayo and Dublin; from Renfrewshire, Aberdeenshire and Perthshire; and from Lancashire, Yorkshire, Sussex, Hampshire, Surrey and East Anglia.

BIBLIOGRAPHY

Laws L 18.

British   Ashton (1), pp. 361–3; *Gardiner MSS*, Hp-552 and Hp-830; Greig, No. 33; *Hammond MSS*, Sm-284; Hugill, p. 411; *JFSS*, vol. I, pp. 142–3; also vol. II, pp. 166–7; Kennedy, p. 573; Kidson, p. 130; MacColl, p. 27; O'Lochlainn (1), pp. 42–3; Ord, pp. 384–5; Petrie, No. 808; Purslow (1), pp. 112–13; Reeves (2), pp. 217–18; Seeger and MacColl, p. 88; Sharp and Karpeles (2), vol. II, pp. 146–8; Sola Pinto and Rodway, pp. 162–3; Williams, pp. 263–4.

Broadsides   *British Museum*, LR 271 a 2, vol. II, p. 161; also vol. V, p. 117 (Such); also vol. VI, p. 176 (Such); also vol. VII, p. 177; also vol. VIII, p. 37 (Catnach).

North American   Hubbard, pp. 269–70.

Australian   Edwards, pp. 1–2; Ward, pp. 28–9.

Alternative titles   The (Gallant) Poachers; Young Henry the Poacher; Young Henry's Downfall; Poor Tom Brown of Nottingham Town (etc.).

'Van Dieman's Land', sung by Charlotte Higgins.

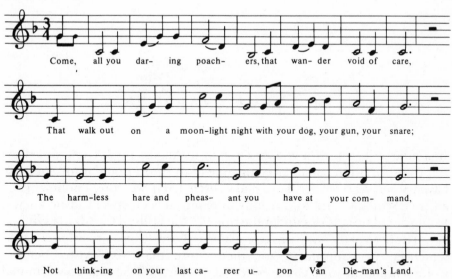

fairly slow, steadily   a M

Come, all you dar-ing poach-ers, that wan-der void of care,
That walk out on a moon-light night with your dog, your gun, your snare;
The harm-less hare and pheas-ant you have at your com-mand,
Not think-ing on your last ca-reer u-pon Van Die-man's Land.

1   Come, all you daring poachers, that wander void of care,
    That walk out on a moonlight night with your dog, your gun, your
        snare;
    The harmless hare and pheasant you have at your command,
    Not thinking on your last career upon Van Dieman's Land.

2   There was poor Jock Brown from Glasgow, Willie Guthrie and
        Monroe,
    They were three daring poachers the country well did know;
    The keeper caught them hunting all with their guns in hand
    They were fourteen years transported into Van Dieman's Land.

3   The very day we landed upon that fatal shore,
    The settlers gathered round us, full forty score or more;
    They herded us like cattle, they sold us out o' hand,
    They yoked us to the plough, my boys, to plough Van Dieman's Land.

4   But there was a lass from Sweet Dundee, Bess Logan was her name,
    She was given a sentence for the playing of the game;
    The captain bought her freedom and married her out of hand,
    She gave us all good usage going to Van Dieman's Land.

5   Our beds were made with rotten straw, our sleep was far from sound,
    We'd to burn fires all round us to keep the wolves away;
    . . . .
    It was hell and damnation upon Van Dieman's Land.

94   JAMIE RAEBURN

In a note written for the *Buchan Observer* of August 1908, Greig described this transportation ballad as being 'one of the most popular folksongs we have'. Seven years earlier, Ford had written that it 'was long a popular song all over Scotland, and sold readily in penny-sheet forms'. Kidson knew it from several broadsides under the title of 'The Hills of Caledonia Oh'.

    The hero of the song was, according to Ford, 'a baker to trade who was sentenced to banishment for theft more than sixty years before'. Commenting on this, Greig refers to a search of the Glasgow criminal records by John Ord, who 'failed to find any person of the name of James Raeburn who had been banished from Glasgow for theft or any other crime during that period'. This cannot be considered conclusive evidence as early nineteenth-century records of transported felons are notoriously deficient. Whatever the facts may be, the song has not lost its popularity in Scotland.

JAMIE RAEBURN

BIBLIOGRAPHY

British Buchan (Norman), p. 40; Ford (2), vol. II, pp. 55–6; Greig, No. 36; *Henry Collection*, No. 151; *JFSS*, vol. II, pp. 180–1; Ord, pp. 357–8; Seeger and MacColl, p. 80.

Alternative titles James Raeburn's Farewell; John Raeburn.

'Jamie Raeburn', sung by Charlotte Higgins.

slow   p π¹

For my name is Ja- mie Rae- burn, in Glas-gow I was born,

From my home and ha- bi- ta- tion I was forced to gang a- wa';

My home and ha- bi- ta- tion I was forced to gang a- wa',

Far fae thon bon- nie hills and dells o' Ca- le-do-ni- o.

1   For my name is Jamie Raeburn, in Glasgow I was born,
     From my home and habitation I was forced to gang awa';
     My home and habitation I was forced to gang awa',
     Far fae thon bonnie hills and dells o' Caledonio.

2   It was early in the morning, O by the break o' day,
     The turnkey he came along and unto us did say:
     'Arise, ye hapless convicts, arise ye ane and a',
     This is the day ye hae to stray fae Caledonio.'

3   We all arose, put on our clothes, our hearts well filled with woe;
     . . . .
     My father stood behind the coach, could grant us no relief,
     For the leavin' o' thon hills and dells o' Caledonio.

4   O fare ye well, my father, I'm vexed for what I've done,

. . . .

Likewise unto my sweetheart, young Katherine is her name,
Nae mair we'll wander doon by the (Cleed), nor yet by the   (Clyde)
    Broomielaw.

5   . . . .

. . . .

. . . .

So fare ye weel, ye hills and dells o' Caledonio.

6   O, fare ye well, my mother, I'm vexed for what I've done,
I hope none will upcast to you the things that I have done,
I hope you'll be provided for when I am far awa',
So, fare ye weel, ye hills and dells o' Caledonio.

7   If ever we do meet again, I hope it will be above,
Where hallelujahs they are sung to Him who dwells in love;
No earthly judge will judge us then, but Him who loves us all,
So fare ye weel, ye hills and dells o' Caledonio.

Note: Mrs Higgins did not falter when singing this song. She progresses without hesitation past the 'missed' lines which we have dotted off so as to indicate which lines of melody are to be used.

95   THE ISLE OF FRANCE

It is extraordinary how the excision of a few stanzas and a rearrangement of those which remain can alter the perspective of a song. A glance at Mr MacDonald's three verses suggests that a convict from the Isle of France is being put aboard a little boat by the Coast Guard in order to be sent from Ireland for unruly behaviour. The longer texts tell a different story: A convict arrives, shackled, on the Isle of France (one of the Channel Islands?). His story is that he was sentenced to seven years' transportation for unruly behaviour. He had completed six years and was on his way home on a ship called *The Shamrock Green*. The hulk, however, is shipwrecked, casting him up on the island, where he is offered sustenance and comfort by the Coast Guard. A speedy letter is sent to the Queen, who grants him his freedom. He blesses the Coast Guard and wishes success to the Isle of France.

The song has been collected chiefly in England and the references all give a melody similar to ours. Kidson had a 'strong suspicion that the ballad was founded on a real escape from a convict transport-ship'.

BIBLIOGRAPHY

British   *JFSS*, vol. I, p. 123; also vol. II, pp. 258–9; Sharp (1), pp. 232–3; Sharp and Karpeles (2), vol. II, pp. 143–5.

Broadsides   *British Museum*, LR 271 a 2, vol. II, p. 219 (Taylor of Spitalfields); also vol. VI, p. 14 (Such); *Madden Collection*, M 11-92 (Hodges); also M 11-826 (Fortey); also M 14–118 (Disley); also M 17–335 (from Carlisle); also M 18–1264 (Harkness of Preston).

Australian   Edwards, pp. 5–6.

Alternative title   The Shamrock Green.

'The Convict Song', sung by John MacDonald.

moderate, steadily   m I/Ly

For the sun was set and the clouds ad-vanced,

When a con-vict came from the Isle of France;

All a-round his legs he wore a ring and chain

And his coun-try was of the sham-rock green.

Note: The singer often creates 5/4 bars by changing the rhythm ♩. ♪ to ♩. ♩ or ♫ ♩.
He also occasionally omits the crotchet rests at the ends of the lines.

1   For the sun was set and the clouds advanced,
When a convict came from the Isle of France;
All around his legs he wore a ring and chain
And his country was of the shamrock green.

2   When the coast guard hailed yon little boat
All on the ocean wi' him to float,
When the birds at night they had a silent rest
When yon poor convict had a wounded breast.

3   When the letter it came from her Majesty Queen,
Saying that young man he's of the shamrock green:
For bein' unruly, I do declare,
He was sentenced there for seven long year.

96   THORNABY WOODS

In Dixon and Bell, the editors comment: 'There is a prevalent idea that the song is not the production of an ordinary ballad-writer, but was written about the middle of the last century by a gentleman of rank and education, who, detesting the English game-laws, adopted a too-successful mode of inspiring the peasantry with a love of poaching.' Thorneyhaugh-Moor Woods is in the Hundred of Newark, Nottinghamshire, and was once part of Sherwood Forest where another band of poachers provided ballad-makers with the raw material of their craft.

BIBLIOGRAPHY

British   Broadwood and Maitland, pp. 50–1; Dixon and Bell, pp. 434–6; *Hammond MSS*, Wr-298; *JFSS*, vol. V, pp. 198–200; also vol. VII, pp. 14–15; Kennedy, p. 570; Mason, pp. 57–8; Purslow (2), p. 88; Sharp and Karpeles (2), vol. II, pp. 235–8.

Broadsides   *British Museum*, LR 271 a 2, vol. V, p. 40; also vol. VI, p. 13 (Such).

North American   Eddy, pp. 154–5.

Alternative titles   Thorneyhaugh-Moor (Thornymoor, Thornyholme, Thornham (etc.) Woods (Fields); The Nottinghamshire Poacher; The Old Fat Buck (etc.).

'Thornymoor Woods', sung by Nelson Ridley.

1   'Twas in Thorneywood Fields near Buckinghamshire,
     Where the keepers' houses stand in squares;
     Not half a mile from one each other's doors,
     Right fol the ri diddle i day.

2   I was going out one moonlight night,
     When one of my best dogs he got shot;
     He came back to me most bloody and lame,
     And wasn't I sorry to see the same.
     O, I'll take my peek-staff in my hand,
     I'll hunt the woods till I find that man;
     And I will tan his old hide quite well if I can,
     Right fol de rol diddle i day.

3   Over hedges and ditches and gates and stiles,
     With my two dogs close after my heels,
     To catch an old buck was in Thorneywood Fields,
     Right fol de ri diddle i day.

4   The very first joint it was all for myself,
     With right fol lol a right fol laddity –
     The very first joint was all for myself,
     Right fol de rol diddle i day;
     The very first joint was all for myself,
     It was through an old woman that sold bad ale,
     She (bloomin') us honest three chaps in the gaol,   (bringing?)
     Right fol de rol diddle i day.

97   BIG JIMMIE DRUMMOND

To the best of our knowledge there is only one other printed version of this strange cant ditty. It is there accompanied by an editorial note: 'a nonsense song with a surprisingly wide distribution, having been noted all over the British Isles with only slight alterations in the words'.

    Our brief text has none of the characteristics of a nonsense song. It is, perhaps, somewhat enigmatic but that may well be the effect of textual lacunae. According to several of our Scots Traveller friends, the three stanzas given here represent only a fragment of the entire song. Our attempts to find a more satisfactory text have so far proved unsuccessful.

BIBLIOGRAPHY

British   Kennedy, p. 768.

Alternative title   The Choring Song.

'Big Jimmie Drummond', sung by Big Willie McPhee.

1   O, my name it is Big Jimmie Drummond,
       My name I will never deny;
       I will moolie the gahnies in dozens,
       And there'll be naebody there for to tell.

2   O, last nicht I lay in a cauld granzie,
       (Last nicht) I lay in the cauld gaol;   (tonight?)
       O, my mort and my kinshins are scattered,
       And I dinna jan whaur they may be.

3   But if ever I dae gang a-chorin'
I'll be sure for to gang by mysel',
I will moolie these gahnies in dozens,
And there'll be naebody there for to tell.

Glossary

moolie	kill
gahnies	hens
granzie	barn, granary
mort	woman
kinshins	children
jan	know
chorin'	stealing

98   THE FIRST DAY IN OCTOBER

The theme and what might be described as the *atmosphere* of these verses appears to be compounded out of three other songs, all of which are concerned with an affray involving poachers and gamekeepers. For our purpose, the most important of these three songs is 'The Bold Poachers', which E. J. Moeran noted from Robert Miller of Sutton, Norfolk, in 1921. Its plot concerns three brothers who are tried for killing a gamekeeper and are sentenced, one to the gallows and the other two to transportation to a penal colony. It is obvious, even from this very brief résumé, that the plot of Mrs Hughes's song differs substantially from the Norfolk piece. Nevertheless, the first two stanzas of her song are full of curious echoes of the second to fifth stanzas of 'The Bold Poachers'. Compare 'The First Day in October' with the relevant stanzas of the Miller song as printed in *JFSS*, vol. VII, p. 15:

1   Concerning of three young men
One night in January
Against our laws contrary
A fortune (a-poaching) went straight way.

2   They were desired to ramble
Amongst the trees and brambles
A-firing at the pheasants
Which brought the keepers near.

THE FIRST DAY IN OCTOBER

3   The keepers dare not enter
To care the woods to venture,
In the outside near the centre
In them old bush they stood.

4   The poachers being tired
To leave they were desired,
At last young Parkins fired
And spilled a keeper's blood.

5   All homeward they were making,
Nine pheasants they got taking
Another keeper faced them –
They fired at him also.

6   He on the ground lay crying
Just like someone a dying,
And no assistance nigh him,
Pray God forgive his crime.

In both this and our song, Parkins is the name given to the poacher who fires the gun and thus precipitates the action. Compare, also, the third and fourth lines of the opening stanza of our song with the second stanza of 'The Bold Poachers'. Mrs Hughes rendered the lines as follows:

O, through briar 'n' bush did he ramble
Both through forest, fen and bonny old Ireland.

This can be viewed either as bowdlerisation or as inspired improvisation, but there is little doubt that the singer is attempting to create the same kind of landscape as the one depicted in the other song.

In the third line of the same stanza we are told that 'he killed nine hares or ten'. Is it too far-fetched to suggest that this is an assonantal rendering of 'nine pheasants they got taken'? One can appreciate how 'they got taken' can become 'hares or ten', particularly if one takes into account the transliterative possibilities involved in a meeting between a somewhat heavy country Norfolk dialect and the equally heavy speech of Hampshire and Dorset gypsies.

The third stanza of 'The First Day in October' is one which occurs frequently in southern English gypsy versions of 'Geordie' (Child 209) and even occasionally in some versions of 'The Knight and the Shepherd's Daughter' (Child 110) and frequently in 'The Braes of Yarrow' (Child 214). It exists also as a solitary fragment in the repertories of many gypsy singers.

The final stanza of Mrs Hughes's song is the one most difficult to place; it could, of course, be a re-working (including a reversal of roles) of the following lines from the fifth and sixth stanzas of 'The Bold Poachers':

> . . . another keeper faced them,
> They fired at him also.

> He on the ground lay crying,
> Just like someone a dying
> (etc.)

On the other hand, it may well have come from a version of 'The Poacher's Fate' (Laws L 14).

BIBLIOGRAPHY

British   Gardiner MSS, Hp-908 and Hp-1293; Purslow (4), p. 63.

Broadsides   British Museum, LR 271 a 2, vol. I, p. 161 (Taylor of Bethnal Green); also vol. I, p. 205; also vol. V, p. 159; also vol. IX, p. 172 (Fortey).

Alternative titles   The Poachers; The Oakham Poachers.

'The First Day in October', sung by Caroline Hughes.

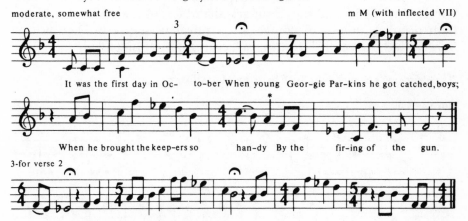

*Note: This is often pitched halfway between A and Ab

1   It was the first day in October
    When young Georgie Parkins he got catched, boys;
    When he brought the keepers so handy
    By the firing of the gun.

2   O, through briar 'n bush did he ramble
    Both through forest, fen and bonnie old Ireland;
    For he killed nine hares or ten
    He was ordered before he now got shot.

3   For all you men give me great orders
I am only one amongst you;
If you'll give my life fair play, my boys,
I'll fight you one 't a time.

4   For young Georgie got up to fight them,
Down through the copse some of them run, love;
When the gamekeeper fired and shot him dead,
Left his poor body lay round.

99   THE PRISONER'S SONG

Scots travelling folk who sing this song all appear to have learned it from the same source – an Irish Traveller named Docherty. Intermittently, over the past five or six years, the editors have questioned Irish singers but have not succeeded in finding any who know the song. That it is Irish is beyond doubt, but that is all that can be said of it with any certainty. The final stanza is one which occurs in many versions of 'The Boston Burglar' (our No. 92). Indeed, the use of the word 'penitentiary' and the 'ball and chain' reference in the second stanza suggest that the song may be of American-Irish origin – unless, of course, the equivalent stanza in 'The Boston Burglar' has been culled from an earlier transportation ballad.

'The Prisoner's Song', sung by Christina MacAllister.

1   One morning fair, I strollèd where the sparrow built its nest,
For to see the liberty of that bird did make me sore oppressed;
It hops along from bush to bush just as same as it could say:
'Cheer up, my lads, and don't be sad, some day you will be free.'

2   It would break the heart of any man, or the heart of any stone
For to see so many strapping fellows reduced to skin and bone;
They're all tied round with iron chains, attached to a ball of lead;
You could hear them praying from their hearts, and a-wishing they
      were dead.

3   So, come all you true-bred fellows, a warning take by me:
O, never you stay out late at night nor keep bad company;
For if you do, you'll sure it rue, you'll bring yourself like me,
For I'm doing seven-and-twenty years in the penitentiary.

100   TWENTY-ONE YEARS
(Laws E 16)

In America where 'Twenty-One Years' originated (the action usually
taking place in Nashville, Tennessee), this is more of a saga than a song.
There are related pieces like 'Down in the Valley' and 'Birmingham Jail',
the subject being a common one. To our knowledge, the song has not been
connected with a specific incident. Morris comments that 'this piece is a
popular barn-dance number used by fiddling bands on radio programs. It
is sung extensively by the rural folk of Florida.'

Most of the reported texts are six to seven stanzas long and are
remarkably consistent. Randolph gives five sets: one of these is a fragment
of two stanzas; another, entitled 'The Answer to Twenty-One Years',
consists of a girl's explanation that brain-fever and general indisposition
have prevented her from visiting her imprisoned lover; the third and
fourth texts, entitled 'Ninety-Nine Years' and 'A Sequel to Ninety-Nine
Years' see the heroine married to the judge and then cast aside (on the
whole these texts do not seem to be related to our song); the fifth set is a
seven-stanza text incorporating four of our stanzas, which appear to be the
core of the song.

BIBLIOGRAPHY

Laws E 16.

North American   Brown, vol. III, pp. 417–18; Davis (1), p. 284.

Alternative titles   Twenty-One Summers; Twenty-One Years is a Mighty Long Time.

A. 'Twenty-One Years', sung by Caroline Hughes.

B. 'Twenty-One Years', sung by Nelson Ridley.

A.

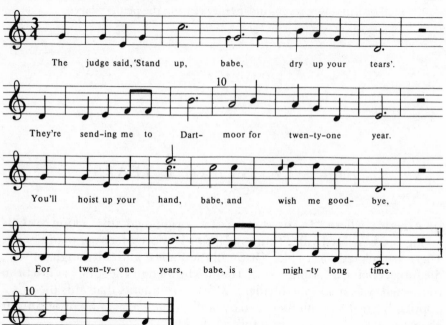

fairly slow, smooth   m I

The judge said, 'Stand up, babe, dry up your tears'.

They're send-ing me to Dart- moor for twen-ty-one year.

You'll hoist up your hand, babe, and wish me good- bye,

For twen-ty- one years, babe, is a migh -ty long time.

1   The judge said, 'Stand up, babe, dry up your tears.'
     They're sending me to Dartmoor for twenty-one year.
     You'll hoist up your hand, babe, and wish me goodbye,
     For twenty-one years, babe, is a mighty long time.

2   Well, six months is gone past, babe, I wish I was dead,
     While the dirty old jailhouse a floor for my bed.
     It's raining, 'tis hailing, the moon gives no light,
     And baby, please tell me why you never write.

3   I've counted the (days), babe, I've counted the nights,
I've counted your footsteps, I've counted the lights;
I've counted your footsteps, I've counted the stars,
I've counted a million of those prison bars.

4   Now, come you young fellows, with hearts brave and true,
Don't b'lieve in a woman, you're beat if you do;
Don't trust any woman, don't matter what for,
For twenty-one years, boys, is a mighty long time.

B.

moderate   m I

The Judge said, 'Stand up, boys, and dry up your tears,

You're sen-tenced to Dart- moor for twenty-one years'.

The Judge said, 'You're guil- ty'. The Judge said, 'It's time'.

Twen-ty -one years, babe, is a might-y long time.

1   The Judge said, 'Stand up, boys, and dry up your tears,
You're sentenced to Dartmoor for twenty-one years.'
The Judge said, 'You're guilty.' The Judge said, 'It's time.'
Twenty-one years, babe, is a mighty long time.

2   The steam from the engine, the smoke from the train,
I know you'll be true, babe, until I come home;
Don't trust any woman, no matter what kind,
For twenty-one years, babe, is a mighty long time.

[303]

3 . . . .
  . . . .
  You look down that railway, boys, you can see,
  They keep all on the waving their farewells to me.

4 I counted the minutes, I counted the stars,
  I counted the footsteps, I counted the stars;
  You look down that railway, boys, you can see,
  They keep on waving, here's farewell to me.

RURAL LIFE

101 JOHN BARLEYCORN

Barley, according to some authorities, is the most ancient of the cultivated grains and goes back to the very beginnings of agriculture. It was the main brew plant of the Hebrews, Greeks and Romans, and as a beer-making cereal it extends back to Neolithic times. Its use in the production of green malt for whiskey probably dates from the Middle Ages.

In the religious festivals of ancient India, North Africa and Greece, and in the European festivals of more recent times, barley was invariably personified as a female deity or grain-mother. If songs celebrating an Anglo-Saxon or Celtic Demeter once existed, they have vanished without trace; we have, instead, the very masculine John Barleycorn.

As far as we know, the earliest printed text of this

> 'pleasant new ballad to sing both even and morne,
> Of the bloody murther of Sir John Barley-corne.'

is a black-letter broadside printed for Henry Gosson (1607–41). The Stationer's Register under 14 December 1624 enters 'Sir John Barleycorn' (beginning 'As I went through the North Country'). William Chappell, in an editorial note on the Gosson broadside, writes: . . . the language is not that of London and its neighbourhood during James's reign. It is either northern dialect – which according to Puttenham would commence about sixty miles from London – or it is much older than any of the printers.' It is possible that the song is a re-make of the Scots ballad 'Allan-A-Maut' (*Bannatyne MSS*, 1568), a piece with an identical theme.

The early broadside versions of John Barleycorn deal symbolically with the ploughing, planting and harvesting of the barley crop and the subsequent malting, roasting and brewing of the beer. Later versions including many recorded from the oral tradition contain verses which describe the effects of the brew on imbibers from various trades. These verses would appear to have been borrowed from 'Master Mault, he is a Gentleman', printed for Clarke, Thackeray and Passenger (c. 1670) on a ballad sheet shared with another printing of 'John Barleycorn'.

BIBLIOGRAPHY

British Baring-Gould and Sheppard (2), pp. 28–9; Barrett, pp. 14–15; Buchan and Hall, pp. 151–2; *The Bullfinch* (a songster published by Wm. McLellan, Glasgow, 1802), pp. 1–4; Christie, vol. I, pp. 134–5; Dick, No. 332; Dixon and Bell, pp. 300–1; *Ewing*, Nos 277, 278, 281, 282 and 283; Evans, vol. IV, pp. 214–20; Ford (2), vol. II, pp. 18–19; Hamer, pp. 8–9; *Hammond MSS*, Dt-364 and Dt-554; Jamieson, vol. II, pp. 231–43; *JFSS*, vol. I, pp. 81–2; also vol. III, pp. 255–7; also vol. VI, pp. 27–8; also vol. VIII, pp. 41–2; Kennedy, p. 608; O'Lochlainn (1), pp. 176–7; *Pepys*, vol. I, No. 426; Purslow (1), pp. 48–9; *Roxburghe*, vol. II, pp. 372–8; Sharp and Karpeles (2), vol. II, pp. 171–9; Williams, pp. 246–7.

References for 'Master Mault': Evans, vol. IV, pp. 220–6; Jamieson, vol. II, pp. 244–50; *Pepys*, vol. I, No. 470; *Roxburghe*, vol. II, pp. 379–82.

Broadsides *British Museum*, LR 407 h 7, pp. 282–3 (A Collection of Ballads).

North American Flanders, Ballard, Brown and Barry, pp. 259–65; Flanders and Brown, pp. 46–8; Fowke, pp. 14–15.

Alternative titles The Barleycorn; The Barley Grain for Me; (Sir) John Barleycorn; There was Three Kings into the East; Alane a-Maut (etc.).

'John Barleycorn', sung by Nelson Ridley.

1   There was three men came from the east
        To mow both hay and corn,
        And one had a beard well down of his face,
        They thought it was John Barleycorn.

Refrain: O, my little John Barleycorn.

2   They wheeled and wheeled him round about
        Till the sorrows came out of his head;
        And then they served him worser than that,
        They ground him between two stones. (refrain)

3   We'll cause the huntsmen to hunt the hounds,
        And never to sound his horn;
        And then they will come back again,
        To see John Barleycorn. (refrain)

102   ALL JOLLY FELLOWS THAT HANDLES THE PLOUGH

The English traditional song repertoire, rich in so many ways, is singularly lacking in ploughmen's songs. The nineteenth-century agrarian revolution which in Scotland gave the impetus for the creation of the bothy ballads, appears to have provided little or no inspiration for the English song-makers.

Greig printed a text of 'All Jolly Fellows', 'for purposes of comparison with our Northeastern ploughman's songs'. His editorial comment is interesting:

If it is safe to found on a single specimen of the Southern ploughman ditty, we should also say that the relations between master and servant appear to be more cordial across the Border than they are with us, judging from the general tone of our local ploughman's songs.

BIBLIOGRAPHY

British   Baring-Gould and Sheppard (2), pp. 130–1; Broadwood, pp. 64–5; Greig, No. 158; Henderson, pp. 117–18; *JFSS*, vol. III, pp. 278–80; Kennedy, p.

549; Kidson and Moffat (2), pp. 54–5; Sharp and Karpeles (2), vol. II, pp. 190–3; Williams, pp. 207–8.

Alternative title   Was Early One Morning.

(untitled), sung by Nelson Ridley.

1   It's four o'clock now, boys, it's time to unyoke,
     You're all jolly fellows that follows the plough;
     You'll get Dobbin ready and groom him down well,
     Then I'll gave you a jug of my bonnie brown ale.

2   It's four o'clock now, boys, to the stable we'll go,
     You're all jolly fellows that follows the plough;
     You've not ploughed your acre, I'll swear and (devow)   (avow)
     You're all jolly fellows that follows the plough.

3   It's four o'clock now, boys, to the stable we'll go,
     You're all jolly fellows that follows the plough;
     When the cocks they're a-crowing, the farmer did say,
     You'll get Dobbin ready and groom him down well.

103   WE DEAR LABOURING MEN

During the years between 1790 and 1816, the English peasant was turned into a wage-labourer. The transformation was not a peaceful one; the intensification of the enclosure system, repressive poor-law legislation, extension of more rigorous application of the game-laws coupled with an unprecedented rise in the cost of living, all combined to produce a new and intense class-consciousness among the labouring poor. It seems to us that this new working-class consciousness is reflected in this song.

'We Dear Labouring Men', sung by Caroline Hughes.

moderate, evenly   a I (with inflected VII)

O, some do say the farm-er's best but I do need say no;

If it weren't for we poor la-bouring men, what would the farm-ers do?

They would beat up all their old odd stuff un-til some new come in;

There's nev-er a trade in old Eng-land like we poor la-bouring men.

1   O, some do say the farmer's best, but I do need say no;
    If it weren't for we poor labouring men, what would the farmers do?
    They would beat up all their old odd stuff until some new come in;
    There's never a trade in old England like we poor labouring men.

2   O, some do say the baker's best, but I've got need say no;
    If it weren't for we poor hard-working men, what would the bakers do?
    They would beat up all their old hard stuff until some new come in;
    There's never a trade in old England like we dear labouring men.

3   O, some do say that the butcher's best but I've got needs say no;
     If it weren't for we poor hard-working men, what would the butchers
        do?
     They would beat up all their old hard stuff until some new come in –
     There's never a trade in old England like we dear labouring men.

4   Let every true-born Englishman lift up a flowing glass,
     And drink a toast to the labouring man, likewise his bonnie lass;
     And when these cruel times are gone, good days will come again;
     There's never a trade in old England like we poor labouring men.

104   THE FEEIN' TIME

In Scotland, the system of engaging farm-labourers was rooted in the Martinmas and Whitsun feeing fairs. These were operated almost wholly in the farmers' interests. Labourers were fee'd (contracted) to farms for periods ranging between six months and a year, wages being paid only at the termination of each period. The result was that active protest against conditions of work was held in check by the farmer's right to withhold the labourer's wages. In this situation, the farm-servant could only put up with his lot and hope that his next place of employment might be a better one. Mr MacDonald's comments on the hiring fairs are interesting: 'In the old days, when you went into a market or a feeing fair (if you were unemployed or if you were in a fairm you didna like) like in Glesca Fair here, that's where they fee'd ye . . . up in George's Square. The fairmers come in and you were up there wi' your suit on and they asked you: "Needin' wark, are ye? Whaur are ye warking'?" And you say that you're feein' such a place but ye dinna like it – the horses is nae use. Generally it's the horses, but noo it's the tractors.'

'The Feein' Time', sung by John MacDonald.

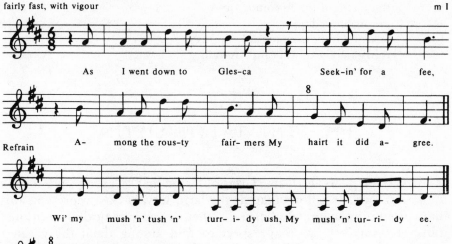

fairly fast, with vigour

As I went down to Gles-ca Seek-in' for a fee,

A- mong the rous-ty fair- mers My hairt it did a- gree.

Refrain

Wi' my mush 'n' tush 'n' turr- i- dy ush, My mush 'n' tur- ri- dy ee.

1 As I went down to Glesca
 Seekin' for a fee,
 Among the rousty fairmers
 My hairt it did agree.

Refrain: Wi' my mush 'n' tush 'n' turridy ush,
 My mush 'n' turridy ee.

2 An auld rousty fairmer
 Cam' steppin' up to me;
 He says, 'My decent chappie,
 Are ye seekin' for a fee?' (refrain)

3 They used to keep the servant maids
 For gi'in' the men their grub;
 And instead o' gi'in it tae the men
 They gi'ed tae the collie dog. (refrain)

4 When I gaed tae the stable
 There's naethin' there at a',
 The auld grey mare lay on her side
 The black yen stood gain' the wa'. (refrain)

5 Noo, Bessy was a black mare,
 They maist are a' the same;
 The only time that she wad wark
 'Twas when her comin' hame. (refrain)

6   But the term-time's comin' on
     I dinna gie a damn;
     Sure, I'll bundle up my auld bit rags
     And gang the road I cam'. (refrain)

105   THE TATTIE-LIFTIN'

More than fifty years ago Gavin Greig observed that 'folksong tends to seek the lowest level. It follows that, as the farm-servant class represents this ultimate stratum in our rural districts where alone, practically, traditional minstrelsy survives, we may expect to find among them the greatest amount of authentic folksong.' The distinction of representing the ultimate social stratum and of acting as custodians for a great amount of authentic folksong is something which, today in Scotland, has become a function of the travelling people.

    The song presented here makes use of a common bothy-song device – the personnel list in which each member of the labour-force is allocated a stanza. But here the *dramatis personae* are not farm-servants but tinkers, that is travellers engaged in harvesting the potatoes. In the course of attempting to get some background information on this interesting piece, we were given the names of four different young men (all under thirty years of age) all credited with its authorship. Whatever the truth of the matter is, one fact is clear – the song is of fairly recent origin.

BIBLIOGRAPHY

British   Kennedy, p. 788.

Alternative title   The Tattie Time.

'The Tattie-Liftin' ', sung by Willie Cameron.

THE TATTIE-LIFTIN'

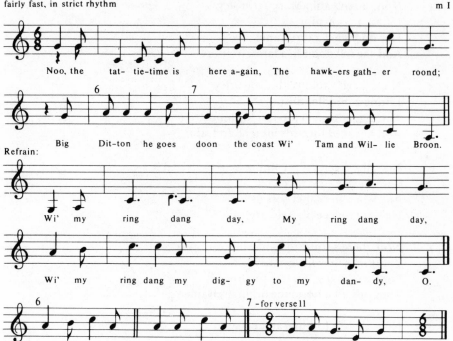

fairly fast, in strict rhythm

Noo, the tat- tie-time is here a-gain, The hawk-ers gath- er roond;

Big Dit-ton he goes doon the coast Wi' Tam and Wil- lie Broon.

Refrain:

Wi' my ring dang day, My ring dang day,

Wi' my ring dang my dig- gy to my dan- dy, O.

7 -for verse 11

1   Noo, the tattie-time is here again,
     The hawkers gather roond;
     Big Ditton he goes doon the coast
     Wi' Tam and Willie Broon.

Refrain: Wi' my ring dang day,
          My ring dang day,
          Wi' my ring dang my diggy to my dandy, O.

2   Noo, the Townsleys gang to collect their squad
     Who're biding near Kinross;
     For the digger's oot upon the field
     And time's too dear to loss. (refrain)

3   Noo, there's auld Willie Townsley
     Living near Gateside;
     I'd advise ye never to wark to him
     For ye wad never be paid. (refrain)

4   Noo, there's auld Mary Townsley
Lifting in oor stint;
Her nose gied a thrummel
And she fell doon in a faint. (refrain)

5   Noo, there's auld Willie Townsley
Lifting a middle stint;
The digger it gaed too fast for him
And he raced towards his tent. (refrain)

6   Noo, the money it is coming in
With the greatest speed;
And when the gaffer sees us
He's apt to lose his heid. (refrain)

7   Noo, there's some that may hae caravans
But others they have nane;
For them that spent it a' on drink,
They pished it doon the drain. (refrain)

8   Noo, there's Johnnie and Betsy
Liftin' oot at Perth;
Johnnie slippit ae morning
And his nose went up her arse. (refrain)

9   Noo, you'll easy ken the gaffer,
For his name is Ron.
He is the ane, O,
Wi' the leggins on. (refrain)

10   There's some of us do awfu' weel,
Like Ditton and Big Tam;
But there's others that they're in the dirt
And hae to push a pram. (refrain)

11   Noo, the tattie-time is come and gane
We're scattered far and wide;
Some are turning tae the north
Ithers tae the Glesca-side. (refrain)

12   Noo, we're turning tae our ither trades
Such as scrap and rags;
For some gae oot with sacks and bills,
Wi' carts and paper bags. (refrain)

13   Noo, if you want anither verse,
    Compose it for yoursel',
    For I'm no' awfu' good at that
    As ye can easy tell. (refrain)

106   THE HASH O' BENNYGAK

This is another typical bothy song of the catalogue type with verses which may be interchanged with those in a dozen other songs.

BIBLIOGRAPHY

British   Kerr (1), pp. 30–1.

'The Hash o' Bennygak', sung by Maggie McPhee.

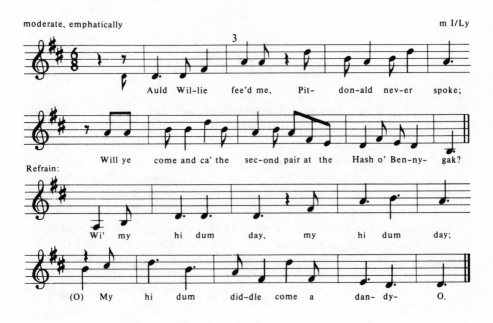

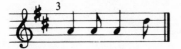

1 Auld Willie fee'd me, Pitdonald never spoke;
  Will ye come and ca' the second pair at the Hash o' Bennygak?

Refrain: Wi' my hi dum day, my hi dum day;
  (O) My hi dum diddle come a dandy-O.

2 O, we fee'd a servant loon he's . . .
  And ilka time he passes by he wad fairly mak you greet. (refrain)

3 Wor Bill is like a policeman, he never falls asleep:
  It's up and doon the neep rigs he maks his barra squeak. (refrain)

4 When we gang to the kitchen a' for to get wor tea,
  We get a bit o' breid and cheese, it's a' that we can see. (refrain)

5 O, we fee'd a servant dame, she comes fae Huntley toon,
  I'll swear it'd tak a horse's girth her middle to gang roond. (refrain)

6 For if you want to ken the writer and the author o' this song,
  You'll get him in a herrin' boat in the pier o' Foggie Loan. (refrain)

107 NICKY TAMS

The original of this very popular piece was the work of G. S. Morris, an Aberdeenshire agricultural worker who in the 1930s became a professional entertainer and song-writer. *Nicky tams* – an indispensable part of a ploughman's attire – are leather thongs which are worn buckled just below the knee in order to prevent the bottoms of the trouser legs from trailing in the mire. In Lancashire and Yorkshire they were called 'yorks' and Cumberland farm-labourers knew them as 'yarks' or 'yaks'. In Aberdeenshire and Perthshire, they were known as 'wull-tams' (Will-tams) until the song became popular, and now throughout Scotland they are known by their Morayshire name from which the song takes its title.

BIBLIOGRAPHY

British Buchan (Norman), pp. 48–9; Kerr (1), Book II, pp. 2–3.

Alternative title A Pair of Nicky Tams.

'Nicky Tams', sung by John MacDonald.

1   When I was a lad o' ten year auld I left the parish school,
       My faither sent me to the mert to choice my milk and meal;
       Wi' a pair o' knickybockers on my legs to hide my spinnel trams,
       But (pibroch) straps or naethin' else can beat your   (breist-straps?)
           nicky tams.

2   O, first I got on for baillie loon and syne I got on for third,
       Of course I had to get noo the horseman's grip an' word,
       A loaf o' breid to be my piece and a bottle for drinkin' drams,
       But ye canna win through the calf-hoose door without your nicky tams.

3   Now, I'm courtin' bonnie Annie, Rab Tamson's kitchie dame,
       She is five-and-forty and I am seventeen;
       She clarts to me a muckle piece wi' several kinds o' jams,
       And ilka night she tells me she admires my nicky tams.

4   Now I gaed tae kirk on Sunday the lassies for to please,
       For in the middle o' the psalm, noo, they workit up my knees;
       A muckle wasp bein' fleein' past got in aboot my thees,
       O, I'll never win tae the kirk again withoot my nicky tams.

5   Noo, I've often thocht I'd like to be a bobby on the beat,
     Or mebbe I'll get on the trams to drive a pair o' horse;
     But whatever it's my luck to be, the bobby or the trams,
     Sure, I'll never forget the happy days I wore my nicky tams.

Glossary

mert	market
spinnel trams	spindle-like legs
baillie loon	the foreman's boy
third horseman's grip and word	the man who drives the third pair of horses the secret handshake and the password used at initiation ceremonies among ploughmen
win through	get through
clarts	probably from 'clort', a Buchan name for a bannock or bread
muckle	large
ilka	every
kirk	church
thees	thighs

108   THE DYING PLOUGHBOY

The bothy, from which the new-type ballads of nineteenth-century northeastern Scotland took their qualifying title, was the name given to the living quarters of male farm-servants. Occasionally the bothy formed part of the main farm structure, but more often it was an out-house adjacent to the stable or byre.

Like the western ranch-house, the lumber camp, the ship, the military barracks and the sheep station of the Australian out-back, the bothy was a masculine community and, like the cowboy, the logger, the seaman, the soldier and the stockman, the ploughman lived a rough, hand-to-mouth existence and occasionally died in harness.

In song, the dying cowboy's last wish is that he should not be buried on the lone prairie, but that (if only in death) he should be close to his parents and sister. The logger, the soldier, the sailor and the stockman all, in their last moments, remember their parents, a lost sweetheart, a sister . . . the dying ploughboy's last thoughts are of his horses, his plough and the land he has turned.

BIBLIOGRAPHY

British   Greig, No. 26; Kerr (2), pp. 57–9; Ord, p. 235.

Alternative title   The Term.

'The Dying Ploughboy', sung by John MacDonald.

1   The winter winds was howling soft
     Aroond yon lonely stable loft;
     When something in my hairt gaed wrang,
     A vessel burst and the blood it sprang.

2   Noo, the doctor left me in good cheer,
     But something tells me death is near;
     For something in my hairt gaed wrang,
     A vessel burst and the blood it sprung.

3*   So, fare ye weel, guid friends and a'

     O, fare ye weel, my dandy pair
     It's you I've lowsed, ay, I'll yoke nae mair.

4   O, fare ye weel until my plough,
     Nae mair fresh land wi' you I'll toil;
     For something in my hairt gaed wrang,
     A vessel burst and the blood it sprung.

*   MacDonald goes without hesitation from the first to third lines of this stanza.

HUMOROUS AND MISCELLANEOUS

109   SHEELICKS

George Bruce Thompson, the author of this and other songs, was a native of the Aberdeenshire parish of New Deer and a friend of the collector, Gavin Greig, who wrote in 1910 in the *Buchan Observer*:

> Although never hitherto printed, these songs have got about and abroad until I begin to get records of them from singers at a distance. It is well that the versions of them should be correct and I am glad to be able, through the courtesy of the author, to print 'Sheelicks' from his own mansucript.

Mrs McPhee's set has crossed with another of Thompson's pieces, 'McGinty's Meal and Ale', from which she has taken her second stanza. The repeated references to 'McGinty's meal and ale' are, of course, one of the main features of the song of that name.

BIBLIOGRAPHY

British   Buchan (David), pp. 204–6; Buchan (Norman), pp. 68–70; Greig, Nos 134 and 136; Kerr (2), pp. 24–5.

'McGinty's Wedding', sung by Maggie McPhee.

fairly fast, emphatically

m I

Pay at- tention to my sang and I'll tell you o' a wad-din',

On the twen-ty third of Ju- ly in a town called Sleep-y Stead-in;

A' the coun-try-side was there, though they did-nae get a oid-din',

go directly to chorus

At M' Gin-ty's meal and ale, noo, we a' come in to see.

The chorus is sung to the same tune as the verse, but with different rhythms:

etc.

The style of singing, half spoken half sung, made it difficult to decide on the meter of the song. It is half-way between 6/8 and 2/4, the rhythm either

1 Pay attention to my sang and I'll tell ye' o' a waddin',
   On the twenty-third of July in a town called Sleepy Steadin;
   A' the countryside was there, though they didnae get a biddin',
   At M'Ginty's meal and ale, noo, we a' come in to see.

Chorus: Hi, hi, went the drum! Diddle, diddle, went the fiddle,
   And the jing-a-ring went up and doon and back and through the
       middle,
   And the jing-a-ring went roond aboot like sheelicks in a riddle
   At M'Ginty's meal and ale, noo we a' come in to see.

2   O, Miss M'Ginty run ben the hoose, the road was dark and crookit,
She fell helster-howdie ower a pig, for there she never lookit;
For she let oot a squeal that wad paralyse a teuchit,
At M'Ginty's meal and ale, noo we a' come in to see. (chorus)

3   O, a tailor wi' a timmer leg, he danced wi' a' was intae't,
In the middle o' a foursome reel, he brak it through and tint it;
He gaed hame wi' a barra-shaft and he was quite contented,
At M'Ginty's meal and ale, noo we a' come in to see. (chorus)

4   For there were a chiel cam ower the field, he min't ye on a arra',
He come there on a bicycle, was hurled hame on a barra;
And of a' the balls I ever was at, I never was at a marra,
O' M'Ginty's meal and ale, noo we a' come in to see. (chorus)

5   We had plenty to eat, we had frost-bitten liver,
As sure as I'm here and as sure as I never;
And the taste o' the beef nearly gied us a' the feather,
At M'Ginty's meal and ale, noo we a' come in to see. (chorus)

6   Noo, there were a chiel come ower the field, his name was Butter Scotty,
He was made up wi' a plaster and a potty;
He come there wi' a hundred pound, he gaed hame wi' but ae notie,
At M'Ginty's meal and ale, noo we a' come in to see. (chorus)

Glossary

sheelicks	husked grain
riddle	sieve
ben	in
helster-howdie	from 'heels ower gowdie', meaning topsy-turvy, head over heels
teuchit	lapwing
tint	lost
barra-shaft	handle of a wheelbarrow
chiel	man
min't	reminded
hurled	driven, carried
marra	equal

110 THE ALE-WIFE AND HER BARREL

The male drunk is a character frequently encountered in Scots traditional song. The drunken wife, though less common, is by no means a stranger there. The song presented here, however, is something of a rarity. Peter Buchan, in 1831, collected a five-stanza version of it which Christie printed with some slight alterations almost half a century later. In 1908, Greig collected a text consisting of two stanzas and a chorus.

We have not succeeded in tracing any English or American variant and must assume that 'The Ale-Wife' is domiciled exclusively in Aberdeenshire.

BIBLIOGRAPHY

British Buchan MSS (from which it was printed in *Illustrated Book of Scottish Songs*, printed by Illustrated London Library, 237 The Strand, London, n.d., pp. 234–5); Christie, vol. I, pp. 190–1; Greig, No. 12.

'The Ale-Wife, the Drunken Wife', sung by Maria Robertson.

Chorus: The ale-wife, the drunken wife,
             The ale-wife she deaves me –
             My wifie wi' her barrelie,
             She'll ruin and she'll leave me.

1   She tak's her barrel on her back,
             Her pint-stoup in her hand,
             For she is to the market gane,
             To set up a stand. (chorus)

2   The ale-wife, the drunken wife,
             Around the folk a' ken,
             I canna keep my wifie
             Oot amang the men. (chorus)

111   HOOLY AND FAIRLY

The earliest printed text of this amusing song appeared in the second volume of *Yair's Charmer* (Edinburgh 1751) under the title of 'The Drucken Wife o' Gallowa''. Under the same title, Oswald published the melody in the tenth book of *The Caledonian Pocket Companion* (1759). Words and music together appeared under the title 'Hooly and Fairly' in Robert Bremner's *Thirty Scots Songs for a Voice and Harpsichord* (1757).

Maria Robertson's text, a refashioning of the original piece, is the work of Joanna Baillie (1762–1851), the daughter of a Lanarkshire minister of the Gospel. Her biographer, the Reverend William Rogers, wrote that she 'had at the very outset of life exhibited a remarkable talent in rhyme-making. She composed verses before she could read.' In addition to writing a number of skilful songs, she served the London Theatre for some forty years as a highly successful dramatist.

BIBLIOGRAPHY

British   Glen, No. 191; *Museum*, vol. II, No. 191; Rogers, p. 43.

General   References for 'The Drucken Wife o' Gallowa'': Allan, pp. 34–7; Ford (2), vol. II, pp. 249–51; Herd, vol. II, pp. 38–40.

'Hooly and Fairly', sung by Maria Robertson.

HOOLY AND FAIRLY

moderate, somewhat free and plaintive

Verse I only

O neigh-bours, what had I a- do for to mar-ry?

My wife she drinks pos- sets o' wine of ca- nar- y-

And cries me her nig- gard- ly, drag- a- bout car- lie;

O, gin my wife wad drink hoo-ly and fair- ly.

Hoo- ly and fair- ly:

O, gin my wife wad drink hoo-ly and fair- ly.

Variant for verses 2-7 (incl.)

1   O, neighbours, what had I ado for to marry?
     My wife she drinks possets o' wine of canary —
     And cries me her niggardly, dragabout carlie;
     O, gin my wife wad drink hooly and fairly.
         Hooly and fairly:
         O, gin my wife wad drink hooly and fairly.

2   She dines wi' her kimmers on dainties enoo,
     Aye bowin' and smirkin' and dichtin' her mou';
     While I sit aside and I'm helpit but sparely;
     O, gin my wife wad spend hooly and fairly.
         Hooly and fairly:
         O, gin my wife wad spend hooly and fairly.

3   Her's to fairs and to bridals and preachin's and a',
     She gangs so licht-hearted and buskit sae braw,
     While I sit aside and she gars me gang barely;
     O, gin my wife wad spend hooly and fairly. (etc.)

4   In the kirk sic a commotion she made,
     Wi' dabs o' red roses and breist-knots o'erlaid;
     The dominie stickit his palm very nearly,
     O, gin my wife wad dress hooly and fairly. (etc.)

5   When, tired wi' her tanters, she lies in her bed,
     The wark a' neglected, the hoose ill-upred,
     When a' oor guid neighbours are stirring richt early;
     O, gin my wife wad sleep timely and fairly. (etc.)

6   A word o' guid counsel or grace she'll hear none,
     She bardies the elders and mocks at Mess John;
     While back in his teeth his ain text she flings rarely,
     O, gin my wife wad speak hooly and fairly. (etc.)

7   I wish I were single, I wish I were freed,
     I wish I were dighted, I wish I were deid.
     Or she in the mould to torment me nae mairly,
     O, gin my wife wad speak hooly and fairly,
         Hooly and fairly,
         Wasting my breath to cry 'hooly and fairly'.

112 ERIN-GO-BRAGH (Ireland Forever)
(Laws Q 20)

The title of this song would suggest that it is an Irish piece built around a
joke, of an Irishman attempting to pass himself off as a Scotsman. In more
complete texts than ours, the fight is sparked off by a police-officer, who
says:

> I know you're a Pat by the cut of your hair,
> But you all turn to Scotchmen as soon's you come here:
> You have left your own country for breaking the law
> And we're seizing all stragglers from Erin-go-bragh.

The song *is*, in fact, a Scots one. The venue is usually given as 'Auld Reekie'
(Edinburgh) and the irony is directed against a lowland Scots policeman
whose ignorance concerning his country's northern inhabitants and their
language, causes him to mistake a highlander for an Irishman. The
highlander, himself a member of a downtrodden minority, expresses his
solidarity with the downtrodden Irish. Most texts contain a stanza
expressing the following sentiments:

> I am not a Paddy, though Ireland I've seen,
> Nor am I a Paddy, though in Ireland I've been.
> But though I were a Paddy, that's nothing ava',
> There's many a bold hero from Erin-go-bragh.

The song is a popular one in Scotland, particularly among Travellers,
and has, in addition, been reported from Nova Scotia and Ireland. Most of
the reported texts have seven to nine stanzas and tell the story rather more
coherently than does ours, the verses of which have had to be rearranged so
as to maintain the narrative. The above-quoted stanzas are missing from
our version, as is also the opening stanza where the hero is introduced:

> My name's Duncan Campbell from the Shire of Argyll
> I've travelled this country for many a mile,
> Through Scotland, through England, through Ireland and all,
> And the name I go under's bold Erin-go-bragh.

The song is well enough known to have produced a number of
parodies. An amusing concluding stanza of one of these is quoted in Greig:

> Farewell to Auld Reekie, policemen and a'
> May the devil be with you, says Erin-go-bragh;
> But I will tell you a guise and I'm sure ye will smile:
> That Erin-go-bragh was the Duke of Argyle.

BIBLIOGRAPHY

Laws Q 20.

British   Buchan and Hall, pp. 141–2; Ford (2), vol. I, pp. 47–9; Greig, Nos 127 and 131; Joyce (1), p. 86; Kennedy, p. 702; Ord, p. 387.

Broadsides   *British Museum*, LR 271 a 2, vol. V, p. 64 (Such); also vol. VII, p. 45 (Such).

North American   MacKenzie (song plus an excellent note), pp. 330–1.

Alternative titles   Duncan Campbell; Bold Erin-go-Bragh.

'Erin-go-bragh', sung by John MacDonald.

moderate, regularly

*Note: These bars are often 9/8 bars with the following rhythm:

1 .   O, as I was a-walking up fair Wackford Street
　　　A saucy (young villain) I chancèd to meet;　　　　　　　　(policeman)
　　　He looked in my face and he tipped me some jaw,
　　　Saying, 'What brought you over from Erin-go-bragh?'

2 Here's a lump of black tarmac I hold in my wrist
And around his great napper I made it to twist.
The blood from his napper I quickly did draw,
And I made him remember bold Erin-go-bragh.

(5) 3 O, they all flocked around me like a flock of wild bees
And says, 'Where is the villain that struckèd the police?
If (I) catch him, (I'll) clap him, (I'll) give him the law
And make him remember young Erin-go-bragh.'

(3) 4 Here's a neat little pack that I've got on my back,
I'll pack up my clothing and soon I'll be off;
For while I've got one thing I'm sure he's got six,
But (I) won't forget Pat nor the weight of his stick. (he)

(4) 5 I've travelled through woodses and copses and fields,
I've travelled through old England a good many miles;
I've travelled through Scotland, through France and through Spain,
And I'll never forget Pat nor the weight of his cane.

113 THE WILD ROVER

In spite of its popularity with nineteenth-century broadside printers, this amiable song appears to be something of a rarity among British traditional singers. It has travelled to Australia, Canada and the United States, from whence Alan Lomax has recorded an interesting analogue called 'The Moonshiner'.

BIBLIOGRAPHY

British Ashton (1), p. 353; *Gardiner MSS*, Hp-346; Kennedy, p. 261; Purslow (1), p. 109.

North American Creighton (4), p. 134; Hubbard, p. 274; Lomax (4), p. 257.

Australia Edwards, p. 264.

'The Wild Rover', sung by Charlotte Higgins.

THE WILD ROVER

1   I've been a wild rover for many long years,
I've spent all my money on whiskey and beer.
But I mean to give over this wild, wild, career,
And I ne'er will be called the wild rover no more.
       I went to an alehouse where I used to get drunk,
       I asked them for credit, but the answerie was 'No'.

Chorus: No no never, never no more,
         I ne'er will be called the wild rover no more.

[330]

2   I'll go home to my parents, tell them what I've done   (E)*
        And ask their forgiveness for their prodigal son.   (F)
        I went back to that alehouse one morning in May   (E)
        Put my hands to my pocket, pulled out silver and gold.   (F)
           You can keep your beer, lady, your whiskey as well   (E)
           For I'll never be called the wild rover no more.   (F)

                         (chorus)

* The letters in parentheses indicate which line of music is used.

114   CREEPING JANE
(Laws Q 23)

The central core of this popular sporting ballad is generally considered to be the three or four stanzas which describe, mile by mile, the fortunes of a horse-race. Mr Ridley's text lacks these important stanzas but possesses several interesting features absent from all the English sets known to us but present in the Donegal text (Hughes). In neither version is Creeping Jane mentioned by name; she is referred to as 'the little dun mare' or the 'wee din mare'.

Again, Mr Ridley's text is unique among English versions in putting a date to the event, the 'twenty-fourth of August last'. The Irish version has it as 'the eighth of October last' and describes the mare as having two split ears – 'two prick ears' in our version.

In all the printed English texts that we have seen, including the Such broadside, the jockey is referred to as 'the rider'. In our version, as in the Irish, he is 'the little boy'. Finally, both the Ridley and the Hughes texts mention the amount of money won on the race, a detail missing from the other versions.

BIBLIOGRAPHY

Laws Q 23.

British   Baring-Gould and Sharp, pp. 40–1; *Hammond MSS*, D-512; *JFSS*, vol. I, p. 233; Hughes, vol. I, pp. 40–5; Kidson and Moffat (2), pp. 114–15; Purslow (1), pp. 53–4; Purslow (3), p. 29; Reeves (1), pp. 76–7; Sharp and Karpeles (2), vol. II, pp. 255–60; Sharp and Marson, pp. 50–1.

Alternative title The Bonnie Wee Mare.

'The Jockey's Song', sung by Nelson Ridley.

1   The twenty-fourth of August last,
     The place we call Newmarket Cross;
     With the little dun mare, she'd two prick ears,
     She led the course for two or three years,
Refrain: Sing la dah-dee, fol the rol diddle i day.
              With the little dun mare, she'd two prick ears,
              She led the course for two or three years,
              Sing la dah-dee fol the rol diddle i day.

2   There was gentlefolks riding all round the racecourse,
     Said one to each other what money they've lost;
     For she's won enough money on this very day
     Six coaches, six horses to carry away,
Refrain: Sing la dah-dee fol the rol diddle i day.
              For she's won enough money (etc.)

3 She caused the jockeys to wiggle their whips,
   She caused the jockeys to wiggle their whips;
   And as they was a-wiggling over the moor,
   My little brown mare stepped in before, (refrain, etc.)

4 'Who's there, who's there?' the little boy cried,
   'Who's there, who's there?' the little boy cried;
   'Who's there, who's there?' the little boy cried,
   I think my mare won't win this time, (refrain, etc.)

115 THE PENNY WAGER

This is a very abbreviated text, much reduced since it first appeared under the title 'Adventures of a Penny'. The full story is as follows: A traveller with one penny in his pocket stakes his purse against five or ten pounds in a pub wager. Fortunately he wins. The next morning he asks the landlord's wife what is to pay and she says, 'Give us a kiss, love, and be on your way'.

  The horse mentioned in the second verse plays a larger part in some of the fuller versions, it being not only our hero's method of conveyance to the inn but also, indirectly, part of the stake in the wager:

   For if them had a-won and I had a-lost,
   I should have to have sold my little Tommy black horse.

The song enjoyed broadside popularity but does not appear to have reached North America.

BIBLIOGRAPHY

British Baring-Gould and Sheppard (2), pp. 52–3; *Gardiner MSS*, H-834; Joyce (2), No. 60; Kennedy, p. 612; Kidson and Moffat (2), pp. 10–11; Purslow (2), p. 68; Sharp and Karpeles (2), vol. II, pp. 243–6.

Broadsides *British Museum*, LR 271 a 2, vol. IV, p. 357 (Catnach).

Australian Edwards, pp. 252–3.

Alternative titles As I Was a-Travelling the North Country; The Hearty Good Fellow; I Bridled My Nag.

'I Called For Some Liquor', sung by Nelson Ridley.

THE PENNY WAGER

not too fast · m D (ending on III)

1   I called for some liquor and that was all brown,
      And it's down by the roadside I sat myself down,

Refrain: With me right fol the lay, way fol the day,
          Here is me, in my pocket is one penny.

2   Now, my old pony's got the wind, now, I'm catched in the storm,
      Now, I'm catched in the storm and I can't pull him in (refrain)

3   Out came the farmer – what is it to pay?
      He said, 'Only a kiss, dear, and take it away.' (refrain)

Following the return of William III from his Irish campaigns, London balladmongers would appear to have been fully employed in creating an acceptable popular image for Ebsworth's 'saturnine' monarch. Old tales and ballads were refurbished with William represented as a roistering up-dated Prince Hal, consorting with sailors, farmers, shepherds and foresters. 'The Loyal Forester or Royal Pastime', printed for C. Bates in Pye Corner (c. 1676) is such a piece. Only five of its twenty stanzas are embodied in the fragment which follows. In spite of this the singer understood the story well enough: 'They laid in await for him. He tried his keepers, see. As I've heard the old travelling men say, they laid a-waiting for him and he done it to see if they would face anyone. When they beat him they told him it was his own fault. He tried his keepers, see.'

BIBLIOGRAPHY

British   Euing, No. 156; *Hammond MSS*, D-99; *Purslow* (2), pp. 49–50; *Roxburghe*, vol. VII, pp. 763–64.

Alternative title   The Bold Forester.

'Suit of Russet Grey', sung by Nelson Ridley.

1   The suit of grey russet King William put on,
        'And now,' said Queen Mary, 'where are you a-going?'
        Do you think I will follow such a very unwise man
        To tell you my council unto a woman?*

2   He ordered his grey horse, likewise his two hounds,
        Likewise for a revolver for to fetch 'em down;
        Now, begone, you bold poachers, you'll hunt no course here,
        Without the leave of King William to hunt the fat deer.

3   Here's fifty bright shillings down to you I will (flow),   (fling)
        If you will impotrace me to William, the King;†
        I don't want your grey horse and not your two hounds,
        And I don't want your shillings if you fling 'em down.

* Purslow gives this couplet:
    Oh it must be a fool or some very unwise man,
    That would tell of his council unto a woman.

† Purslow gives this line: If thou'll not betray me to William, our King.

117   THE SAILOR CUT DOWN IN HIS PRIME
(Laws Q 26)

A single stanza of this very popular lament is given in Joyce (2), 'from Mr. W. Aldwell of Cork (Dec 17, 1848) who heard air and song sung in Cork about the year 1790.' The earliest complete texts are those issued as broadsides during the eighteenth century, though 'The Buck's Elegy' (*Madden*) may be of an earlier date.

    Broadside texts are fairly explicit in pointing out the cause of the young man's death:

    Had I but known what his disorder was,
    Had I but known it and took it in time,
    I'd took *pila cotia*, all sorts of white mercury
    But now I'm cut off in the height of my prime.

The third line of this stanza has been considerably altered in Mr Ridley's third stanza! References to drugs once used in the treatment of venereal infection are rarely encountered in traditional versions of the lament and the 'gallows whores' of 'The Buck's Elegy' are now merely 'flash girls'.

In most of the versions reported from English country singers in the early part of this century, the central roles were reversed and the lament was for 'A Young Girl Cut Down in Her Prime'. In the intervening period two world wars have established the supremacy of the male soldier/sailor form. In North America, on the other hand, 'The Bad Girl's Lament' (Laws's title) would appear to have achieved a degree of co-existence with innumerable variants of 'The Cowboy's Lament'.

BIBLIOGRAPHY

Laws Q 26.

British Gardiner MSS, H-582 and Wt-1431; *Hammond MSS*, D 349; *Henry Collection*, No. 680; Holloway and Black, No. 17; *JFSS*, vol. I, p. 254; also vol. IV, pp. 325–6; also vol. V, pp. 193–4; Joyce (2), No. 442; *Madden*, vol. IV, p. 227; Purslow (2), p. 102; Purslow (3), p. 114; Reeves (2), p. 188; Sharp and Karpeles (2), vol. II, pp. 122–4.

North American Bulletin, No. 7, pp. 16–18; Carey, p. 116; Lomax (3), 193–4; Peacock, vol. II, pp. 420–1; Thorp and Fife, pp. 148–90 (for detailed analysis of American variants and extensive bibliography).

General The Unfortunate Rake (edited by Kenneth Goldstein), Folkways disc FS 3805, a Study in the Evolution of a Ballad (20 versions, analogues and parodies of 'The Sailor Cut Down in His Prime').

Alternative titles The Whore's Lament; Trooper (Young Man, Soldier) Cut Down in His Prime; St James' Hospital; One Morning in May; The Streets of Laredo (etc.).

'The Sailor Cut Down in His Prime', sung by Nelson Ridley.

slightly free

p I (with inflected IV)

Now, as I was a- walk-ing down through the dark ar-ches,

Dark was the morn-ing and dark was the night;

Who should I spy then was one of my ship-mates,

He was wrapped up in flan-nels, much cold- er than clay,

1   Now, as I was a-walking down through the dark arches,
Dark was the morning and dark was the night;
Who should I spy then was one of my shipmates,
He was wrapped up in flannels, much colder than clay.

2   We will carry him to the churchyard, three valleys over,
Play the dead march as we carry him along;
Now, never go courting flash gels in the city,
Flash gels in the city are the ruin of me.

3   Now, beat the drum slowly and play the dead march now,
Beat the drum slowly as we carry him along;
That's sweet Billy Caution as I said to Marjorie,
I'm in a deep sitivation, I'm sure I will die.

4   It's yonder, round the corner there's three maids a-standing,
One to each other they whispered and said:
'Here comes the young sailor, what money he squandered –
He's the young sailor cut down in his prime.'

5   Now beat the drum slowly and play the dead march now,
       Beat the drum slowly as we carry him along;
       Never go courting flash gels in the city,
       Flash gels in the city are the ruin of me.

118   THE JOLLY HERRING

Mrs Hughes's version of this popular song is unusual in that four of its six stanzas make use of hunting images. The version recorded by Cecil Sharp from Mrs Louie Hooper of Hambridge, Somerset, in 1904, has for its refrain:

> So it's beagles and long legs
> And a man to whip in,
> And don't you think I done well
> With my jolly red herring?

It is, we think, from this refrain that Mrs Hughes's version is derived.

    The song is fairly widespread throughout England and several sets of it with cumulative refrains have been reported. In a Cumberland version, the herring has been supplanted by 'T'Oald Boar', and in North America by 'The Old Cow' and, more commonly 'The Old Sow'. A solitary Scots version, 'The Soo's ta'en the Measles', reported from Kirkcudbrightshire in 1917, would appear to be directly related to the Lomax and Randolph versions.

BIBLIOGRAPHY

British   Baring-Gould, pp. 13–15; Hamer, pp. 16–17; *Hammond MSS*, S-283; *JFSS*, vol. V, pp. 283–6; *JEFDSS*, vol. IX, pp. 79–80; Kennedy, p. 651; Purslow (3), p. 52; Reeves (1), pp. 219–20; Reeves (2), pp. 179–80; *Rymour*, vol. II, p. 52; Sharp and Karpeles (2), vol. II, pp. 436–9; Williams, p. 167.

North American   Brown, vol. III, p. 218; Davis (1), p. 147; Fuson, p. 185; Gordon, pp. 105–6; *JAFL*, vol. 66, pp. 51–2; Linscott, pp. 253–4; Lomax (4), p. 31; Randolph, vol. III, pp. 149–50.

Alternative titles   The Herring Song; The (Jolly) Red Herring; The Old Cow; The Old Sow (Sow's Nose); Sow Took the Measles.

(untitled), sung by Caroline Hughes.

THE JOLLY HERRING

Now, 'tis hunt- ing, 'tis hunt- ing I did want to go,

I could- n't find no hor- ses, nor hounds nor no dogs;

I made it me mind out to catch a large ship,

I done it my du- ty right out of my head.

first interpolation

second and third interpolations

O yes, if it's true what you says O yes, if its true now, what

you have told me.

1 Now, 'tis hunting, 'tis hunting I did want to go,
   I couldn't find no horses, nor hounds nor no dogs;
   I made it me mind out to catch a large ship,
   I done it my duty right out of my head.

2 Now what do you think that I made of his head?
   I made the finest large ship that ever were sail;
   There was life-boats and little boats and sailors, quite true,
   Don't you think I done well with my jolly herring?

3 Now, what do you think that I made of his tail?
   I made the finest pack hounds that ever was made;
   There was footmens and whipmens and horses, nice things,
   Don't you think I done well with my jolly herring?

(O yes, if it's true what you says.)

4   O, what do you think that I made of his back?
     I made the finest lot of ridin' horses that ever you seen;
     There was little ones and big ones and all things like that,
     Don't you think I done well with my jolly herring?

(O yes, if it's true now what you have told me.)

5   Now, what do you think that I made of his legs?
     I made the finest lot of whipmens that ever you seen;
     There was little ones and big ones and all things like that,
     Don't you think I done well with my jolly herring?

(O yes, if it be true now what you have told me.)

6*   Lie, tooral lie, di diddle, lie dee dee, dee;
     Lie, die dee dee, lie dee dee, deedle ee, day.
     Lie, die dee dee, dee dee dee, lie did dee, dee –
     But I'm not such a fool as you take I to be!

*   In this verse the commas placed in the diddling section indicate the placement of bar-lines in the music.

119   PADDY BACKWARDS

Anne Gilchrist has used the title of the Irish song 'Amhran na mBreag' (Song of Marvels) as a group designation for that family of songs 'whose motif is the invention of as many picturesque or preposterous marvels, declared to have been seen by the singer, as can be strung upon successive verses'. 'The Derby Ram', 'Kingston Hill', 'Martyn Sayd to His Man', 'The Man to the Green Jo', 'Wha's Fu'?' and 'The Thrawn Song' – all belong in this group. 'Paddy Backwards' is probably one of the most recent additions to the family and appears to be rather more at home in the United States and Canada than in Britain.

BIBLIOGRAPHY

British   Gardiner MSS, Hp-236 and Hp-1016; Purslow (4), pp. 65–6.

Broadsides   'Paddy's Ramble to London' (Pitts).

North American Creighton (4), pp. 177–8; Creighton and Senior (2), pp. 240–1; Leach, pp. 274–5; Randolph, vol. III, pp. 201–2; Sharp and Karpeles (1), vol. II, p. 270.

General JEFDSS, vol. IV, pp. 113–21 ('Song of Marvels or Lies', by Anne Gilchrist); *Rymour*, vol. I, p. 67 (note only).

Alternative titles Nottamun (Nottingham) Town.

'All You Paddies Lay Down', sung by Caroline Hughes.

1   O, as I went to market, I vow and declare,
     As I went to market, 'twas all on a cow;
     The cow was so lazy she chucked all my O,
     She dirtied my shoes and she dirtied my clothes,

Refrain: And sing ay, ay; sing ay to meself,
           O 'tis ay, O you paddies, lay down.

2   I looked all up to my magistrates well,
I asked him the place if he knowed it quite well.
When he got there nothing could he see
But a thousand potatoes growing on a pear tree,

Refrain: And sing down, down; sing down, down;
Sing down, all you paddies, lay down.

120 THE HOP-PICKERS' TRAGEDY

The tragic event described in the following two stanzas took place on 20 October 1853, when a horse-drawn brake carrying a party of hop-pickers plunged over Hartlake Bridge into the River Medway. The memorial in the graveyard at Hadlow (Addlehouse?) says that thirty people, four of whom were children, were drowned. Three members of the Herne family and Comfort, Charlotte, Alice, Selina Leatherhand, all Travellers, were among the dead. Of the twenty-three remaining names, eight are Irish and the rest English. In spite of being very well known among Kent and Surrey Travellers, the song does not appear to have been printed at any time.

'There Was Four-and-Twenty Strangers', sung by Nelson Ridley.

very free   m I (-VI)

There was four- and- twen- ty strang-ers there hop- ping they had been,

Re- plied to Mis- ter Cox- es all near old Gol- den Green;

All in the par- ish of Ad- dle-house, all near old Ton- bridge town,

That lit- tle did those poor souls thought that they were go- ing down.

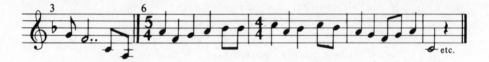

1. There was four-and-twenty strangers there, hopping they had been,
    Replied to Mr Coxes all near old Golden Green;
    All in the parish of Addlehouse, all near old Tonbridge Town,
    That little did those poor souls thought that they were going down.

2. Some was men and women and the others girls and boys,
    They kept in contact to Larklake Bridge till the horses they took shy;
    They kept in contact to old Larklake Bridge till the horses they took shy,
    That to hear the screams from those poor souls as they were going down.

121   THE LITTLE CHIMNEY SWEEP

In spite of its popularity with nineteenth-century broadside printers, this piece does not appear to have established itself among traditional singers. We are informed by Robert Thompson of Huntingdon that the *Madden Collection* contains a slip by an anonymous London printer where it is stated that the song was written by a Mr Upton. The text below is an assembly of lines and stanzas recorded on the Hughes site on three different occasions.

BIBLIOGRAPHY

British   JFSS, vol. III, pp. 273–4.

Broadsides   Madden, M 15–228; also M 8–1096 (Pitts); also M 12–265 (T. Birt, London).

Alternative title   The Lost Child Found.

(untitled), sung by William Hughes.

1 It was down at Stony Bottom in a place called Derby Shore,
  A woman sat in the window a-spinning of the yarn;
  All in the street that little boy contentedly did play,
  When along did come a chimney-sweep and stole her child away.

2 When three long years had gone and past and he could not be found,
  That chimney-sweep came by that way again;
  This lady called out to him: 'There's work for you,' she said,
  'Now my chimney wants a-sweeping, I'm stifled out with smoke.'

3 My little boy got ready, her chimney for to sweep,
  She viewed him, yes she viewed him up and down;
  Her spirits they was lifted up when she viewed his tender face,
  'It is the hour of Providence, my lost dear child is found!'

4 Now that little boy upstepped and her chimney for to sweep,
  She viewed him, yes, she viewed him up and down;
  'Now you are my long lost child,' his tender mother cried,
  'For I marked you with that cherry under your left eye.'

5   Come, all you motherly women, a warning take by me,
Never let your children wander from your knee;
Never let your little one now wander far at play,
Or along will come a chimney-sweep and steal them right away.

122   THE LITTLE BEGGAR BOY

The opening stanza of this piece echoes the fourth stanza of Randolph's A-text of 'The Drunkard's Lone Child':

Hungry an' tired, I've wandered all day,
Askin' for work, but I'm too small, they say,
All day long I been beggin' for bread,
Father's a drunkard an' mother is dead. (vol. II, p. 298)

Our fourth and fifth stanzas are almost identical with the chorus used in an Edinburgh children's singing game:

Ding dong! castle bells, Tell me where my mother dwells;
Bury me in the old churchyard, Beside my oldest brother.
My coffin shall be black, Six angels at my back;
Two to sing, and two to pray, And two to carry my soul away.

BIBLIOGRAPHY

British   Chambers (1), p. 150; Northall, pp. 144–7; *Rymour*, vol. I, p. 150.

'The Little Beggar Boy', sung by Emily Baker.

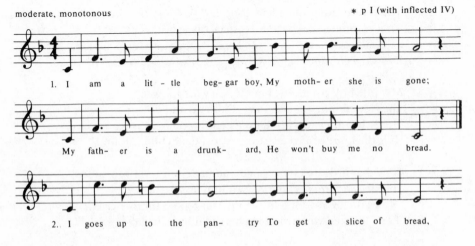

moderate, monotonous   * p I (with inflected IV)

1. I am a lit-tle beg-gar boy, My moth-er she is gone;

My fath-er is a drunk-ard, He won't buy me no bread.

2. I goes up to the pan-try To get a slice of bread,

My dad-dy come be-hind me And whip me up to bed.

3. I set be-side the win-dow To hear the or-gan play,

God bless my dear old mom-my Who is dead and far a-way.

4. Ding-dong, my cas-tle bell, Fare-well, my mom-my;

You bur-y me in the same church-yard A-long the side of ny mom-my.

5. My cof-fin shall be black, Six white an-gels at the back,

Two to pray and two to watch And two to car-ry my soul a-way.

Lines 2-⌐ (incl) seem to enter another mode: a M (with inflected II

1   I am a little beggar boy,
       My mother she is gone;
       My father is a drunkard,
       He won't buy me no bread.

2   I goes up to the pantry
       To get a slice of bread,
       My daddy come behind me
       And whip me up to bed.

3 I set beside the window
   To hear the organ play,
   God bless my dear old mommy
   Who is dead and far away.

4 Ding-dong, my castle bell,
   Farewell, my mommy;
   You bury me in the same churchyard
   Along the side of my mommy.

5 My coffin shall be black,
   Six white angels at the back,
   Two to pray and two to watch
   And two to carry my soul away.

123 LITTLE POPPA RICH

This was another favourite jingle with the children of the Hughes family. Gomme quotes a Derbyshire version which was 'said or sung in a game called "T' Bull's i' t' Barn"'.

BIBLIOGRAPHY

British Gomme, vol. II, p. 51; Gullen, p. 119; Opie (1), pp. 127–8.

'Little Poppa Rich', sung by Caroline Hughes.

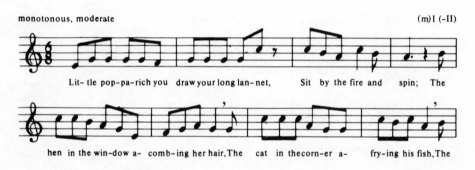

monotonous, moderate   (m)I (–II)

Lit- tle pop-pa-rich you draw your long lan-net, Sit by the fire and spin; The

hen in the win-dow a- comb-ing her hair, The cat in the corn-er a- fry-ing his fish, The

bull in the barn a- sheen-ing his corn; Cock-a-pen dun-gle a- blow-ing his horn, The

wind was high and it blowed him a- way.

*This is almost spoken, then swooped down an octave.

1   Little poppa-rich you draw your long lannet,
       Sit by the fire and spin;
       The hen in the window a-combing her hair,
       The cat in the corner a-frying his fish,
       The bull in the barn a-sheening his corn;
       Cocka-pen dungle a-blowing his horn,
       The wind was high and it blowed him away.

124   TWA AND TWA

Scattered like exclamation points throughout the Scots traditional repertoire are innumerable short pieces frequently set to pipe and fiddle tunes and often consisting of a single stanza. The following is a typical example.

BIBLIOGRAPHY

British   Robert Burns, *The Merry Muses of Caledonia* (London, 1965 edn), p. 131.

'Twa and Twa', sung by Jeannie Thompson.

TWA AND TWA

p I (–VI, ending on lower V)

fast, with a snap

Twa and twa made the bed,
Twa and twa lay the- gith- er;

When the bed be- gun to heat, The
one got up a- bune the oth- er.

(this section is diddled without words)

1   Twa and twa made the bed,
    Twa and twa lay thegither;
    When the bed begun to heat,
    The one got up abune the other.

TRAVELLING LIFE

125   THE TWO GYPSY GIRLS

We heard Mrs Hughes lilt this dandling song on several different occasions. It always proved marvellously effective when any of her infant grandchildren (or great-grandchildren) needed pacifying. The chorus is from 'The Galloping Major', a popular music-hall song written and composed by Fred W. Leigh and George Bastow between 1900 and 1910.

BIBLIOGRAPHY

British ('The Galloping Major') Gammond, Peter, *The Music Hall Songbook* (London, 1975).

'The Two Gypsy Girls', sung by Caroline Hughes.

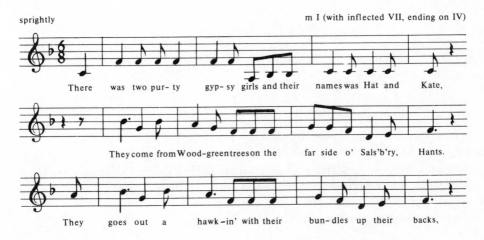

sprightly   m I (with inflected VII, ending on IV)

There was two pur-ty gyp-sy girls and their names was Hat and Kate,

They come from Wood-green trees on the far side o' Sals'b'ry, Hants.

They goes out a hawk-in' with their bun-dles up their backs,

And bub-bies in their arms suck-in' an' cry- in' all day long.

La de de la de de doo-dledeela de de Bum-pe-tybum-pe-ty bum-pe-ty bump!

Comes the gal-lop-ing ma-jor. All the boys de-clare, O he's a gay old sta-ger

O boys, clear the road, here comes the gal-lop-ing ma-jor.

Bum- pe- ty bum-pe-ty bum- ty bum-pe-ty Straight-a-way in- to me char-ger,

All the boys de- clare, I think you're a gay old sta-ger O boys,

clear the road, here come's the drunk- en sai- lor! (kisses her fingers)

126   DIDDLING SONGS

These two lilts were used to provide music for dancing. Sheila Hughes explained: 'Of a Sunday when the men come back from having a few drinks, there's sometimes a bit of a dance. All the women sit down in a ring and sing and keep time while the men dance in the middle.'

Two diddling songs, sung by Caroline Hughes.

quite fast

m D

1. O, it's me and me broth-er took a peej in the shov-el And a- we were all the lot

O, to the hole in the wall in the hole in the wall, With the hob-nail boots your fath-er wore.

2. Till a lod-dle dee-dle all the dee-dle all the deed-le all the did-dle all the did-dle

um a did-dle all a dear dol the li-dle the doo li- dle the dear dol the li- dle the

dee-dle de de da dee dum. 3. Till the lod-dle dee-dle um a dee-dle all the dee-dle

um a did-dle all the dee-dle all the did-dle all the dear dum a did-dle all

lum a did-dle all the dee-dle dum a well- a done-a girl-a when you shows good time.

4. Skip-pin 'a- way, you pret-ty boys, skip-pin 'a-way your time, now, Skip-pin 'a-way, you pret-ty

boys, skip-pin a-way your time now, Skip-pin 'a-way, you pret-ty boys, skip-pin 'a-

way your time, now, This time now shows good time. 5. Till the lod-dle dee-dle all the

dee-dle all the dee dum, Till the lod-dle dee-dle all the dee-dle all the dear dol a lid-dle

all the did-dle all the dee-dle all the dear dol   Well done, girl, when you shows good time.

* **Breathing points**

brisk, quite fast   p I/M (-VI, with inflected VII)

O for I axed me girl to   come a- gee, She come at me te- nar- i- ty

And the I- rish girl stepped up to me And I   look for John o Me-   Car- i- ty.

Till a la da dum dee-dle a   la da dum dee-dle a   lad-di- ty dee-dle de   dee,

Dun te da   de de la dee-dle de dee-dle   de dum was bounced to gin o me car-i- ty.

*Here the singer takes a short, quick breath.

127   THE MOSS O' BURRELDALE

A charter of 1591 refers to the great yearly fair called St Serf's, or St Sair's, by Keith Hall but later held at nearby Kirkton-of-Culsalmond, Aberdeenshire. The moss referred to in our song is less easily identified. There is a Burreldale some eighteen miles to the north of Culsalmond and another situated twelve to thirteen miles northwest of it. Neither of these, however, has a moss associated with it and both places are situated too far away from the venue of the fair to be considered as suitable camping sites. Travellers whose memories of the fair go back to the beginning of the present century say that the main camping place was the Moss of Wartle, five miles west of Kirkton-of-Culsalmond.

In Mrs McPhee's text, the fair has been moved south to Kinkell, a village located on the Crieff-Auchterarder road in Perthshire. Kinkell is not mentioned in the *List of Markets and Fairs*. Kinkell Brig, however, was for a long time a traditional camping site for travellers.

BIBLIOGRAPHY

British   Buchan and Hall, pp. 106–7; Kennedy, pp. 779–80; Kerr (1), Book I, pp. 32–3.

General   *List of Markets and Fairs Now and Formerly Held in Scotland* (prepared for the Royal Commissioners of Market Rights and Rolls by Sir James Marwick, 1890).

A.   'The Moss o' Burreldale', sung by John MacDonald.

B.   'The Moss o' Burreldale', sung by Maggie McPhee.

A.

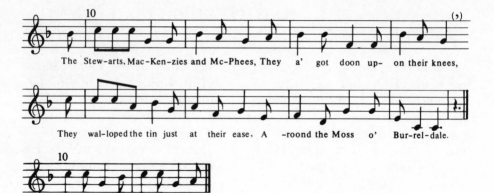

The Stew-arts, Mac-Ken-zies and Mc-Phees, They a' got doon up- on their knees,

They wal-loped the tin just at their ease, A -roond the Moss o' Bur-rel-dale.

1 It was on the night of old St Sairs,
 I had an old braxtie for to sell;
 The women they got on the ale,
 Aroond the Moss o' Burreldale.
  The Stewarts, MacKenzies and McPhees,
  They a' got doon upon their knees,
  They walloped the tin just at their ease,
  Aroond the Moss o' Burreldale.

2 Noo, the auld sweep bein' on the booze,
 To yon dykeside to hae a snooze,
 When somebody come to him wi' the news
 Aboot the row in Burreldale.
  The heather merchant ca'd MacQueen,
  Wi' silver buckles on his sheen
  He swore that night he'd clear the green
  Aroond the Moss o' Burreldale.

3 Big Frank Kelby he come up,
 All in his hand a loadin' whip;
 He says, 'MacNeill, ye papist pup,
 Ye'll die this nicht in Burreldale!'

B.

fairly fast, slightly free   a D

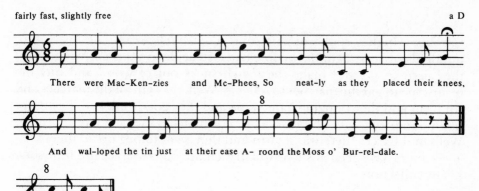

There were Mac-Ken-zies and Mc-Phees, So neat-ly as they placed their knees,

And wal-loped the tin just at their ease A- roond the Moss o' Bur-rel-dale.

1 There were MacKenzies and McPhees,
  So neatly as they placed their knees,
  And walloped the tin just at their ease
  Aroond the Moss o' Burreldale.

2 O, the women fought wi' jug and pail,
  So neatly as they faced the gale,
  To see if they could get good sale
  Aroond the Moss o' Burreldale.

3 O, it was on a day o' a' Kinkell,
  The tinkers had their old nyags to sell,
  They filled their bellies full o' ale,
  And trampit back to Burreldale.

4 O, some o' them did gather rags,
  And some o' them blew up their bags,
  And some o' them noo dealt in nyags
  Aroond the moss o' Burreldale.

5 O, the brawest laddie upon the green
  Was a heather merchant ca'd MacQueen,
  He had silver buckles on his sheen
  Aroond the Moss o' Burreldale.

128   JAL ALONG

Caroline Hughes spoke of this song thus: 'Well, years and years ago, hundreds of years ago, the people had a struggle to get their living. Well, they used to go and make the match-sticks out of wood and buy the brimstone to gilt the matches to sell 'em. Well, they gilt all the matches and sold 'em and they bought champagne and they got drunk and they never had no money to get no bread with, nor matches the next day-morning. Well, in the trees there was a farm and they went to beg bread there. . . .' The editors have been unsuccessful in their attempts to trace this little song in any collection.

'Jal Along', sung by Caroline Hughes

1   O, a-beggin' I will go, my love,
    And a-beggin' I will go;
    But a kushti cant among you
    At the farm all in the trees.

2   Jal along, jal along, my kushti cant,
    Jal along, jal along, jal along;
    But if our matches ain't gilted
    I'm sure we're to get no scran.

3   O, since we been to bed all night
    We been rolling in champagne,
    But there isn't a penny amongst us
    To buy a brimstone pot.

4   Jal along, jal along, my ravvle of a nee,
    Jal along, jal along, jal along;
    But a kushti cant among you
    At the farm all in the trees.

Glossary

kushti cant	probably meaning a good house for food (kushti: pretty, decent, good; cant: a mispronunciation of ken, for house?)
jal	to go, walk
scran	bread, scraps of food
ravvle of a nee	possibly a mispronunciation of 'rakli', meaning girl

129   MANDI WENT TO POOV THE GRAIS

Miss Gillington's New Forest gypsy version of this song has a fairly complicated plot. It tells how a gypsy, putting the horses out to graze, has a violent argument with a policeman. She finally strikes him and runs off to hide in a barn where she spends the night. The following morning she begs or steals a cart belonging to 'a house in the trees' and is once again set upon by a policeman, who theatens her life. The song ends with 'what a kushti bit of fun' it was with the Romani girls.

There is a slightly different story in Kennedy. The girl merely looks at the policeman and says she can't get away. The farmer comes up threatening to impound the mares. 'My aunt' then chases a mare around a haystack and the policeman moves the Travellers on.

There is no doubt that Mrs Hughes's version is not only an abbreviated one but the Romani itself is somewhat run-down. The three stanzas given here contain a much higher percentage of English words than do either of the other texts.

BIBLIOGRAPHY

British   Gillington, pp. 24–5; Kennedy, p. 777.

Alternative title   Mandi Jalled to Puv a Grai.

'Mandi Went to Poov the Grais', sung by Caroline Hughes.

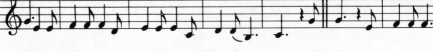

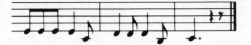

1   O, 'tis mandi went to poov the grais
     All around the stiggers to kai
     The gavver's arter mandi
     To lel me oprey.

2   'Ma,' says the rakli
     Pickin' up a shovel,*
     ''Tis like your dear old daddy says
     You can't kor well.'

3   Well, all around the stiggers
     Stealin' a bit o' kas,
     The gavver said, 'Whaddaya got?'
     I had to put it down.†

* The first time Mrs Hughes sang this line as 'kicking up the godli'.
† The last line was spoken.

Glossary

mandi	I
poov	field; *poov the grais*, put the horses to grass
grais	horses
stiggers	hedges, stacks
to kai	probably should be *akai*, meaning here
gavver	probably short for *gavmush*, policeman

lel me oprey	take me away
rakli	girl
godli	noise
kor	fight
kas	hay

130   THE ATCHING TAN SONG

'We're just like the Indians, only the Indians have reservations and we don't. We're just hunted frae pillar to post by the police' (Scots Traveller, recorded in Marshall's Field, New Alyth, Perthshire, 1963).

'Move on, move on! You'd think *gorgios* didn't know any other words. Move on! And that's all they ever say' (English Traveller, Cobham, Kent, 1963).

This dramatic half-chanted, half-sung account of one of the most common experiences in the life of a Traveller has an urgency which a more formally constructed song might find difficult to achieve. We have been unable to discover the meaning of 'chadders in the bottlers'.

Nelson Ridley's recitation of the piece is completely lacking in Romani terms:

> When it's raining the first thing in mind
> Is it's tent rods and ridge poles, hay for to find;
> The old pony to hobble I turned him on grass
> But where shall I find him, good Lord only knows.
> I hunted all round, no horse could I find
> I went to the farm door and gave a sound knock;
> Out came the farmer, what is it to pay?
> He said, 'Take your old pony and clear right away!'

BIBLIOGRAPHY

British   Kennedy, p. 763.

(untitled), sung by Caroline Huges.

THE ATCHING TAN SONG

recitative style

We packed up our tent rods, our ridge-poles, our pots and kit-tles We

went a-long the road so nice. We pulled off to camp, to have a cup-pa tea,

Long come the p'lice-man, he said You got-ta move. Where's your hors-es? In the

slightly faster

poov, get 'em out! We have to shift at one o'clock in the morn-ing to get on.

Ridge-poles and tent rods and all things like that Chad-ders in the bottlers they

got to lel out Broad day in the morn-ing at four, O, p. m.

Get the grais in their burd- les †and jell straight- a- way.

*It is difficult to give an overall mode for this tune as it changes key several times internally. Without these transitions it is essentially a p I tune (with inflected IV, ending on lower V).

†Bridles

131   HI, BARA MANISHEE

Among Scots Travellers, canting songs appear to be limited to odd lines
and stanzas interpolated into otherwise Scottish texts. Charlotte Higgins
translated her song thus:

> Hi, bonnie lassie, will you go with me?
> Hi, bonnie laddie, I dinna ken your face.
> Will you come, will you hurry, will you come to the camp?
> If you don't get food, you'll get some drink.

'Hi, Bara Manishee', sung by Charlotte Higgins.

Hi, bara manishee, will ye bing wi' me?
Hi, bara gadgie, I dinna jan your fee;
Will ye bing, will ye ja, will ye bing tae the wattle?
If ye dinna get habben you'll get some peeve.

GLOSSARY

abune (from Anglo-Saxon *abufan*) – above.

ae (Scots) – one, only, particular.

awa' (Scots) – away.

bairn (Scots and northern English, from the Saxon *bearn*) – a child, baby.

bardie (Scots) – to be rude, petulant, often applied to female contentiousness.

birse (from Anglo-Saxon *byrst*) – the act of pressing; also to warm at a lively fire; also to push or drive; as a noun, a bristle (as of a sow).

bit (Scots) – commonly used in conjunction with a substantive in place of a diminutive, as 'a bit bairn', a little child.

blaw (Scots) – to blow.

blue-buck (slang) – a Traveller, both of whose parents were *gorgios*; a tramp, etc.

bothy (from Gaelic *bothag*, or *bothan*, meaning a cot) – a place where male farm-servants are lodged (see notes to Nos 104–108).

brae (Scots) – the side of a hill, an acclivity.

braw (from the Icelandic *braer*, meaning splendid) – fine, handsome, pleasant, agreeable, richly clad.

braxty (Scots) – of or pertaining to a sheep which has died of disease (braxy, braxes, bracks).

brig (from Anglo-Saxon *bricg*) – bridge.

brose (Scots) – a kind of pottage made by pouring water or broth onto meal, which is stirred while the liquid is poured.

bubbies (Scots slang, plural) – the female breasts.

buck (slang) – a *gorgio* man who marries a Traveller woman.

bugger-all (slang) – nothing.

burn, burnie (Scots) – a brook, a small stream.

busk (from Germanic *butzen*) – to dress, attire oneself; make ready.

byre (Scots) – a cow-house.

carle (Scots and northern English) – a man; also a clown, boor, a person of low extraction.

claes (Scots dialect) – clothes.

cuddy (Scots) – an ass.

daurna (Scots dialect) – dare not.

deaves (Scots dialect) – deafens.

dell (from Anglo-Saxon *dael*) – part, a quantity; therefore double-dell = everything.

dicht (from Anglo-Saxon *diht*, to set in order) – has many meanings: to prepare or make ready; to array, to deck; to prepare food; to polish, make clean, wipe; to scourge or exercise discipline; to rub in order to remove moisture.

dighted (Scots dialect) – made an end of, destroyed.

dole (slang) – to be 'on the dole' is to draw unemployment benefits.

dominie (Scots slang) – a pedagogue or schoolmaster.

double-dells (see dell, above).

e'en (Scots) – eyes.

fae (Scots dialect) – from, away from.

fecht (from the Germanic *fecht-an*) – to fight.

foy (from the French *voye*, a way) – a celebration marking the term of an apprenticeship or an entertainment given to a friend who is about to leave a particular place of residence or go to another country.

fu' (Scots dialect) – full, meaning drunk or intoxicated.

gaberlunzie man (Scots) – a beggarman, itinerant, or a tinker.

gadgie (slang, from *cadger*) – a beggar.

gaffer (slang) – a master, an employer, foreman.

gar (Scots dialect) – to cause, make, force, compel.

gey (Scots dialect) – considerable, worthy of notice; tolerable; middling.

gied (Scots) – gave.

gin (Scots dialect, pronounced with a hard *g*) – if, against (in relation to time).

gleid (Scots dialect) – squint-eyed or blind of an eye; also used to denote moral delinquency.

gorgi(o) (from the Romany *ganjer*, *ganjo*) – one who is not a gypsy.

greet (greit) (from Germanic *greit-an*) – to weep or cry.

hairst (Scots dialect) – harvest.

hap (Scots dialect) – to cover, defend from the cold; a covering of whatever kind.

hooly (Scots dialect) – slowly, softly, gently.

kame(d) (also kaim(ed)) (Scots) – comb(ed).

ken (from Old English) – to know.

kimmer (Scots dialect) – a gossip, a gossiping woman.

kirk (Scots dialect) – church.

knowe (from Anglo-Saxon *cuolle*) – a small hill.

kye (from Old English *kie*) – kine.

lannet (from Middle English *linnet*, the flax plant) – also flax refuse.

lift (from Germanic *lufte*) – the firmament, the sky.

loon (Scots dialect) – a fellow; a low or lazy person; a boy or young fellow.

marrow (Scots dialect) – a companion, equal, mate, associate.

muckle (Scots dialect) – great, much; also proud, haughty, pretentious.

napper (slang) – obsolete term for the head.

neep (Scots dialect) – a turnip.

neeprigs (Scots dialect) – turnip rows.

owsen (from Germanic *auhsne*) – oxen.

pintle (Scots dialect) – the penis.

pint-stoup (Scots) – tin measure containing two quarts.

plack (Scots) – a small copper coin formerly circulated in Scotland, equal to four pennies Scots or the third part of an English penny.

pram (slang, abbreviation for perambulator) – baby-carriage for an infant.

quean (northeastern Scots dialect) – a young woman.

root (slang) – the penis.

rossety-end (Scots) – a shoemaker's thread; thread tipped or smeared with rosin.

rousty (from the Icelandic *raus*) – hoarse, having a rough voice.

sae (Scots) – so.

sark (Scots and northern English dialect) – a shirt.

scran (cant word) – victuals, bread, scraps of food.

sheen (Scots dialect) – shoes.

shoola (slang, probably from shoal or shule, to beg or scrounge) – a *gorgio* girl who has married a Traveller man. Often used in a pejorative sense.

speir(ing) (also spier) (from Anglo-Saxon *spyrian*) – to ask or enquire.

tanters (Scots dialect) – tantrums.

tatties (slang) – potatoes.

thon (from Anglo-Saxon *thon*) – yonder.

thrummel (Scots dialect) – tremble, twitch.
    twa (from Anglo Saxon *twa*) – two.

wadna (Scots dialect) – wouldn't.
  wiled (from Suio-Gothic *wel*) – enticed.

BIBLIOGRAPHY

FOLKSONG AND FOLKLORE

Aarne and Thompson	Antti Aarne and Stith Thompson, *The Types of the Folktale* (Helsinki, 1961).
Allan	David Allan, *Songs of the Lowlands of Scotland* (Edinburgh, 1799).
Arnold	Byron Arnold, *Folksongs of Alabama* (Birmingham, Alabama, 1950).
Ashton (1)	John Ashton, *Modern Street Ballads* (London, 1888).
Ashton (2)	John Ashton, *Real Sailor Songs* (London, 1891).
Bagford	*The Bagford Ballads*, edited by Joseph Woodfall Ebsworth (Hertford, 1878, 2 vols).
Bannatyne MSS	The Advocate's Library, Edinburgh (1568).
Baring-Gould	S. Baring-Gould, *A Book of Nursery Songs and Rhymes* (London, 1895).
Baring-Gould and Hitchcock	S. Baring-Gould and Gordon Hitchcock, *Folksongs of the West Country* (Newton Abbot, 1974 edn).
Baring-Gould and Sharp	S. Baring-Gould and Cecil J. Sharp, *English Folksongs for Schools* (9th edition, London, 1906).
Baring-Gould and Sheppard (1)	S. Baring-Gould and H. Fleetwood Sheppard, *A Garland of Country Song* (London, 1895).
Baring-Gould and Sheppard (2)	S. Baring-Gould and H. Fleetwood Sheppard, *Songs of the West* (London, 1905).
Barrett	William Alexander Barrett, *English Folksongs* (London, 1891).
Barry	Phillips Barry, *The Maine Woods Songster* (Cambridge, Massachusetts, 1939).
Barry, Eckstorm and Smyth	Phillips Barry, Fanny Hardie Eckstorm and Mary Winslow Smyth, *British Ballads from Maine* (New Haven, Connecticut, 1939).
Belden	H. M. Belden, *Ballads and Songs* (Columbia, Missouri, 1940).

Bell (John)	John Bell, *Rhymes of the Northern Bards* (Newcastle-upon-Tyne, 1812).
Bell (Robert)	Robert Bell, *Early Ballads* (London, 1877).
Botkin (1)	Benjamin A. Botkin, *The American Play-Party Song* (Lincoln, Nebraska, 1937).
Botkin (2)	Benjamin A. Botkin, *A Treasury of New England Folklore* (New York, 1947).
Botkin (3)	Benjamin A. Botkin, *A Treasury of Western Folklore* (New York, 1951).
Brand	Oscar Brand, *Bawdy Songs and Back-Room Ballads* (New York, 1960).
Brewster (1)	Paul G. Brewster, *Ballads and Songs of Indiana* (Bloomington, Indiana, 1940).
Brewster (2)	Paul G. Brewster, 'The Two Sisters' (*Folklore Fellows Communication* No. 147, Helsinki, 1953).
British Museum	British Museum, London (see section at the end of this bibliography).
Broadwood	Lucy E. Broadwood, *English Traditional Songs and Carols* (London, 1908).
Broadwood (John)	John Broadwood, *Sussex Songs* (London 1890).
Broadwood and Maitland	Lucy E. Broadwood and J. A. Fuller Maitland, *English County Songs* (London, 1893).
Bronson	Bertrand Harris Bronson, *The Traditional Tunes of the Child Ballads* (Princeton, New Jersey, 1959–72, 4 vols).
Brown	*The Frank C. Brown Collection of North Carolina Folklore* (Durham, North Carolina, 1952, 7 vols).
Bruce and Stokoe	John Collingwood Bruce and John Stokoe, *Northumbrian Minstrelsy* (Newcastle-upon-Tyne, 1882).
Buchan (1)	Peter Buchan, *Ancient Ballads and Songs of the North of Scotland* (Edinburgh, 1828, 2 vols).
Buchan (2)	Peter Buchan, *Gleanings of Scotch, English, and Irish Scarce Old Ballads* (Peterhead, 1825).
Buchan (David)	David Buchan, *A Scottish Ballad Book* (London, 1973).
Buchan MSS	The manuscripts of Peter Buchan, British Museum, c. 1828.
Buchan (Norman)	Norman Buchan, *101 Scottish Songs* (Glasgow and London, 1962).
Buchan and Hall	Norman Buchan and Peter Hall, *The Scottish Folksinger* (London, 1973).
Bulletin	*Bulletin of the Folksong Society of the North-east* (Cambridge, Massachusetts, 1930–7).
Butterworth	George S. K. Butterworth, *Folk Songs from Sussex* (London, 1913).

Caledonian	*The Caledonian Musical Repository* (Edinburgh, 1809).
Campbell	Alexander Campbell, *Albyn's Anthology* (Edinburgh, 1816–18, 2 vols).
Carey	George G. Carey, *Maryland Folk Legends and Folksongs* (Cambridge, Maryland, 1971).
Chambers (1)	Robert Chambers, *Popular Rhymes of Scotland* (Edinburgh, 1841).
Chambers (2)	Robert Chambers, *Scottish Songs* (Edinburgh, 1829, 2 vols).
Chambers (3)	Robert Chambers, *The Songs of Scotland Prior to Burns* (Edinburgh, 1862).
Chappell (1)	William Chappell, *A Collection of National English Airs* (London, 1838–40, 2 vols).
Chappell (2)	William Chappell, *Popular Music of the Olden Time* (London, 1855–9, 2 vols).
Chappell (Louis)	Louis W. Chappell, *Folk-Songs of Roanoke and the Albemarle* (Morgantown, West Virginia, 1939).
Child	Francis J. Child, *The English and Scottish Popular Ballads* (Cambridge, Massachusetts, 1882–98, 5 vols).
Christie	William Christie, *Traditional Ballad Airs* (Edinburgh, 1876–81, 2 vols).
Coffin	Tristram P. Coffin, *The British Traditional Ballad in North America* (Philadelphia, 1950).
Colcord	Joanna C. Colcord, *Songs of American Sailormen* (New York, 1938).
Collection	*A Collection of Old Ballads* (edited by Ambrose Phillips?) (London, 1723, 3 vols).
Combs	Josiah H. Combs, *Folksongs of the Southern United States* (Austin, Texas, 1967).
Cowell	Sam Cowell, *120 Comic Songs* (London, 1850).
Cox (1)	John Harrington Cox, *Folk-Songs Mainly from West Virginia* (New York, 1939).
Cox (2)	John Harrington Cox, *Folk-Songs of the South* (Cambridge, Massachusetts, 1925).
Cox (3)	John Harrington Cox, *Traditional Ballads Mainly from West Virginia* (New York, 1939).
Crawhall	Joseph Crawhall, *Olde Tayles Newlye Relayted* (London, 1883).
Cray	Edward Cray, *The Erotic Muse* (New York, 1969).
Creighton (1)	Helen Creighton, *Folklore of Lunenburg County, Nova Scotia* (National Museum of Canada, Bulletin No. 117, Ottawa, 1950).
Creighton (2)	Helen Creighton, *Folksongs from Southern New Brunswick* (Ottawa, 1971).

Creighton (3)	Helen Creighton, *Maritime Folk Songs* (Toronto, 1962).
Creighton (4)	Helen Creighton, *Songs and Ballads from Nova Scotia* (Toronto, 1933).
Creighton and Senior (1)	Helen Creighton and Doreen H. Senior, *Twelve Folk Songs from Nova Scotia* (London, 1953).
Creighton and Senior (2)	Helen Creighton and Doreen H. Senior, *Traditional Songs from Nova Scotia* (Toronto, 1950).
Cunningham	Allan Cunningham, *Songs of Scotland* (London, 1825, 4 vols).
Davis (1)	Arthur Kyle Davis, Jr, *Folksongs of Virginia: A Descriptive Index and Classification* (Durham, North Carolina, 1949).
Davis (2)	Arthur Kyle Davis, Jr, *More Traditional Ballads of Virginia* (Chapel Hill, North Carolina, 1950).
Davis (3)	Arthur Kyle Davis, Jr, *Traditional Ballads of Virginia* (Cambridge, Massachusetts, 1929).
Dean-Smith	Margaret Dean-Smith, *A Guide to English Folk Song Collections* (Liverpool, 1954).
Dick	James C. Dick, *The Songs of Robert Burns* (London, 1903).
Dixon and Bell	James Henry Dixon and Robert Bell, *Ancient Poems, Ballads and Songs of the Peasantry of England* (London, 1877).
Doerflinger	William M. Doerflinger, *Shantymen and Shantyboys* (New York, 1951).
D'Urfey	Thomas D'Urfey, *Wit and Mirth: or Pills to Purge Melancholy* (London, 1719–20, 6 vols).
Dusenbury MSS	*The Dusenbury Songs* (transcribed and notated by Laurence Powell), from the singing of Mrs Emma Dusenbury of Mena, Arkansas, between August 1933 and August 1936.
Eckstorm and Smyth	Fannie H. Eckstorm and Mary Winslow Smyth, *Minstrelsy of Maine* (Boston, 1927).
Eddy	Mary O. Eddy, *Ballads and Songs from Ohio* (New York, 1939).
Edwards	Ron Edwards, *The Overlander Songbook* (Adelaide, 1971).
Euing	*The Euing Collection of English Broadside Ballads* (Glasgow, 1971).
Evans	Thomas Evans, *Old Ballads* (London, 1810, 4 vols).
Farmer (1)	John S. Farmer, *Merry Songs and Ballads* (1897, 5 vols).
Farmer (2)	John S. Farmer, *Musa Pedestris* (1896).

Finger	Charles J. Finger, *Frontier Ballads* (New York, 1927).
Firth	C. H. Firth, *Naval Songs and Ballads* (London, 1908).
Fitzwilliam	*The Fitzwilliam Virginal Book*, edited by J. A. Fuller Maitland and W. Barclay Squire (London, 1899).
Flanders (1)	Helen Hartness Flanders, *Ancient Ballads Traditionally Sung in New England* (Philadelphia, 1960–5, 4 vols).
Flanders (2)	Helen Hartness Flanders, *Country Songs of Vermont* (New York, 1937).
Flanders (3)	Helen Hartness Flanders, *A Garland of Green Mountain Songs* (Northfield, Vermont, 1934).
Flanders, Ballard, Brown and Barry	Helen Hartness Flanders, Elizabeth F. Ballard, George Brown and Phillips Barry, *The New Green Mountain Songster* (New Haven, Connecticut, 1939).
Flanders and Brown	Helen Hartness Flanders and George Brown, *Vermont Folksongs and Ballads* (Brattleboro, Vermont, 1931).
Flanders and Olney	Helen Hartness Flanders and Marguerite Olney, *Ballads Migrant in New England* (New York, 1953).
FMJ	*Folk Music Journal* of the English Folk Dance and Song Society (1965–).
Folklore Fellows	*Folklore Fellows Communications*, Helsinki, Suomalainen Tiedeakatemia, Academia Scientiarum Fennica.
Forbes	John Forbes, *Cantus, Songs and Fancies* (Aberdeen, 1666).
Ford (1)	Robert Ford, *Children's Rhymes* (Paisley, 1903).
Ford (2)	Robert Ford, *Vagabond Songs and Ballads of Scotland* (Paisley, 1899–1901, 2 vols).
Ford (Ira)	Ira W. Ford, *Traditional Music of America* (New York, 1940).
Fowke	Edith Fowke, *Traditional Singers and Songs from Ontario* (Hatboro, Pennsylvania, 1965).
Fowke MSS	Edith Fowke MSS of unpublished collected material, Toronto.
Frazer	Sir James George Frazer, *The Golden Bough* (London, 1955, 13 vols).
Fuson	Harvey H. Fuson, *Ballads of the Kentucky Highlands* (London, 1931).
Galvin	Patrick Galvin, *Irish Songs of Resistance* (New York, 1962).
Gardiner	George B. Gardiner, *Folk Songs from Hampshire* (London, 1909).
Gardiner MSS	George B. Gardiner Manuscripts (Cecil Sharp House, London, 1905–9).

Gardner and Chickering	Emelyn E. Gardner and Geraldine Chickering, *Ballads and Songs of Southern Michigan* (Ann Arbor, Michigan, 1939).
Gerould	Gordon Hall Gerould, *The Ballad of Tradition* (Oxford, 1932).
Gillington	Alice E. Gillington, *Songs of the Open Road* (London, 1911).
Glen	John Glen, *Early Scottish Melodies* (Edinburgh, 1900).
Gomme	Alice Bertha Gomme, *The Traditional Games of England, Scotland and Ireland* (reprint, New York, 1964, 2 vols).
Gordon	Robert W. Gordon, *Folksongs of America* (National Service Bureau, New York, 1927).
Gray	Roland Palmer Gray, *Songs and Ballads of the Maine Lumberjacks* (Cambridge, Massachusetts, 1924).
Greenleaf and Mansfield	Elizabeth B. Greenleaf and Grace Y. Mansfield, *Ballads and Sea Songs of Newfoundland* (Cambridge, Massachusetts, 1933).
Greig	Gavin Greig, *Folksongs of the Northeast* (reprint, Hatboro, Pennsylvania, 1963).
Greig and Keith	Gavin Greig and Alexander Keith, *Last Leaves of Traditional Ballads and Ballad Airs* (Aberdeen, 1925).
Gullen	F. Doreen Gullen, *Traditional Number Rhymes and Games* (London, 1950).
Halliwell (1)	James Orchard Halliwell, *The Nursery Rhymes of England* (reprint, London, 1970).
Halliwell (2)	James Orchard Halliwell, *Popular Rhymes and Nursery Tales of England* (reprint, London, 1970).
Hamer	Fred Hamer, *Garners Gay* (London, 1970).
Hammond	H. E. D. Hammond, *Folksongs from Dorset* (London, 1908).
Hammond MSS	The manuscripts of Henry and Robert Hammond, collected between 1905 and 1910 (Cecil Sharp House, London).
Harland	John Harland, *Ballads and Songs of Lancashire* (London, 1875).
Hecht	Hans Hecht, *Songs from David Herd's Manuscripts* (London, 1904).
Henderson	W. Henderson, *Victorian Street Ballads* (London, 1937).
Henry (1)	Mellinger Edward Henry, *Folk-Songs from the Southern Highlands* (New York, 1938).

Henry (2)	Mellinger Edward Henry, *Songs Sung in the Southern Appalachians* (London, 1934).
Henry Collection	Sam Henry Collection, Central Library, Belfast, Northern Ireland.
Herd	David Herd, *Ancient and Modern Scottish Songs* (Edinburgh, 1776, 2 vols).
Hogg	James Hogg, *The Jacobite Relics of Scotland* (Edinburgh, 1819, reprint Paisley, 1874, 2 vols).
Holloway and Black	John Holloway and Joan Black, *Later English Broadside Ballads* (London, 1975).
Hubbard	Lester A. Hubbard, *Ballads and Songs from Utah* (Salt Lake City, 1961).
Hudson and Herzog	Arthur Palmer Hudson and George Herzog, *Folk Tunes from Mississippi* (New York, 1937).
Hughes	Herbert Hughes, *Irish Country Songs* (London, 1914, 2 vols).
Hugill	Stan Hugill, *Shanties from the Seven Seas* (London, 1961).
Huntington	Gale Huntington, *Songs the Whalemen Sang* (Barre, Massachusetts, 1964).
Ingersoll	Ernest Ingersoll, *Birds in Legend, Fable and Folklore* (New York, 1923).
Ingledew	C. J. Davison Ingledew, *The Ballads and Songs of Yorkshire* (London, 1860).
Jackson	George Pullen Jackson, *Spiritual Folk-Songs of Early America* (New York, 1937; reprint, New York, 1964).
JAF	*Journal of American Folklore* (Philadelphia, 1888–).
Jamieson	Robert Jamieson, *Popular Ballads and Songs*, (Edinburgh, 1806, 2 vols).
JEFDSS	*Journal of the English Folk Dance and Song Society* (London, 1932–64).
JFSS	*Journal of the Folk Song Society* (London, 1899–1931).
JIFS	*Journal of the Irish Folksong Society* (Dublin, 1904–10).
Joyce (1)	Patrick Weston Joyce, *Ancient Irish Music* (Dublin, 1873; reprints, 1912).
Joyce (2)	Patrick Weston Joyce, *Old Irish Folk Music and Songs* (Dublin, 1909).
Karpeles (1)	Maud Karpeles, *Folksongs from Newfoundland* (London, 1934).
Karpeles (2)	Maud Karpeles, *Folksongs from Newfoundland* (London, 1971).

Kennedy	Peter Kennedy, *Folksongs of Britain and Ireland* (London, 1975).
Kerr (1)	James S. Kerr, *Buchan Bothy Ballads* (Glasgow, n.d.).
Kerr (2)	James S. Kerr, *Cornkisters* (Glasgow, 1950).
Kidson	Frank Kidson, *Traditional Tunes* (Oxford, 1891).
Kidson and Moffat (1)	Frank Kidson and Alfred Moffat, *Children's Songs of Long Ago* (London, n.d.).
Kidson and Moffat (2)	Frank Kidson and Alfred Moffat, *A Garland of English Folksongs* (London, 1926).
Kidson and Neal	Frank Kidson and Mary Neal, *English Folk-Song and Dance* (Cambridge, 1915).
Kinloch (1)	George R. Kinloch, *Ancient Scottish Ballads* (London, 1827).
Kinloch (2)	George R. Kinloch, *The Ballad Book* (Edinburgh, 1827).
Kirkpatrick Sharpe	Charles Kirkpatrick Sharpe, *A Ballad Book* (Edinburgh, 1823).
Korson and Emrich	George Korson and Marion Vallat Emrich, *The Child's Book of Folklore* (New York, 1947).
Laws	G. Malcolm Laws, Jr, *Native American Balladry* (Philadelphia, 1964 revised edition) for Laws numbers A–1 to I–20, incl. Also: *American Balladry from British Broadsides* (Philadelphia, 1957) for Laws numbers J-1 to Q-39, incl.
Leach	MacEdward Leach, *Folk Ballads and Songs of the Lower Labrador Coast* (Ottawa, 1965).
Leigh	Egerton Leigh, *Ballads and Legends of Cheshire* (London, 1867).
Linscott	Eloise Hubbard Linscott, *Folk Songs of Old New England* (New York, 1939).
Logan	W. H. Logan, *A Pedlar's Pack of Ballads and Songs* (Edinburgh, 1869).
Lomax (1)	John A. and Alan Lomax, *American Ballads and Folk Songs* (New York, 1934).
Lomax (2)	John A. and Alan Lomax, *Cowboy Songs and Other Frontier Ballads* (New York, 1946).
Lomax (3)	Alan Lomax, *Folksongs of North America* (London, 1960).
Lomax (4)	John A. and Alan Lomax, *Folksong: U.S.A.* (New York, 1948).
Lomax (5)	John A. and Alan Lomax, *Our Singing Country* (New York, 1941).

MacColl	Ewan MacColl, *Scotland Sings* (London, 1953).
MacKenzie	W. Roy MacKenzie, *Ballads and Sea Songs from Nova Scotia* (Cambridge, Massachusetts, 1928).
Madden Collection	The Madden Collection of Broadsides and Slip-songs, Cambridge University Library, Cambridge.
Maidment	James Maidment, *A North Country Garland* (Edinburgh, 1824).
Mason	M. H. Mason, *Nursery Rhymes and Country Songs* (London, 1878).
Merrick	W. Percy Merrick, *Folksongs from Sussex* (London, 1912).
Moeran	E. J. Moeran, *Six Suffolk Folk-Songs* (London, 1932).
Moore	Ethel and Chauncey O. Moore, *Ballads and Folk Songs of the Southwest* (University of Oklahoma Press, 1964).
Moore (Frank)	Frank Moore, *Songs and Ballads of the American Revolution* (New York, 1856).
Morris	Alton C. Morris, *Folksongs of Florida* (Gainsville, Florida, 1950).
Morton	Robin Morton, *Folksongs Sung in Ulster* (Cork, 1970).
Motherwell	William Motherwell, *Minstrelsy: Ancient and Modern* (Glasgow, 1827).
Museum	*The Scots Musical Museum*, edited by James Johnson (Edinburgh, 1787, 6 vols).
Neeley	Charles Neeley, *Tales and Songs of Southern Illinois* (Menasha, Wisconsin, 1938).
Newell	William Wells Newell, *Games and Songs of American Children* (New York, 1883).
New Suffolk Garland	*New Suffolk Garland*, edited by John Glyde, Jr (Ipswich, 1866).
Niles	John Jacob Niles, *Songs of the Hill-Folk* (New York, 1934).
Northall	G. F. Northall, *English Folk-Rhymes* (London, 1892).
O'Lochlainn (1)	Colm O'Lochlainn, *Irish Street Ballads* (Dublin, 1939).
O'Lochlainn (2)	Colm O'Lochlainn, *More Irish Street Ballads* (Dublin, 1965).
Opie (1)	Iona and Peter Opie, *The Oxford Dictionary of Nursery Rhymes* (London, 1951).
Opie (2)	Iona and Peter Opie, *The Lore and Language of Schoolchildren* (Oxford, 1959).
Ord	John Ord, *The Bothy Songs and Ballads of Aberdeen, Banff and Moray, Angus and the Mearns* (Paisley, 1930).

Owens	William A. Owens, *Texas Folk Songs* (Dallas, Texas, 1950).
Peacock	Kenneth Peacock, *Songs of the Newfoundland Outports* (Ottawa, 1965, 3 vols).
Pepys	Pepys Broadside Collection (c. 1650), Magdalen College Library, Oxford.
Percy	Thomas Percy, *Reliques of Ancient English Poetry* (London, 1765).
Petrie	George Petrie, *The Complete Petrie Collection of Irish Music*, edited by Charles Villiers Stanford (New York, 1902–5).
Playford (Henry)	Henry Playford, *Wit and Mirth: or, Pills to Purge Melancholy* (London, 1699).
Playford (John)	John Playford, *Choice Ayres and Songs* (London, 1679).
Pound	Louise Pound, *American Ballads and Songs* (New York, 1922).
Purslow (1)	Frank Purslow, *The Constant Lovers* (London, 1972).
Purslow (2)	Frank Purslow, *Marrowbones* (London, 1965).
Purslow (3)	Frank Purslow, *The Wanton Seed* (London, 1968).
Purslow (4)	Frank Purslow, *The Foggy Dew* (London, 1974).
Ramsay	Allan Ramsay, *The Tea-Table Miscellany* (Edinburgh, 1876, 2-vol. edition).
Randolph	Vance Randolph, *Ozark Folksongs* (Columbia, Missouri, 1946, 4 vols).
Ravenscroft	Thomas Ravenscroft, *Deuteromelia* (London, 1609; reprint, Philadelphia, 1961).
Reeves (1)	James Reeves, *The Everlasting Circle* (London, 1960).
Reeves (2)	James Reeves, *The Idiom of the People* (London, 1958).
Ritchie (1)	James T. R. Ritchie, *Golden City* (Edinburgh, 1965).
Ritchie (2)	James T. R. Ritchie, *The Singing Street* (Edinburgh, 1964).
Ritson (1)	Joseph Ritson, *The North Country Chorister* (London, 1810).
Ritson (2)	Joseph Ritson, *Northern Garlands* (London, 1810). *The North Country Chorister* is incorporated in this work.
Ritson (3)	Joseph Ritson, *Scottish Song* (revised edition, Glasgow, 1869, 2 vols).
Rogers	Charles Rogers, *The Scottish Minstrel* (Edinburgh, 1870).
Rollins (1)	Hyder E. Rollins, *Old English Ballads, 1553–1625* (Cambridge, 1920).
Rollins (2)	Hyder E. Rollins, *The Pepys Ballads* (Cambridge, Massachusetts, 1929–32, 8 vols).

Ross — Peter Ross, *The Songs of Scotland Chronologically Arranged* (Paisley, 1893).

Roxburghe — *Roxburghe Ballads*, edited by J. Woodfall Ebsworth and William Chappel (Hertford: printed for the Ballad Society, 1871–99, 9 vols).

Rymour — *Rymour Club Miscellanea* (Edinburgh, 1911–28, 3 vols).

Sandburg — Carl Sandburg, *The American Songbag* (New York, 1927).

Scarborough (1) — Dorothy Scarborough, *A Song Catcher in the Southern Mountains* (New York, 1937).

Scarborough (2) — Dorothy Scarborough, *On the Trail of Negro Folk-Songs* (Cambridge, Massachusetts, 1925).

Scott — Sir Walter Scott, *Minstrelsy of the Scottish Border* (3 vols: vols 1 and 2, Kelso, 1802; vol. 3, Edinburgh, 1803; revised edition, Edinburgh, 1902, 4 vols).

Scottish Studies — *Scottish Studies*, Journal of the School of Scottish Studies (University of Edinburgh, 1957–   ).

Seeger and MacColl — Peggy Seeger and Ewan MacColl, *The Singing Island* (London, 1960).

Sharp (1) — Cecil J. Sharp, *English County Folksongs* (London, 1912; reprint, London, 1961).

Sharp (2) — Cecil J. Sharp, *English Folksongs* (London, 1920, 2 vols; reprinted in one book, London 1959).

Sharp and Karpeles (1) — Cecil J. Sharp and Maud Karpeles, *English Folk Songs from the Southern Appalachians* (London, 1932, 2 vols).

Sharp and Karpeles (2) — Cecil J. Sharp, *Cecil Sharp's Collection of English Folk Songs*, edited by Maud Karpeles (London, 1974, 2 vols).

Sharp and Marson — Cecil J. Sharp and Charles L. Marson, *English Folk Songs from Somerset* (1st Series, London, 1904).

Sharp (Cuthbert) — Cuthbert Sharp, *The Bishoprick Garland* (Newcastle-upon-Tyne, 1834; reprint, 1969).

Smith — Laura Alexandrine Smith, *Through Romany Songland* (London, 1889).

Smith (Reed) — Reed Smith, *South Carolina Ballads* (Cambridge, Massachusetts, 1928).

Sola Pinto and Rodway — Vivian de Sola Pinto and Allan E. Rodway, *The Common Muse* (New York, 1957).

Spaeth — Sigmund Spaeth, *Weep Some More, My Lady* (New York, 1927).

Swainson — Charles Swainson, *Provincial Names and Folklore of British Birds* (London, 1885).

Swann — H. Kirke Swann, *A Dictionary of English and Folk-Names of British Birds* (London, 1913).

Stokoe and Reay   John Stokoe and Samuel Reay, *Songs and Ballads of Northern England* (Newcastle-upon-Tyne, 1892).

Thomas   Jean Thomas, *Devil's Ditties* (Chicago, 1931).

Thomas and Leeder   Jean Thomas and Joseph A. Leeder, *The Singin' Gatherin'* (New York, 1939).

Thompson   H. W. Thompson, *Body, Boots and Britches* (Philadelphia, 1940).

Thompson (Stith)   Stith Thompson, *Motif-Index of Folk-Literature* (Helsinki, 1932–6, 6 vols).

Thomson   William Thomson, *Orpheus Caledonius* (London, 1725, 2 vols; facsimile of 1733 edition, Hatboro, Pennsylvania, 1962).

Thorp and Fife   N. Howard Thorp, and Austen E. and Alta S. Fife, *Songs of the Cowboys* (New York, 1966).

The Thrush   *The Thrush: A Choice Selection of the most Admired Popular Songs* (London, 1827).

Ward   Russel Ward, *The Penguin Book of Australian Ballads* (London, 1964).

Wells   Evelyn K. Wells, *The Ballad Tree* (New York, 1950).

Whall   W. B. Whall, *Sea Songs and Shanties* (Glasgow, 1910).

Williams   Alfred Williams, *Folk-Songs of the Upper Thames* (London, 1923).

Wimberly   Lowry C. Wimberly, *Folklore in the English and Scottish Ballads* (Chicago, 1928; reprint, New York, 1965).

Zimmerman   George Denis Zimmerman, *Songs of the Irish Rebellion* (Pennsylvania, 1967).

BRITISH MUSEUM
shelf numbers for broadside collections

LR 31 b 19   A collection of ballads chiefly printed in Newcastle-upon-Tyne by J. White and in London (1730–1830). Two volumes.

LR 271 a 2   A collection of ballads, chiefly Catnach and Pitt, 1800–70. Ten volumes, collected by Baring-Gould.

1871 f 13   A collection of ballads printed on single sheets, 1750–1840.

1875 d 5   A collection of ballads and broadsides, chiefly London, by J. Pitts, 1790–1875.

1875 d 16   A collection of ballads and other broadside sheets published by J. Pitts and others.

1875 f 19   A collection of ballads, London 1800–50.

1876 e 2   A collection of ballads printed 1830–75.

1876 e 20   A collection of ballads and broadsides, 1770–1830.

11602 gg 28   A collection of ballads on single sheets, 1850–5.

11602 gg 30   A collection of ballads printed chiefly by L. Croshaw of York and J. Pitts of London, 1820–40.

11621 i 12   A collection of ballads collected by Thomas Bell, 1780–1820.

WORKS DEALING WITH TRAVELLERS

Acton   Thomas Acton, *Gypsy Politics and Social Change* (London, 1974).

Barrère and Leland   A. Barrère and C. G. Leland, *A Dictionary of Slang, Jargon and Cant* (London, 1897).

Black   George F. Black, *A Gypsy Bibliography* (Edinburgh, 1909).

Boswell   S. G. Boswell, *The Book of Boswell* (London, 1970).

Brockie   William Brockie, *The Gypsies of Yetholm* (Kelso, 1884).

Clébert   Jean-Paul Clébert, *The Gypsies* (London, 1963).

Crabb   James Crabb, *The Gipsies' Advocate* (Edinburgh, 1831).

Fairley   John A. Fairley, *Bailie Smith of Kelso's Account of the Gypsies of Kirk Yetholm in 1815* (Hawick, 1907).

Gillington   Alice E. Gillington, *Gypsies of the Heath* (London, 1916).

Groome   Francis H. Groome, *In Gypsy Tents* (Edinburgh, 1880).

Hoyland   John Hoyland, *The Gypsies* (York, 1816).

Journal   *Journal of the Gypsy Lore Society* (1st series, 1888–92; 2nd series, 1907–16; 3rd series, 1922–   ).

Leland   Charles G. Leland, *The English Gypsies and Their Language* (London, 1873).

McCormick   Andrew McCormick, *The Tinkler Gypsies* (London, 1907).

MacRitchie   David MacRitchie, *Scottish Gypsies Under the Stewarts* (Edinburgh, 1894).

Morwood   Vernon S. Morwood, *Our Gypsies in City, Tent and Van* (London, 1885).

Sampson   John Sampson, 'English Gypsy Songs and Rhymes' (Gypsy Lore Society *Journal*, vol. 2, Edinburgh, 1891).

Simson   Walter Simson, *A History of the Gypsies* (London, 1865).

Smart and Crofton   B. C. Smart and H. D. Crofton, *The Dialect of the English Gypsies* (London, 1875).

Sutherland   Anne Sutherland, *Gypsies: the Hidden Americans* (London, 1975).

Wood   Manfri Frederick Wood, *In the Life of a Romany Gypsy* (London, 1973).

INDEX OF TITLES

Roman type indicates working title.
Italic type indicates singer's title.

INDEX OF FIRST LINES